world
wild
vet

world
wild
vet

Encounters
in the Animal
Kingdom

Dr. Evan Antin
with Jana Murphy

HENRY HOLT AND COMPANY
NEW YORK

Henry Holt and Company
Publishers since 1866
120 Broadway
New York, New York 10271
www.henryholt.com

Henry Holt® and 🏛® are registered trademarks of Macmillan Publishing
Group, LLC.

Distributed in Canada by Raincoast Book Distribution Limited

Library of Congress Cataloging-in-Publication Data

Names: Antin, Evan, author.
Title: World wild vet : encounters in the animal kingdom /
by Dr. Evan Antin with Jana Murphy.
Description: First edition. | New York : Henry Holt and Company, 2020. |
Includes bibliographical references.
Identifiers: LCCN 2020018959 (print) | LCCN 2020018960 (ebook) |
ISBN 9781250314482 (hardcover) | ISBN 9781250314499 (ebook)
Subjects: LCSH: Veterinarians—Biography. | Exotic animals—Anecdotes. |
Wildlife conservation.
Classification: LCC SF613.A58 A3 2020 (print) | LCC SF613.A58 (ebook) |
DDC 636.089092 [B]—dc23
LC record available at https://lccn.loc.gov/2020018959
LC ebook record available at https://lccn.loc.gov/2020018960

ISBN: 9781250314482

Our books may be purchased in bulk for promotional, educational, or
business use. Please contact your local bookseller or the Macmillan
Corporate and Premium Sales Department at (800) 221-7945, extension
5442, or by e-mail at MacmillanSpecialMarkets@macmillan.com.

First Edition 2020

Designed by Meryl Sussman Levavi

Printed in the United States of America

1   2   3   4   5   6   7   8   9   10

The information provided within this book is for general informational
and educational purposes only. It is based on the experience of the author
and is not meant to provide instruction or training on viewing or handling
wildlife. Many of the animals described in this book can be dangerous
and must be handled (or avoided) appropriately for their safety and for
yours. Do not attempt to handle or approach wildlife or any other animal
without proper training and equipment.

To the rangers and conservationists
who work on the front lines to
protect the world's wildlife.

I see you on every continent and in
every country, quietly, heroically
putting your time, energy, and
even your lives on the line to
defend wild animals and habitats.
Because of you, future generations
will be able to continue to
appreciate our natural world.

From the bottom of my heart,
thank you for your incredible,
inspiring work.

We don't own the planet Earth, we
belong to it. And we must share it
with our wildlife.

—STEVE IRWIN

Contents

Introduction

In the fall of 2019, while helping relocate a small seed population of giraffes to Uganda's Pian Upe Wildlife Reserve, I sprinted across the savannah with a crew of rangers, biologists, and other veterinarians to subdue a fifteen-hundred-pound semi-sedated giraffe. As the beautiful, graceful giant reached the ground, I moved in to administer a series of injections at the base of his neck. All around me, other members of the team were laser focused on their own jobs—covering the animal's head to help calm him, injecting a reversal for the sedative, taking tissue samples, monitoring his heart rate, and securing a series of long lead lines that would help us guide the giraffe into a travel trailer. I'd watched the process once before, but this was my first hands-on participation, and I was mindful as I crouched down of the number one rule of giraffe wrangling: *Stay away from the legs*. A giraffe can kick with enough force to kill—and potentially decapitate—all but the hugest mammal. I glanced to my right, doing the math as I assessed his powerful body and all four legs. He was on his right side, not peaceful, but no longer wildly flailing. I turned my attention to the job at hand.

Seconds later, the giraffe struggled a bit. As I glanced up, I saw his right rear hoof—wide as a plate, dense as an anvil, and propelled by all the force this massive animal could muster—cannonballing toward my face. As I snapped my head back, my Ugandan adventure flashed by—how eager I'd been, how carefully I'd studied this process, how much this was gonna hurt (if I survived it). One second that hoof had been fifteen feet away; the next it was inches from my eyes.

Mercifully (because there was not a damn thing I could have done to stop it) the kick stopped just before crushing my head. My nerves reset, and I got back to work. After that, I reminded each person working in that general area that against all odds, a giraffe can reach you *there*.

This goes to show that no matter how much experience you have as a vet out in the wild, there's *always* a learning curve, even if it gets a little less steep as time goes by.

My own learning curve to understanding and caring for wildlife started when I was just a kid. Growing up in Kansas, I spent my days flipping rocks in a creek, climbing trees, and constantly running my hands through leaves and dirt, always looking for wild animals in the woods near my house. I was hooked on the feeling of adventure, the sense that any minute could bring my next big find, and the fascination that came with each discovery. I guess I was easily amused back then, because even a giant earthworm sighting could make my day.

Over the years, for reasons I can't fully explain, I developed a huge soft spot for creatures most of my peers found gross or scary. Spiders, lizards, snakes—the gnarlier, the better. I loved to study how they moved, to see what they ate, to understand how they sheltered and protected themselves. The more dangerous the creature, the closer I wanted to get to it.

The same boyhood passion that found me out in the woods every day after school led me to become a student of evolutionary and ecological biology. It gave me the ability to let excitement overrule any reservations as I traveled farther and farther afield: driving through the Australian outback, trekking the Tanzanian savannah, bushwhacking my way across the Amazon, and hiking the jungles of Southeast Asia. It led me to veterinary school, where I became a wildlife, exotics, and small-animal vet. And it helped me grow into the conservation-minded eco-traveler I am today. It's been a long progression, and I've made a few mistakes along the way. Mostly, though, I've had amazing, inspiring experiences that make me want to reach more people with what I've learned, and step up as a voice for wildlife conservation.

Thanks to social media, I get to share my encounters with an audience of millions, but there are still things you don't see in my feed, like the fact that a lot of my travel is really freaking uncomfortable—hot, cramped, smelly, and dangerous. It's a simple equation for me, though: if I want to see the animals and the people and places and the cultures, I've got to do what it takes to get there. If that means a fourteen-hour ride on a sweltering bus with as many goats and chickens as humans, bring it on. If I have to fly through a lightning storm on a prop plane to a remote airport with one poorly lit, too-short runway, fine. I will walk, bike, row, swim, climb, or hitchhike. I'll ford a river teeming with leeches—I've done it before—or slash my way through a jungle (even if it's home to one of the most powerful drug cartels in the world).

I'll do just about anything to get where I want to be: Nose-to-trunk with a once-abused temple elephant who's finally found a peaceful home in Southeast Asia. Swimming beside a gentle thirty-five-foot behemoth of a whale shark along a pristine Australian coastline. Holding a gorgeous snake whose neck is as wide as my wrist at a South American serpentarium, watching its venom pour along the handle of my snake hook. Sitting on a rocky Rwandan cliff beside a silverback gorilla who has chosen the place *right next to me* to flop down, belly-up, and watch the world go by.

Those moments are the payoffs, and they're worth every minute of being hungry, tired, blistered, sunburnt, dirty, or uncomfortable I've endured to get to them.

The very best part of my experience is that many times along the way, I've been entrusted to roll up my sleeves and help some of these animals. When I was in college, I got a volunteer opportunity as the official squirrel and raccoon intern at the Greenwood Wildlife Rehabilitation Sanctuary in Colorado. That led me to take volunteer trips of my own across South America and Southeast Asia. With little to offer but enthusiasm and time, I'd show up at a place I'd found on the Internet and trekked to on my own, asking if there was anything I could do to help—and there always was. By the time I earned my veterinary degree, I'd gotten pretty good at figuring out ways to get invited (or at least to get in the front door) to wildlife rescues and preserves all over the world. I've done every job, from bottle-feeding bears and koalas to shoveling shit out of a tamandua's enclosure; from standing guard over endangered sea turtles to performing delicate surgical procedures on monkeys, lizards, rhinos, turtles, and, of course, dogs and cats. At this writing, I've volunteered my services on six continents and in dozens of countries, and every year brings new opportunities and challenges.

This book is the story of how a guy from Kansas ended up getting to do all the things that would make his curious, overenthusiastic boyhood self proud. Thank you for taking the time to share it with me.

world
wild
vet

PART ONE

✧

See the World

1

Australia

I was twenty-one years old when I set out on the trip that would give me my first glimpse of my professional destiny. In Australia, I spent the first two weeks of my semester abroad taking a crash course in marine biology on a coral island on the Great Barrier Reef. Lady Elliot Island is the ocean's answer to a desert mirage—a tiny dot of vibrant green land in a vast expanse of blue sea.

The ring of white-sand beach around the island was stunning, but whenever I think of this place, I see and smell the water. I'd only just gotten scuba certified, and every single dive opened up a new world for me. The first time I slipped beneath the surface, I saw a loggerhead turtle cruising over coral directly below me, his giant spotted flippers stroking through the water. My pulse raced and I held my breath (a no-no in scuba diving, by the way). A giant loggerhead. In the wild. Next to me. His carapace was at least three feet long, and he must have weighed 350 pounds, but he was gliding with total grace, his heavy-lidded eyes steady and somber. He was so majestic and peaceful, my impulse was to fall in behind him and trail around for as long as he'd let me.

Other dives opened my eyes to the diversity of reef life: nurse sharks and reef sharks so close I could have touched them; striped humbugs and bright blue surgeonfish darting around the reef; a giant grouper with beady little eyes and a gaping maw of a mouth who swam right up and brushed against me. I saw an octopus gliding from coral to rock, morphing at each stop to match the color and pattern of his surroundings. It blew my mind. I was so overstimulated by what I was encountering on those dives that I couldn't stop thinking about it, dreaming of technicolor fish and all-knowing turtles at night, and waking up ready to see more every morning.

A few days in, my class was out in the water, listening to our instructions as we got ready to dive in pairs. When I glanced to the side, manta rays—at least three of them—were soaring through the ocean under the power of their massive aquatic wings, only twenty yards from me.

Mother Nature outdid herself with these spectacular creatures in their scale, beauty, and incredible aerodynamics. The reef manta rays I saw that day have wingspans reaching up to fifteen feet and can weigh more than two thousand pounds. Despite their crazy-powerful build, they are peaceful, harmless creatures that eat plankton—they don't even have stingers. These rays are often loners, but they gather in groups to get their gills and skin scrubbed by little cleaner wrasse fish that bite off the dead skin and parasites. The natural "cleaning stations" they visit are found at coral reefs, and Lady Elliot Island is one of the most active in the world.

I'd read that mantas sometimes interact with scuba divers, swimming around and over them, touching them with a wing, almost playing with them. I knew I was in their habitat, and I'd been waiting and hoping. So the minute I spotted them, I was *on my way*. Honestly, I didn't mean to break protocol or abandon my dive partner. It was kind of like when a dog sees a squirrel—I didn't think; I just bolted toward them.

Bad idea. One of the biggest rules in observing underwater animals is that you've got to move slowly. You have to be watchful and patient, not (ahem) abrupt and frantic. You have to be willing to wait.

I would get to see the manta rays another day—and even get up close—but that morning I blew it. I took off in such a hurry, stroking through the water straight for my new friends, that I startled them. The other divers in my group were not loving me as I treaded water and scanned the horizon, looking all around for the rays, which were long gone.

I'd always loved animals. I'd always been fascinated with how they live and what they think and how each species is so different from the next, but my two weeks on that tiny island on the Great Barrier Reef changed me. Swimming in the crystal water and seeing a kind of nature we sure didn't have back in Kansas or Colorado made me a little crazy, a little overeager, and a lot in love with the idea of doing something with my life that would bring me back to the animals there. And I knew that many of the creatures I'd fallen in love with were endangered—which only added fuel to my desire to keep the connection I felt to them alive.

Kangaroo Beach

Back on the mainland I worked hard in my classes, but on my days off I surfed, snorkeled, and explored the coast. One weekend my friends and I set up camp in Murramarang National Park, at Pebbly Beach, sometimes called Kangaroo Beach due to the frequent sightings of eastern grey kangaroos in the area. I couldn't wait to go looking for them.

It turned out no search was needed. These kangaroos are super habituated to people. The very first evening a group of them (a "court" of kangaroos) showed up right on the beach and sat at the perimeter of the site, observing *our* behavior.

Kangaroos on the beach—no joke. These guys had lean faces,

big eyes and ears, and soft coloring. From the neck up, they looked a lot like the deer from back home. But they were standing on two legs. The white-tailed deer in Kansas never did that.

One of the roos kept staring at me, waggling his ears and crossing and uncrossing his little arms in front of him, like a fidgety kid who wants to raise his hand in class but can't quite work up the nerve. His eyes stayed on the sandwich I was eating, so I figured we could make a deal. There are a lot of reasons not to offer people food to wildlife, but these kangaroos interact with humans every day, so I figured a bit of bread from me wasn't going to have a lasting impact on this guy's diet. I put a small piece in my hand and held it out, saying, "Want a bite?" His friends took a step back, but my new pal was brave. He leaned in, then hopped a little closer. I waited, keeping my posture steady, speaking softly. My friends waited, too, probably thinking I was pushing my luck. The roo kept looking from the bread in my hand to my face and back again. The ears twitched; the arms waved.

"It's okay man," I said. "I'm not gonna hurt you. You can have this one."

I set the bread on the ground and withdrew a few inches, and he stepped right up and took it. He ate the next one out of my hand. And then another. After that, we were compadres. That day, this guy and I hung out, sharing snacks, while his friends watched from a few feet away, not quite brave enough to get close.

Did I mention that I was a twenty-one-year-old college kid at this time? No veterinary degree. No experience with the species. Just an avid, goofy fan of wildlife, feeding a friendly kangaroo and having the time of my life. Of *course* I couldn't leave well enough alone. On the second day I had to push the envelope. I took a bread crumb and put it in my lips, then pursed them in the kangaroo's direction. No, you don't have to tell me that was stupid. I know. My furry friend hopped over, leaned in, and planted one on me. Actually, it may have been more of a bite than a kiss, but I don't like to remember it that way. He grabbed his bread crumb, and also both my top and my lower lip, giving them a rough tug, enough to say, "I could take these off if I wanted to." Thank God he wasn't in the mood for a fight—I could be lipless today.

After that we stuck to hand-feeding, which was ill-advised enough. If I met that kangaroo now, I'd know better than to feed him and encourage his potentially dangerous comfort level with people, but back then I couldn't see past the opportunity to make that connection. I still had a lot to learn about safely and responsibly interacting with wildlife.

A Big Idea, and One Giant Fish

As the end of the in-class session neared, I used my days off from class to travel as far as the northern Great Barrier Reef and to Tasmania, Melbourne, and New Zealand. I'd covered a lot of ground, but two or three days at a time didn't feel like enough.

In the Australian university system, there's a long gap between the end of classes and finals—time to study for exams and complete research projects. There was nearly a month on my calendar for studying, but to me it looked a lot like an invitation to get out and see the country. I'd been thinking about the animals I was encountering, and about how I wished I'd been able to capture those moments on film, so I called my mom and asked if she would send me a camcorder, a tripod, and a box of mini DV videotapes from home. Then I got out my map and calendar and hatched a plan.

To be honest, I had no idea who, if anyone, would ever see the videos I wanted to make. This was 2006. I was just an undergrad. I knew nothing about filmmaking, production values, marketing, social media—all the stuff that brings content to people. I was newly (and rarely) on Facebook. What I did know was that this was my first time exploring a foreign country and its wildlife completely on my own, and I was experiencing things I never wanted to forget. These moments were changing my life. I at least wanted to be able to share them with my mom.

The picture I had in my head was of me out in some remote area, filming short takes with amazing wildlife. Just like Steve Irwin.

I had seen a tape where Steve Irwin set up a tripod and camera on the bank of a river teeming with crocodiles, pushed Play, and ran to the other side of the lens. Then he pointed to the water and said, straight into the camera, something like "Crikey, he's a big bloke, but we need to rescue him from this ditch and get that untangled from him." And then he waded right in, all the while talking about the beasts and how *amaaazing* they were. Those were beautiful moments between me and Steve (and, you know, wildlife aficionados around the world).

Fourteen years later, I'd have the opportunity to spend time with Steve Irwin's family at their Australia Zoo. In the aftermath of historic wildfires that devastated millions of acres of land and countless animals, I was honored to be able to help raise awareness about the heroic work the zoo was doing. The trip also gave me the chance to tell the Irwins in person what a crucial role Steve played in motivating me toward the career I have today. I usually don't get starstruck, but meeting Terri Irwin was a huge moment—one that took me back to the raw excitement and insatiable curiosity I'd felt during my first, unforgettable trip to Australia.

Back in 2006, I decided to head out into Irwin's country to experience it for myself. Capturing something even a little bit like the videos my idol made was on my mind as I laid out a route that would take me to destinations all over Australia. I wanted total freedom to make the most of the trip, so I decided I would do it by myself. Just a man and a camera on the open road.

I rented a four-door compact car and loaded it up with an atlas, my field guides to Aussie wildlife, my camera and tripod, a homemade snake hook, cans of beans, crackers, and peanut butter. I also brought along a pillow and a sleeping bag, and I filled almost the entire trunk with water bottles. At that point, pretty much all I had left was gas money, but I didn't care.

The first item on my agenda was to go swimming with whale sharks. The Ningaloo Reef, on the northwest coast of Western Australia, is one of the best places in the world to see them. It was a thirteen-hour drive from where I got the car, but I was so excited I covered the entire distance in a straight shot. I lost track of time as I cruised along, with the turquoise waters of the Indian Ocean on one side of the road and lush, open landscape on the other.

Whale sharks are the biggest extant fish species in the ocean. They are humongous—as long as forty feet or more. For reference, a seventy-two-passenger school bus is thirty-five feet, so we're talking a bus length and change worth of shark. People often spot these fish from planes flying overhead. Despite their size, whale sharks are filter feeders who basically spend their lives scooping up krill and plankton and other small sea life, so they don't pose any danger to humans (unless maybe you swim into one's mouth or get slapped by its enormous tail). The combination of their peaceable nature and their preference for shallow depths makes them ideal to observe in their natural habitat with little more than some luck and a snorkel.

I arrived in Ningaloo late, ate some beans from a can, slept in my car, and was standing on the shore with snorkel in hand at daybreak. My camera stayed stowed. This was going to be an experience I'd just have to remember in my mind's eye—my equipment was basic grade and definitely not waterproof.

To catch a ride on a small boat going whale sighting, I forked over the price of a few days' beans and water. Fifteen minutes out, we spotted the polka-dotted pattern of a whale shark out ahead of us in the crystal-clear East Indian Ocean. He was bigger than an elephant, bigger than a car, bigger than my childhood bedroom.

Just. Massive. I was so thrilled I kept turning to strangers on the boat, shouting, "DO YOU SEE IT?!" As if anyone could possibly miss it.

What happened next remains one of my favorite wildlife experiences of all time. (Fair warning: you're going to hear me say those words a few times in this book.) Our boat stopped, the captain gave us the nod, and I was over the side, in the sea, and cutting across the water with the most powerful stroke I could manage. Yeah, I'll admit it: I wanted to get to him first. Unlike the manta rays, this was an animal not easily spooked by a swimmer.

This was the biggest animal I'd ever seen up close and personal. A behemoth with the telltale anatomical structures of a shark—classic dorsal fin and tail fins, smooth white lines down his body. I could see his massive fins but not his face. I quickly realized that if I was going to get a look at him—or observe any part of him for long—I was going to have to pick up the pace. The whale shark appeared to be making zero effort to cut through the water, but I was paddling my ass off and barely keeping up. Ten minutes in, I was gasping and sputtering, trying to gain just enough on him to see the front. Twenty minutes and my lungs were on fire, my heart pounding out of my chest, my mind blown by the experience. And then he finally decided he wasn't in such a hurry (or took mercy on me).

The shark slowed in the water and began a gradual, gentle turn in my direction. This was my chance. I swam even harder, pulling away ahead and off to one side, so I'd be waiting for him. You're not supposed to get out in front of them. A whale shark won't eat you, but it could bump you. It could open its crazy-wide mouth (up to five feet across!) to catch some krill and stop your heart with a display of its hundreds of rows of tiny teeth. You could disturb its peaceful swim. Even as excited as I was, I knew better, and I moved a bit farther to the side and swam on, ahead now, periodically glancing back.

And that's when he turned just enough for his whole face to come into view. He was the biggest adorable thing I'd ever seen. His eyes were spaced far apart, and his big mouth was open slightly, so that it looked like he was flashing me a giant, floppy grin.

Hello, friend! I waved a tired, leaden arm at him and thought to myself, *You're never, ever gonna forget this moment.*

The whale shark kept gliding forward; I stayed put. I couldn't swim anymore. Even fully immersed in the water, I was sweating profusely and physically spent. Fitness experts say swimming works nearly every muscle in the body—and I was already feeling most of them. I lazily made my way back to the boat and crawled aboard, exhausted and completely satisfied.

Monitor Moment

After swimming with the whale sharks, I doubled back up the coast and headed to an area called the Kimberley. The northernmost of the nine Western Australian regions, the Kimberley is huge—about the size of California. It's remote and sparsely populated, with only around thirty-five thousand permanent residents. Imagine California with thirty-five thousand people instead of nearly forty million and you start to get the idea of just how far it is between towns in this region and how long you can go without laying eyes on another soul. I was there to visit the region's national parks, including Tunnel Creek, Purnululu, El Questro Wilderness, Mitchell River, and Windjana Gorge.

The scenery at Tunnel Creek, at the top of my list, is not what most people come to Australia expecting to see. Rather than desert or beach, it's composed of craggy, steep-sided mountains. Sandstone and limestone form jagged peaks and deep, rocky gorges. Inside the park, its namesake creek has carved a massive tunnel through the center of a mountain. It's a land of rock and water, with sunny ledges and sweet hiding places—a perfect environment to look for some of my favorite creatures on the planet: lizards and snakes.

Toting my camera bag and snake hook, I climbed up a boulder-strewn path to the entrance of the cave. I made my way inside, wading through the areas where the creek had no bank. The trek was about a half a mile in all, and I had to break out the flashlight a few times to find my way. When I exited the cave at the far side of the mountain and let my eyes adjust to the sunlight, the first thing I focused on was a massive sand monitor resting on a rock.

I *love* monitors. I had a pet savannah monitor for years. She was my first lizard love. (I had an iguana before that, but I was crazy about that monitor lizard.) I got her when I was in high school, and I named her Rex because she looked so much like a dinosaur, but I swear she had the personality of a teddy bear. Rex was always by my side when I was home. She loved to hang out anywhere warm, so if I fell asleep on my back, she'd sprawl out on my stomach and doze there. I'm still the only person I know who's been willing to sleep with that particular kind of pet.

The monitor I was looking at was gorgeous, black and yellow with thick scales running along the inside of his forelegs, which ended in thin fingers and long, sharp claws. This big male was more than five feet long and easily over twenty pounds.

I remember thinking, *This is where it starts.* This was the kind of opportunity I'd been looking for: my first subject, first video. I ran toward the monitor. He dove for a burrow, but he was too big to fit. The last third of his tail was sticking out.

I couldn't believe my luck. I frantically set up my camera, keeping one eye on the big guy because I knew I had only seconds. Then I squatted down beside the burrow, braced myself, and wrapped my hands around that big scaly tail. I slowly worked my way up until I could pull his entire body out.

A note about capturing reptiles: they may not like it, but they don't react the way mammals do. Typically, after a quick burst of energy, lizards and snakes, crocs and turtles settle down and become passive and tolerant. In many cases, as long as you aren't hurting them, they'll put up with a little handling and you can part ways with no harm done. Mammals, in contrast, panic and stay terrified for too long. Many really think they're going to die. Fight or flight kicks in and their heart rates rise, their respirations become deeper and faster, and they completely freak out. I never want to cause that kind of panic in an animal unless I have to (for instance, to perform a veterinary procedure or take necessary conservation measures), so even though I admire and treat all kinds of animals, I almost never go out looking to catch a mammal.

But the monitor wasn't a mammal, and he was too fascinating to ignore. Back on the ledge, he was staging a protest at being so rudely taken from his comfy hole. I waited out the hissing and clawing and trying to bite my face off, holding him just firmly enough and far enough away that he couldn't do me any harm. All the while I marveled at the heft of him—I'd never held a monitor nearly that large (or any reptile that large). When he stopped trying to kill me, I gripped him with one hand and started setting up my shot with the other. I was about to make my first wildlife video!

What I hadn't anticipated as I stood there looking at my camera was how uncomfortable it would feel to know the film was finally running. I had so much I wanted to say, but I couldn't seem to spit it out. Three or four times I tromped back to the camera, fifteen-pound monitor still in hand, to start again. Finally I did a take where I talked about his size, habitat, and diet—me in absolute awe of this beautiful creature, him occasionally trying to mangle my face.

The entire process probably took ten, maybe twelve minutes, but it felt much longer. At the end I left the camcorder running as I put my new Aussie buddy on the ground, took a couple giant steps back, and watched him scuttle off into the wild.

I was so damn proud and happy in that moment I could have climbed that craggy mountain and pounded my chest. I had *done*

it! The search. The catch-and-release. The setting up of equipment and stringing enough words together to tell the story of an
amazing animal. And I had the tape to prove it.

The Road

Given that I was nature hunting in the country believed to be
home to more deadly species than any other, there were times
when I probably should have been scared. I wasn't. I was too
excited to be there. One of the rare exceptions was a night early
in the trip when I woke up in the passenger seat of my rental car
(which was also my bed) thrashing around and soaked in sweat.
I'd had a nightmare in which two guys jumped into the back
of the car and were holding me at gunpoint. That was so many
years ago, but I still remember what those dudes looked like. I'm
no psychoanalyst, but it seems to me that deep down I was more
afraid of people than of any other creature.

I headed south toward the middle of the country—the outback—to see Uluru (Ayers Rock), Kings Canyon, and the domed
rock formations collectively known as the Olgas. I've taken a lot
of road trips in different countries since that one in Australia, but
I've never been anywhere where you can see a car coming from
so far away. Once you get out of the cities, the roads are broad and
expansive, the land is flat, and there are no streetlights or fences
along the highways. It's so dark it's almost eerie. In such total
darkness, sometimes you can see headlights from fifty miles off.

Because the roads are so remote and so dark, there was road-
kill everywhere. In the mornings, I'd often come upon the carcasses of wallabies, kangaroos, emus, lizards, and snakes being
eaten by buzzards and other birds of prey. I even saw buzzards
that had been hit by cars while mindlessly gorging on the victims of the road. One night, driving in the wee hours, I spotted
a kangaroo in the distance—a common occurrence. I slowed and
stayed focused on where it was, my eyes scanning the periphery of

the headlights. As I got closer to the spot, I lost sight of it. Then, without warning, it darted back into the road a few feet in front of me. I instinctively swerved and slammed on the brakes, sending the car into a skid. It didn't have anti-lock brakes, so it kept skidding for at least fifty feet.

The only evasion I could muster wasn't enough. I was still skidding forward at around twenty miles an hour when I clipped the kangaroo. It went flying into the air, then crumpled to the road.

When the car stopped, I jumped out and ran to check on the kangaroo. It wasn't moving. I crouched next to it, feeling for a pulse. Nothing. I waited a minute and tried again, probing under the soft, woolly fur, but there was no heartbeat.

I knew I had to drag the kangaroo off the road, or its presence might wreck the next driver speeding down that wide-open highway, so I hoisted it up and hauled it a few feet from the shoulder. Then I got back into the car, my mind replaying the last minutes, wishing I'd seen the animal sooner, swerved faster, stayed five more minutes the last time I'd stopped for gas. I hadn't been to vet school yet. I hadn't learned how to coexist with death. I felt wrecked, more alone than I'd been since I'd started the whole trip, and guilty. I was out there to appreciate nature and see Australia's beautiful animals, and I had killed one.

After a few minutes, I started the car, put my hands on the wheel, and pulled away. I figured the buzzards would arrive at dawn to clean up the mess I'd made. This wasn't the kind of memory I'd come to Australia to make, but I knew it was one that would stick with me.

Kakadu

From the middle of the country, I drove to a region in the Northern Territory that locals call the "Top End." The area is kind of like a massive wetland, with endless swamps and waterways and waterfalls to boot. I was there during the wettest time of year, when all the plains are flooded—perfect conditions to find crocodiles, lizards, and snakes.

Top End's Kakadu National Park is the largest of Australia's national parks. It spans more than seven thousand square miles and has been home to the Aboriginal people for over fifty thousand years. I could spend a year in this park and not begin to explore all the facets of its waterfalls and woodlands, plains, rivers, and coastline. With only a few days available to me, I chose to focus on the animals. In the daylight, I encountered marsupials and saltwater crocodiles and wildly exotic tropical birds, including hundreds of unbelievably loud groups of cockatoos. But it was at night that I really found what I came for. Kakadu was the site of some of the best night cruising I've ever done. Night cruising to a reptile lover means getting behind the wheel in the dark, taking it slow, and keeping your eyes on the road for creatures to meet.

They were everywhere. The road actually serves as a hot rock for reptiles. The asphalt retains heat, so cold-blooded animals seek its warmth. A reptile's metabolic function is dependent on the external temperature, so if you put a reptile in sixty-degree weather, its entire system will slow down. In ninety-degree weather, with some exceptions, it'll be in go mode, as if it's had a shot of espresso. For the cold-blooded, temperature changes everything—making the difference between a snake or lizard that's easy to catch and handle and one that's alert, fast, and snappy.

Each time I spotted a new species of wildlife, I tried to make a video, so I was steadily getting more comfortable with the camera. One night as I drove slowly down a deserted road, I came to a section littered with debris from an overhanging tree. Among the straight and angular lines of the branches and twigs, I spied the curves of a smooth, rounded S: *Snake!* Practice had taught me that the best way to do this was quickly. As soon as I saw the snake, I stopped the car, leaving the headlights on, grabbed the hook from the passenger seat, and ran toward the figure on the pavement. At six feet out I could see it was a python, between four and five feet long. Pythons aren't venomous, so I dropped the hook and scooped the snake up in my hands before it could slither away.

My find was a beautiful olive python, and she felt smooth, heavy, and cool as I picked her up. She was calm, and we checked each other out for a second before I supported her midsection with my palm, giving her enough room to move her head, then guided her to coil herself around my arm so she'd feel secure. With the snake on my left arm, I got back into the car and eased it off the road, grabbed my camera and tripod, and proceeded to set up, one-handed, in front of my headlights.

When the camera was ready, I hit Record and stepped back in front of it, holding the gorgeous snake up to the lens and then pulling her back toward me to get both of us in the shot.

"*Look* at this beautiful girl," I said. "She's an olive python, and she and I are in the only place in the world where you can find a snake like this. This one is about five feet long, but the species can grow to more than twice that length—they're *big* snakes. This one probably eats ducks and other water birds, small- to medium-sized mammals like rodents and wallabies, and even the occasional reptile. She's a crafty hunter who can catch prey in water or on land. She may look intimidating, but this snake poses absolutely no threat to people. She's not venomous, and she's not aggressive. Look at what a sweetheart she's being for me, and we only just met. I just found her and picked her up, and she's content to hang. It's a tragedy that olive pythons like this are often victims of mistaken identity—to the untrained eye, they look an awful lot like the venomous king brown snake, and many people kill them on sight."

As I wrapped up my summary, the python started unwinding, looking to move her head farther up my arm. Time to let her go. I packed up my gear, labeled the tape, and added it to the growing collection I had in a box on the backseat.

Much as I loved the outback, it was time to head back to school and my exams. I eased back onto the pavement and in a few miles turned onto the wide-open, pitch-dark highway that would return me to the east coast and civilization.

After putting more than five thousand miles on my rental and using it as my ride, my hotel, my production studio, and occasionally my creature keeper, I returned the filthy, beat-up vehicle in Darwin, then flew back to Sydney to take my final exams. A week later, I was on a flight home, a box full of videotapes in my carry-on and a host of first and once-in-a-lifetime experiences under my belt.

I wasn't sure what I was going to do next, but my time in Australia had shifted my perspective. My road trip had given me confidence and made me hungry to see more of the world and its wildlife. The travel bug inside me was gnawing away, eager for the next opportunity.

2

Tanzania

After my semester in Australia, I sifted through the University of Colorado Boulder's semester abroad options until I found a program in what sounded like the next most exotic place in the world: Tanzania. A few months later, I arrived in the regional capital of Arusha, ready to dive into a four-month wildlife ecology and conservation program.

For me, going out on a safari in Africa for the first time felt like being turned loose in a world that existed only in fiction or movies—like landing smack in the middle of *The Lion King*. There I was in Tarangire National Park at dawn, riding in the back of a Range Rover and trying to use the few Swahili phrases I'd learned with a guide who spoke little English. My digital camera dangled on a wrist strap, and my camcorder hung from my pinkie. No matter that my entire collection of AV equipment was budget basic: I was prepared to document the world in photo *and* video.

The scenery was everything I'd imagined Africa would be—open plains, wide grasslands, brushy vegetation, and a landscape punctuated by baobab trees, with their barrel-shaped trunks crowned by angular, nearly bare branches. These trees can live more than a thousand years, and their massive trunks (so big that people have carved out shelters in them) can store tens of thousands of gallons of water in the dry season. Because they're a source of water when it's scarce, baobabs have become the center of entire ecosystems. Insects, birds, snakes, small mammals, primates, and elephants are just a few of the creatures that rely on this "tree of life" to get through the dry season. If you're hoping to spot wildlife on an African safari, these trees are a great place to start looking.

Over the years I've been lucky enough to travel with some incredible, intrepid, and knowledgeable guides. This particular guide, though, seemed like he was none of those things. From the moment he pointed out a "hyena" up ahead that was clearly just a big rock with a mottled pattern, I figured I was on my own for spotting. Turns out, expertise wasn't necessary to see what I'd come for.

This was the beginning of the wet season, so the vegetation was getting a little green, and when I spied a group of black-and-white-striped bodies out on those plains, I knew we were in for an amazing day. At first I thought we were nearing just a few zebras, but there turned out to be hundreds of them. When we stopped to take pictures, I switched back and forth between my two cameras, narrating for video and taking still shots.

I was in video mode the first time one of the zebras, the one closest to us, opened his mouth and started to . . . bark? laugh? hiccup? cry for help? I wasn't sure what the hell he was doing. As a newbie to zebra sounds, I guess I'd been expecting the kind of sound a horse makes—a whinny, maybe. Or a neigh. A snort. But this guy stretched his neck forward, opened his mouth wide, curled his top lip just enough that I could see some teeth, and started making a high-pitched, stuttered, coughing sound. His whole body seemed to be involved. I didn't know whether to laugh or take cover or get ready to resuscitate him.

"Is he sick?" I asked my guide, without taking my eyes off the zebra.

"Oh no," he replied. That kind of answer is a little problematic. Even with my limited travel experience, I knew that a generic *no* to a question asked in English might mean *no*, but it might also mean *I have no idea what you're saying.*

I rummaged around among the Swahili words I'd learned and landed on the only other one that mattered to me at that moment.

"*Hasira?*" Angry?

"No, no," the guide answered, shaking his head.

A moment later another zebra in the herd answered my question with a similar call, and then a third chimed in. Turns out that this strange, strained sound is just run-of-the-mill zebra talk. I'd like to think that in the years since then, I've gotten good at mimicking a lot of animal calls, but zebra-speak remains way beyond my skills.

Thirty minutes into the trip we approached a wide, low hill with a worn path that led up over its crest. It was still early, and the sun cut across the hill and shone into my eyes. I blinked a couple times to be sure I was seeing what I thought I was seeing. Walking up the hill, single file, each equidistant from the next, was a herd of giraffes. They were cruising along on a majestic morning parade. The scene was so beautiful it looked staged, but only Mother Nature could stage something that spectacular.

When you see giraffes at a distance in the wild, the first thing you notice is how gracefully they glide along—all legs and necks. Their bodies are shaped like one big taper, from the tops of their heads to the bottoms of their tails, and at a walk they move both right legs together, then both lefts. The gentle, loping gait is mesmerizing to watch. I sat with my mouth open for a minute before swinging my camcorder into position to film the show and wing a narrative for it.

"This is one of the most gorgeous scenes in the African wild," I began. "The first people to try to classify these creatures seem to have struggled with what they were, ultimately landing on the species name *camelopardalis.* 'Camel leopard.' These majestic animals look like they're hardly moving this morning, but once they get going, even at a casual trot giraffes can move at twenty to twenty-five miles an hour. And if they feel threatened? Thirty miles per hour or more.

"Speed is not the giraffe's only defense. They may look spindly and vulnerable at a distance, but a giraffe is a fierce fighter when it needs to be. When the only animal that dares to prey on an adult—the lion—attacks, a well-planted kick from those powerful hooves can be deadly. That's why, for the most part, these giraffes have the run of sub-Saharan Africa. They go where they like, do what they want, and fear almost nothing."

I dropped the camcorder and started taking pictures, capturing as many as I could before the last of the giraffes cleared the rise and moved out of sight.

As we drove away, I spotted a brown snake eagle on a low, bare tree branch and motioned for the guide to stop. Flipping the camcorder up again, I talked while I admired the big tobacco-colored eagle with the hard-looking yellow eyes.

When we think of predators in the African wild, usually lions, leopards, and hyenas come to mind, but when you get right down to it, the snake eagle is as hard-core as anything on the continent. It may look like other raptors, but this bird has a special skill set. The snake eagle doesn't just eat snakes; it eats venomous snakes. It spots its quarry, then swoops in and grabs it, relying on the extra-thick scales that cover its feet and legs to buy it a few seconds before the snake can attempt a bite. Even as it soars into the air with its prize, this bird protects itself from bites and venom in the most brutal way possible: it uses one powerful talon to shear the snake's head off and drop it to the ground. Once that nasty job is done, the snake eagle makes a quick meal of what's left—usually swallowing the body of the snake whole—often while still on the wing.

That is one big, bad bird.

I swung the camera down and caught a movement in my peripheral vision. A hundred yards behind us, an elephant stepped out from a thicket and onto the road. It was a massive bull, wider and taller than the Range Rover, with a single tusk. He stopped moving and stood staring at us, and I couldn't believe my luck as I started snapping pictures. A full-on view! The elephant took a few lumbering steps forward and lifted his huge ears, flapping them slowly back and forth. Elephants do that to cool off, but there was nothing casual about this move. This guy was trying to get big and, man, was he pulling it off.

I was beside myself with excitement. Without looking away, I started filming. Behind me, I heard my guide mutter under his breath, and then I felt the truck slip into gear. At that moment, the bull's walk turned into a trot and he started making a low, ground-shaking growling sound. The truck lurched forward. I was too caught up in what I was getting on my camera to think about being in danger and shouted, *"Stop!"* but we kept picking up speed. I said it again in Swahili: *"Kouacha!"* Dude, *Kouacha!* No response. The guide was hauling ass, the bull was giving chase, and there was nothing I could do but look back at the charging behemoth and keep filming.

When the bull ceased chasing us, the guide slowed to a stop, then turned around and looked at me like he was seeing me for the first time—and realizing I was out of my mind. The bull could have stomped us and our vehicle to a pulp if he'd caught us—and by the looks of him, he'd been in the mood to do just that. I realized that day that there are more important qualifications in a safari driver than the ability to tell a hyena from a rock—like making sure your passenger lives to tell the tale.

It had been a peaceful day until we'd met the bull, but he'd changed the whole vibe. In the few minutes we'd interacted, he'd vividly, forcefully reminded me of the order of things in his world. "You're in Tanzania now," he seemed to say, "and this is MY territory."

Houseguest from Hell

I try to be a considerate traveler, to be respectful of all cultures, and to learn something from everyone I meet along the way. Despite my best intentions, though, I suspect the family that had the mixed fortune of getting me as their visiting student probably doesn't look back fondly on my stay.

After arriving in Arusha, my classmates and I moved on to Bangata, a small town of about seven thousand people in northern Tanzania. Each student was assigned to the family who would host them for a few weeks. Some of the families gave their students more responsibilities than others. A couple of my peers even ended up cooking and cleaning around the clock. I got lucky. My family was composed of a grandmother, her daughter, and her three kids. There were two boys, one slightly older than me, the other younger, and a three-year-old girl named Clara. The grandmother was nurturing and kind, and she took care of the children and the house. She also took care of me and didn't make me do any chores—very much like my own grandmother.

The living quarters were spartan. The house was a cinder-block rectangle with metal sheeting covering the exterior, an iron gate for a door, and windows with mesh screens but no glass. We had limited electricity and no running water inside. The water source was a curved metal pipe coming out of the ground in the backyard, operated via the spigot on its end. We drew the water into buckets and carried it inside to bathe and cook. Locals who had grown up drinking there had the digestive flora to handle it just fine, but I had to drop iodine tablets into my glass to keep from getting sick.

The kitchen was a separate hut constructed from a haphazard mix of clay, brick, and metal sheets. The heat source was an open wood-burning fire that was kept going day and night, with a couple of iron pots placed directly on the fire. Someone was always tending the fire, and a pot of something was always cooking. Most of the time it was a carb source, such as rice or *ugali*, a corn-based starchy substance that has the consistency of puffy Styrofoam mixed with mashed potatoes. It tastes as bland as it sounds, but it keeps you from feeling hungry.

All the beds in my family's house were raised off the dirt floor, which was a plus. Many people in that part of the world sleep on mats on the floor, risking encounters with the scorpions and venomous snakes that can easily make their way into the houses. Elevating the bed off the floor even a foot makes you ten times safer. The bathroom was a separate structure about twenty feet from the house, and the "toilet" was a hole in the ground, as are most toilets in that part of the world.

Our teacher told us from the beginning that as per the local culture, we'd be associated with who we hung out with. If you hung out with the women, they'd think you were feminine. If you hung out with a leader, they'd associate you with leadership. If you hung out with just the other students, you'd remain an outsider. Looking back on my time there, I realize that my early choices—innocent as they were—set up my host family to see me in a questionable light. I love kids and am playful by nature, so I started almost every day by horsing around with little Clara and the other small children who lived near us. I'd race them, wrestle with them, chase them around, and toss Clara up in the air and catch her—which made her squeal with laughter every time. When I wasn't playing with the kids, I spent a lot of my time out looking for reptiles, many of which were feared by the locals. After a few days, I'm pretty sure the people of Bangata had me pegged as a giant tree-climbing, rock-flipping American man-baby.

Not exactly the image I'd hoped to project. Unfortunately, it gets worse.

When I realized how fearful the local kids were of some of the harmless wildlife in their environment, I set up a two-pronged plan to teach them about it. First, I did some hands-on stuff, showing them that the creatures they'd been told were dangerous were safe to get close to and even handle if they use proper technique. Second, I started making short videos of local wildlife, narrating the facts about each creature's history and dangers. I would eventually translate my narratives into Swahili, and they'd be my big independent project for the semester.

I thought I was working for a noble cause. I started by trying to save the reputation of the much-maligned chameleon. Maybe because they look so exotic, chameleons are the focus of a lot of fear and superstition in much of Africa. The family I stayed with believed they were venomous, and legends about them range from suggesting that they control the rain to believing they can cause a miscarriage.

I wanted to show the kids that these creatures are harmless, so I caught a chameleon in a tree. Since Clara was my favorite, I took him over to her to show her. Her eyes got huge; then she jumped back, screamed, and ran away. That was one time I got the evil eye from the sweet grandmother. Rather than bring the chameleon any closer to the house, I moved a little farther away and filmed a short video with him in which I explained that these beautiful, colorful creatures are neither venomous nor dangerous. When I was done, I put the lizard back exactly where I had found him in the tree, keeping my disruption of his day to a minimum.

A couple days later, I walked back to my host family's house after class to find the chameleon's tree gone, chopped down so only a low stump remained.

There's a lesson here, one it took me some time to learn. Sometimes it's better to offer education about wildlife in small steps (rather than, say, taking the chameleon straight to the baby). Not only had I upset my host family, I'd made life worse for the creature I'd thought I was helping. I still feel bad that I unintentionally screwed that chameleon over and cost him his home.

The next step in making myself the houseguest from hell was the result of a mistake I'll never make again: failing to purify water from a questionable source before drinking it. If you've never had dysentery (and I hope you haven't), it basically boils down to having a case of diarrhea that is so horrific, painful, and unending you wish you could hurry up and die.

I carelessly drank the unfiltered "tap" water one day at dinner, started getting terrible cramps by morning, and went downhill from there. It is a challenge to significantly foul a hot outhouse like my host family had, but as I sat in there, doubled over and moaning, sunlight streaming through the cracks in the walls and flies lighting on me like I was already decomposing, I pulled it off. I stepped outside to find the kids who loved playing with me every morning watching from a distance, looking concerned. I was too damn sick to be embarrassed or care what anybody thought. I summoned every bit of strength I had left, oriented myself toward the school building—the only place I knew of that had air-conditioning and clean running water—and started walking.

There was one guest room in the school, with a single mattress, reserved for visiting teachers and honored guests. My semester leader took pity on me and let me stay there. While I was in residence, I destroyed the men's bathroom first, then moved on to the women's (the use of which was a first for me). I had never been so sick in my entire life, and after hours of relentless misery, I started to think I might actually not survive.

Finally, the leader tracked down an antibiotic, and after the first couple doses I was able to sleep, then drink, then eat. I was going to live.

I did what I could to clean up the disaster I'd made of the school's restrooms, showered, and walked back to my host family's house. Clara came running, and I tossed her high in the air while she squealed, *"Tena! Tena! Tena!"* "Again! Again! Again!"

As a veterinarian, I often see animals who are desperate to tap out. When they're sick or injured, they want nothing to do with the animal hospital, the exam table, or me. Thanks to my merciless bout of dysentery during my semester abroad in Tanzania, I know just how that feels.

Grumpy, Grumpy Hippo

Finding yourself between a hippo and water can be a death sentence—and that's exactly where I ended up when my semester abroad group visited Serengeti National Park. We'd been divided into groups to study indigenous species, and I was in the group devoted to what is one of the most temperamental animals of the Serengeti: the mighty hippopotamus.

Camping was amazing. At night, we could hear hyenas laughing and lions roaring. Sometimes baboons would come around when we were cooking, but they kept a respectful distance. One night a giant bushpig was less polite, racing through the campsite. He slit open a tent with his tusk, stole my classmate's midnight snack, and dashed out of sight. Mercifully, the only casualty was the tent.

By day I spent my time studying hippo behavior, which is surprisingly deceptive. At first glance, these animals look like big ol' lumps in the water—fat, lazy, and vaguely friendly. Fact check: Fat? Yes. Lazy? Sometimes. Friendly? Hell no.

Hippos are unpredictable, can be highly aggressive, and are the deadliest mammals in Africa. Not only are they a threat to other wildlife; they're a huge threat to humans, killing on average more than five hundred each year. In fact, other than venomous snakes and mosquitoes, they kill more people than any other creature in Africa. In a single incident in Niger, an unprovoked hippo attacked a boat and killed thirteen people. His motivation probably had to do with real estate. Hippos are deeply possessive of their watering holes, and when they perceive a threat to that territory (all too often from a fisherman), they can go berserk—flipping boats and tearing people to pieces. They've even been known to eat their conquests, which is especially terrifying because *hippos are herbivores*. Surprise: Mother Nature doesn't always go by the book.

In summary: Hippos are scary and should be regarded with

caution and respect, from a distance. Even a guy like me, who was too busy taking pictures to be alarmed at being charged by an elephant, knew better than to mess with these guys.

Our time observing them had reinforced my desire to keep a healthy distance. The hippos were constantly, aggressively claiming territory. They yawn—not like "I'm tired"; like "Look at my teeth." They grunt. They lunge. They stake out their space by fanning, which means they take a massive dump and then use their tail to spread the feces and odor—thus informing all other hippos to stay away in a ridiculous display of a "This is mine" mentality.

We were wrapping up our fieldwork one day when I walked to a small creek to relieve myself before packing up the truck. The creek bed was at the base of a ravine, with high rock-and-dirt walls along the sides. Though water sometimes raged to its top, on this day it was just a stream, barely a foot deep. Seeing a perfect environment to spot snakes and small crocodiles, I walked along the bed for what I figured was a great herping opportunity.

I rounded a bend and stopped dead. Not thirty feet in front of me was an adult male hippo staring back at me, the stranger on his turf.

I was shocked to see him, but he'd obviously been expecting me. Whether he'd heard me or smelled me (or both), he was squared up in my direction—waiting.

A robust male hippo can weigh five thousand pounds, with a bulky body as long as fourteen feet perched on short, stumpy legs. He has wicked teeth—his lower canines (tusks) can be as long as a foot and a half—so you know at first sight that he's deadly. Still, if you're looking him over and mentally calculating the weight, the girth, the long days spent half-submerged in rivers and ponds, you'll probably conclude that this is a slow beast. You might figure you could outrun him; no problem.

Thank God I knew a little about hippos. An average, healthy human runner moves along at between ten and fifteen miles per hour, maybe twenty in top shape and full panic. But a charging hippo can easily hit twenty-five miles per hour, and probably thirty. If I ran and he chased, I'd likely wind up a dead man.

I stood frozen, cursing the high, rocky walls around me and regretting every choice I'd made that day that had brought me to this moment. I should have been on the antelope team. I should have stayed out of the ravine. I should have peed and headed straight back to the truck.

The hippo made a huffing, grunting noise. You know the sound your dad makes when he's about to blow a gasket? Like that times a hundred.

Suddenly, the sky that had been comfortably overcast started looking darkly ominous. My heart was slamming in my chest as I weighed my options. Run? No. Climb? Too steep. Get in the face of the deadliest herbivore on the planet and see if I can scare him away? No way. I felt a rush of warmth to my extremities— adrenaline kicking in and prepping me for fight or flight. I may not have been sure just what the best action for me was in that moment, but I was damn certain this was a "flight" situation, not a "fight" opportunity.

The hippo seemed pretty clear on how *he* was going to handle the situation. He tucked his head, lifted his front right foot, and began to scrape the creek bed with it, kicking back dirt. It was like a bull in a cartoon that's getting ready to charge, only so not funny.

I had to get away from the water. His water. Keeping my head down, avoiding eye contact but with my peripherals focused on the hippo, I inched back to the ravine wall. I tried to look casual, neutral, like part of the scenery. Just a harmless critter getting out of the way. When I was flush with the edge, I started slowly creeping backward in the direction of the bend I'd come around. The hippo watched, but he didn't move.

It took me about a heart-pounding minute to get around the corner, out of his sight line—probably the longest minute of my life. I listened for half a second, and when the hippo didn't imme-diately come thundering my way, I ran, far and fast, not stopping to look back until I was clear of the ravine, the creek, and any other water.

I've intentionally put myself in harm's way plenty of times, especially when I was a young, overeager student and newbie traveler. But my hippo encounter wasn't trouble I went looking for. I was minding my own business, walking around the African bush, enjoying the scenery. The incident was a powerful reminder that when you're out in the wild, anything can happen.

Maasai Welcome

In the second half of my semester in Tanzania, I had a not-in-Kansas-anymore experience unlike any other. I spent a week in the home of a Maasai family in a portion of the Great Rift Valley, which runs along northern Tanzania and southern Kenya. The meager creature comforts of my homestay in Bangata seemed opulent when I arrived in the valley, where there was no electricity or running water. Water had to be fetched from a nearby river and carried in buckets, a task delegated to the tribeswomen. The homes were made of mud, sticks, and grass and looked like large domed tepees with flattish roofs. Cot-like beds were laid out around the periphery inside the structure. Mine was the size of a coffee table, about four and a half feet long and two feet wide. I'm six foot two, so in order to stay on it every night, I had to curl up in a fetal position.

I tried to take the hardship in stride. After all, I was staying with people who are defined the world over by their strength and resilience. Over the last century and a half, the Maasai have endured ruinous droughts, epidemic diseases that wiped out half their population and half their livestock, and endless appropriations by the British and the Kenyan governments of the land that was once theirs to roam. Through all of it they have stood tall and proud, draped in bright red, respected, charismatic, and independent.

I had the honor of being placed with the chief and his family. He had a wife and a son who was about my age. Upon arrival, I was given the traditional Maasai daily wardrobe, which consisted of a checked cloth for my outer garment, a chest piece, several handmade bracelets, and a herding staff. This was a moment of mixed emotions. Part of me was thrilled, even proud, to have the privilege of dressing like one of these great, iconic tribesmen. But the rest of me felt unworthy of the honor. I was a kid who'd grown up with a roof over my head, dinner on the table each night, cable TV, good schools, and clean water every time I turned on the tap. By comparison, the Maasai people are among the world's most notorious warriors. Everything about their environment challenges them—harsh land, harsh sun, even the harshly alkaline water of Lake Natron. Despite it all, they seem indomitable.

The chief's wife was strikingly beautiful, with wide, dark eyes and pronounced cheekbones. She had a quintessentially Maasai beauty, and she dressed in traditional Maasai colors, deep reds and royal blues, and wore large hoop earrings and strands of colorful, intricately woven beads.

I'll never forget her name, because for the life of her, she couldn't pronounce mine. She couldn't enunciate the *v*. It became like a comedy routine. She would mispronounce my name, calling me "Effen." I would slowly correct her: "*Ev*-an." Then she would smile and say, "Ebben."

Since she couldn't quite pronounce my name, I made a special effort to get hers right, something that became an inside joke between us. It was, spelled phonetically to the best of my ability, Nor-deh-kee-teh-wee-pee. I'm sure that spelling is plus or minus a few letters.

The Maasai are a nomadic, self-sufficient people, so livestock is a key part of their livelihood. There were animals everywhere. Most of them, including chickens and goats, were part of the food supply for eggs, milk, or meat. The house was basically surrounded by a goat farm. All night long, I'd hear them grunting and farting just inches away from me. Occasionally, they'd even nudge me. I got used to the smell of them after a couple days, but not to the constant, booming sounds of their flatulence.

Although the chickens and goats are utilitarian, Maasai life revolves around their cattle. The Maasai believe that when the earth and sky split, centuries ago, their rain god left the cattle for their use. The young men are taught to protect the family's cattle at all costs.

My days with the tribe were long and full. I woke before sunrise to the sounds of crowing roosters and the family gathered around the fire, talking and preparing the morning meal. I'd unfold myself from my balled-up sleeping position, put on my tribal costume, and be off and running to herd the goats and work alongside the tribesmen.

In my free time, I roamed the nearby desert, looking for snakes and lizards. Like my hosts in Bangata, the Maasai tribe believed every reptile was venomous. Most are not, but I could understand the cultural trend toward steering clear of all of them, since the few truly venomous native snakes in the area include black mambas, puff adders, boomslangs, and massive spitting cobras. All creatures most people are wise to avoid confrontation with.

I wasn't about to try to convert my hosts' feelings about snakes when they were rooted in reasonable caution, but there were no venomous lizards in that environment. It seemed pretty unfair to paint the lowly gecko with the same brush as the black mamba.

I decided to teach my Maasai brother and his friends that most of these reptiles can't hurt you. I caught a small gecko, and with a crowd looking on, I let it bite my top lip. It clamped on pretty hard, and there was an audible gasp from the dozen or so kids (and the adults) watching. The bite was a little uncomfortable but not at all dangerous, so I let the gecko hang there by its jaws. Nobody screamed or ran away, which I thought was progress after the chameleon debacle with Clara.

In my mind, that bite was a small price to pay in order to show my new friends that the lizards they saw every day and had been taught to fear were harmless. Unfortunately, judging by the stares I got and the wide berth I was given after my demonstration, I don't think I changed many minds about the geckos. Instead, I may have set myself further apart as an outsider.

On the second day of my stay, the chief hosted a party in my honor and that of another student staying with a tribe family. There was a significant language barrier between me and the tribe—they spoke neither English nor Swahili—but I somehow got the idea that they were going to barbecue a goat. I was grateful. I was also completely naïve about the variety of ways a goat might be prepared and served at a party in one's honor. I was about to face the single biggest trial of my manners, and of my gag reflex, in my entire life.

Turns out that for this ceremony the goat isn't prepared ahead of time. The killing is part of the event. For our party, two tribesmen suffocated the goat. The poor creature grunted and flailed, trying fruitlessly to escape while we all watched. I sat silently, focused on being respectful of my hosts and their culture, trying to keep my expression neutral.

Once the goat was dead, the tribesmen laid it on its back and cut the abdomen open. As soon as an animal dies from asphyxiation, large blood clots begin forming in the major vessels and the heart. I would not have noticed what was happening to the dead goat's blood, but one of the men reached his bare hand inside the carcass and pulled out several clots. He then turned to present them to me. The guest of honor.

To eat.

This was a gift, and it would have been insulting for me to reject it. This was not my choice. Not my goat. It was also not my moment to distance myself from my hosts and offend them. I slurped a blood clot from the tribesman's hand and swallowed, concentrating on nothing but getting the warm blob down. One of my classmates was next, and he, too, accepted a clot with a pained, focused expression and nodded his thanks.

Okay, I thought, *initiation over.* We had passed.

Not so fast. A moment later one of the tribesmen reached into the carcass, fished around the back of the abdomen with his knife, and extricated a single kidney. He held the dull pink organ aloft, then smoothly cut a slice from it and extended it to me.

As the guest of the chief, it turned out, I would be the only one receiving this gift from the slaughter. And so I accepted it, thinking of how my mom always told me to mind my manners at the table, and began chewing the still warm, flavorless tribute.

I nodded to the tribesmen, then to the chief. *Now* I had passed.

After that the goat was butchered, barbecued over an open fire, and shared with the entire tribe. Parts unsuitable for barbecuing were taken to a community kitchen and stewed. The hide would be tanned and used for clothing, bags, and drum skins; and the bones would be used in traditional medicine or boiled to make stock. Nothing would be wasted.

For the Maasai, offering up that goat was a significant gesture that said, "Thank you for staying with us; we welcome you as our guest." It was their way of showing gratitude to me for experiencing their culture. To an American kid, it was a dark ritual, but it was also a sincere one, and when I look back on that experience I remember it with gratitude to the people who welcomed me, dressed me in their traditional clothes, fed me their most choice food, and allowed me to feel like a part of an entirely different world for a few humbling, thought-provoking, unforgettable days.

The Elephant Hour

For the last weeks of our semester in Tanzania, each student got to pursue an independent project. I wanted to wander instead of staying in one place, so I plotted out bus routes, arranged rides with other students, and set out to add to my growing repertoire of animal education videos.

I spent those weeks on the road filming lizards, crocodiles, snakes, and the big and small mammals and birds of the savannah, but there is one animal that lives large in my memories. I came to think of an elephant named Ncarsis as a friend.

I was camping at Ndarakwai, a private ranch and wildlife sanctuary in Kilimanjaro, hoping for some snake sightings. The eleven-thousand-acre reserve is home to three different ecosystems—savannah, grasslands, and woodlands—as well as to puff adders, spitting cobras, and the extremely venomous black mambas. As highly toxic as black mambas are, they're even more dangerous than most venomous snakes because in some cases they can be extremely aggressive without any prompting.

Besides the snakes I was looking for, elephants, impalas, antelopes, and troops of baboons roamed around the sprawling preserve. The camping area was a flat piece of barren land surrounded by a wooden slat fence. The fence was something of a formality to deter large animals, but smaller ones could easily slip through the gaps in search of food. We slept in tents, and there were fire pits nearby for cooking our nightly meal of rice and beans.

I'd been told that an eight-year-old female elephant lived on the grounds and that we might see her around. She'd been orphaned as a baby and rescued by the reserve, so she was wild but habituated to people. Her name was Ncarsis. Late one afternoon, I was hanging out with a classmate near the fence when a juvenile elephant walked up and began scoping us out. It had to be her. Though not fully developed, she stood about six feet tall and weighed at least six thousand pounds.

I wasn't sure what to expect. I'd never interacted with an elephant (unless you count being chased by one on safari). This one, though, didn't seem to be looking for a fight. She stopped a few feet from the fence, raised her trunk, and sniffed around. I stood stock-still, eyes averted and head down, hoping I wouldn't scare her away.

She inched forward. Then she pointed her trunk directly at me. She was so close I could clearly see the two nostrils at the end of her trunk. She seemed to be reaching for me, so I took one cautious step closer, then another.

The first time I encounter any animal, I want to connect (or not) on their terms. I waited before taking one more step and putting myself close enough that she could touch me. The trunk came closer, and she smelled my hand, then my arm. She rubbed her trunk against the back of my neck and pushed it through my hair.

I was in a weird kind of elephant-induced ecstasy, thinking, *She LIKES me!* and trying not to mess it up. After a few minutes, she dropped her trunk, inched all the way up to the fence, and stood waiting. I took her posture to mean it was my turn, and I gently reached out to pet her trunk. I knew that any sudden moves or noises would freak her out, so I kept my voice low and my movements slow and easy. Her skin was rough and leathery, covered in coarse, whisker-like hairs that stood straight out, like pins along her skin.

I talked to her for a while, and she casually flapped her enormous ears, occasionally reaching out to poke me with her trunk. The whole encounter lasted about a half hour, and then my new friend turned and wandered back into the bush.

I doubted I'd ever see Ncarsis again. The reserve is massive, and she had the run of the place. The next evening, though, she came back and pointed at me again. I made my way to the fence and let her sniff me and check my pockets. I didn't have anything for her, but she didn't seem to care.

On day three, I walked right up and called her "Sweetheart." We were pals. There was no question. For a week and a half I camped at Ndarakwai, and every single day after that first encounter, Ncarsis stopped by to hang out with me.

Back home, if anyone had told me I might have that experience, I would have rowed a boat to Africa and stood by that fence for a month. And yet, it had happened by chance. Awesome, perfect, and totally unexpected. If I'd had any remaining doubts about the career I wanted to pursue and the animals that made it my calling, they were long gone by the time I boarded my flight back to Colorado.

PART TWO

✧

Welcome to the Jungle

3

Ecuador

If you're a film buff, you've got to see *Citizen Kane*. If you're an architect, you'll eventually find your way to a Frank Lloyd Wright house. And if you're an evolutionary biology student, your professional mecca is the Galápagos Islands, the volcanic archipelago sprinkled along the equator hundreds of miles off the South American coast and made world-famous by Charles Darwin and the tortoise Lonesome George.

Traveling to Ecuador between college and veterinary school gave me a chance to check off two of the biggest items on my travel and wildlife bucket list: making my first trek into the Amazon (a.k.a. the Ultimate Jungle I'd Been Dying to See Since I Was Four) and visiting the Galápagos Islands. I was lucky enough to be sharing the experience with one of my best friends in the world, Tim Diggs. The two of us grew up together in Overland Park, Kansas, and though our adult lives have taken us on different paths, we still hang out and travel together when we can.

I'd read about Darwin's finches, about his notebooks, and about the studies he conducted that defined evolution as we still understand it today. Arriving in the place where it all happened

felt like making a pilgrimage. The way these islands are protected suggests that the whole world agrees they're something
sacred. Ninety-seven percent of the land is national park, and
this isolated region teems with rare and unique wildlife. The
islands are home to a higher percentage of endemic species (animals and plants not found anywhere else) than almost any place
in the world, with 97 percent of the local reptiles, 80 percent of
the land birds, and 20 percent of the marine species living only
on or around the islands. Evolutionary isolation has fostered some
highly unusual creatures here, including the pink land iguana,
the Galápagos penguin (the only penguin that lives in the tropics),
the blue-footed booby, and the one and only Galápagos batfish. (If
you've never seen one of these in the flesh or in a photo, imagine
an underwater bat crossed with a ray, with its lips painted ruby
red. Add some whiskers and ask it to scowl like Grumpy Cat and
you've got yourself a batfish.) Sooo neato—and so weird.

Despite their fame and the fantastical nature of some of these
species, I was excited to study something much, *much* bigger. As
soon we arrived on Santa Cruz Island, I hopped a water taxi to a
tortoise sanctuary. I'd imagined big dinosaurs romping around,
eating grass, craning their necks to see who'd arrived all the way
from Colorado to get a look at them. First impression in real life:
super-sleepy tortoises, chilling in the mud. It might have been
uneventful encountering them in their own environment, except
for the fact that they were *so* much bigger than I'd expected. I'd
seen pictures. Yeah, yeah—big. But the first thing I thought of
when I spied one in person was a VW bug. The carapace (the top
half of a turtle or tortoise's shell) is so massive, it's a miracle of
nature that any creature can haul it around.

Because the Galápagos have a lot of rules about what you can
and can't touch for the protection of the animals and the environment, I expected a hands-off day out among the tortoises. What
I forgot in those plans was one of Darwin's observations about
island wildlife—that many of these species, isolated and unhab-

ituated to predators, are surprisingly docile. Some people call it "island tame." Evolutionarily, these animals haven't developed adaptations to guard against what less-isolated species perceive as stranger danger. Basically, since they haven't had much reason to expect people or other large, predatory animals to harm them over the course of thousands of years of evolution, they don't worry about it.

So as I sat on a rock, watching the massive tortoises, one of these slooooowww-moving giants turned my way and started inching closer. I didn't move toward him, but I didn't back away. I sat still, admiring his incredible size, his sleepy eyes, and his hefty legs. I was mesmerized by the way he hauled each foot forward, top down, then righted it in front of him. It looked like a ridiculously labor-intensive way to get from point A to point B. I thought he'd stop moving or turn another way, but after what seemed like hours, his sluggish, lumbering trek put him right at my feet. I was point B. He pushed his head toward me, first just a little, and then—wow—until he was almost touching me, his neck extended at least a foot. Then he cocked his head, raised his neck a bit farther, and gazed at me eye to eye. His head was huge, his skin rough and grimy from the mud. His eyes looked ancient. It was like coming face-to-face with Yoda. I couldn't help thinking, *What does he know?*

I didn't want to presume, but everything about this tortoise's relaxed, leaning-in body language said it was okay to touch him. Animals are always honest about how they feel, and this guy seemed to feel like making friends. I cautiously stretched my hand out toward the top of his head. He had other ideas, gently bobbing so that my hand ended up under his chin. Then he lowered his neck just a little. It didn't take a mind reader to get the request. *Scratch, please?*

Not a problem. I would have been happy to sit there in the hot sun scratching his leathery skin indefinitely. I made a tentative rub against the bottom of the outstretched neck, and this great big guy leaned in. The only way he could have been clearer about how this was what he'd dragged himself over to me for would have been for him to say, "That's the spot." So I scratched.

When it became evident that my new friend wasn't going to wander off anytime soon, I took out my camera, trying to get both of us in the shot whenever possible. (I was way ahead of the curve on the "invention" of the selfie.) With tape rolling, I explained that the islands had once been covered with more than 250,000 of these primeval-looking creatures. When Darwin arrived, tortoises were a major food source for whalers, pirates, locals, and even the naturalist and his crew. The defenseless giants were easy to catch and easy to kill. Sailors swore their meat was a delicacy. Ships' crews not only slaughtered tortoises throughout the islands but also loaded them on ships alive so they'd have fresh meat when they needed it later on. It would take six men or more to carry a five-hundred-pound behemoth, but tortoises were a far more practical food source to take to sea than any mammal because they could survive for months without food or water.

By 1970, some of the islands had no tortoises left. In all, only around three thousand remained. That was the year Ecuador made capturing them or removing them from the Galápagos illegal.

Today, the longest-living terrestrial vertebrates in the world spend their days grazing and napping, protected throughout the islands, and their numbers are slowly climbing. At last count the population was approaching twenty thousand—a far cry from their once-abundant presence, but a step in the right direction.

Each time I pulled my hand back to adjust the camera or make a gesture, my new pal waved his head at me, craning a little farther my way. *Scratch!*

Even as it was happening, I knew this was an interaction I'd never forget. The thing about reptiles is that no matter how much you love them—and, man, I do love them—they're not cuddly. They don't have those kind of relationships, not even within their families. Nature programs mammals with systems that release endorphins to make them feel good when they're cuddling, or grooming, or having other affectionate interactions with their companions. This evolutionary adaptation benefits them by facilitating their being part of a family unit, which gives them better chances of survival in the wild. Reptiles just don't have that, because they are hatched or born prepared to survive independently, already hardwired with the instinct to survive. So I have to think that this guy simply had an itch and I'd happened along at the right time to help him out. No matter what the reason, I was grateful for the moment.

When I finished filming, I stowed my gear, then reached out to scratch my friend's chin one more time. He was sound asleep, his neck stretched out on the ground, his giant head extended between his broad front feet. It was a shockingly vulnerable position to fall asleep in, but this guy was island tame, and he looked like he believed that nothing in the world would ever want to hurt him.

See Sea Lions

Before I arrived, I shortsightedly pictured the Galápagos mostly in terms of their tortoises. But the highlight of my visit turned out to be the spectacular snorkeling and diving. To really see this place, you've got to get into (and out of) a boat. Tim and I made the biggest splurge of our trip (maybe of our lives up until that point) to book a live-aboard stay on a fourteen-person boat. Each day we went out to one or two different islands, and each island brought new surprises below the surface of the water. Hammerhead sharks beneath us. Tiny, brightly colored seahorses suspended in the water. Green turtles zipping past at speeds that defied everything I thought I knew about turtles.

And you know you're not in Kansas anymore when you dive under the water's surface and see a huge iguana swimming right beside you. These lizards are the only known marine iguanas in the world. Somewhere in their ancestry they developed a taste for seaweed, and in the absence of many natural predators on the land or in the water, they learned to swim. The water in the Galápagos stays in the seventies Fahrenheit most of the time, so these guys have to forage quickly before their body temperature drops so far that they get too sluggish to swim. When you see a wet iguana on the seashore in the Galápagos, chances are it's waiting for the sun to bring its body temperature back up and energize it again. This post-swim warming is the time when marine iguanas are most vulnerable, and the wild dogs introduced to the islands in the past century sometimes take advantage of that moment of weakness to prey on them.

The clear blue sea around the islands was the stage for some of the most amazing fish and reptile sightings of my life, but the creatures I will forever associate with my snorkeling days in the Galápagos are the sea lions. I had never interacted with marine mammals before, and they were about to give me a lesson in just how curious, quick, and quirky an animal can be.

The first time we saw them, Tim and I were snorkeling near a tiny, rocky outcrop of a small island. The group on our boat was only ten people total, so we had plenty of autonomy and no tight time constraints. Since Tim and I are both adventurous and strong swimmers, we typically tried to cover a lot of real estate on each snorkel. On this day, we swam around to the far side of the island and spotted a cave along the shore with a single stream of natural light breaking in through an opening somewhere overhead. The walls were steep, smooth stone, and the water was quiet inside. No way were we just going to swim on by.

Seconds after we entered the cave, two sea lions slipped in behind us. I'd thought *we* were swimming, but these creatures quickly made us feel about as agile in the water as a pair of plodding ogres. Ogres in boots.

Sea Lion One and Sea Lion Two swam circles around us, gliding forward and backward, diving, flipping, and rolling—a nonstop flow of movement. They were crazy fast, zipping just inches from us, doing their unique brand of underwater acrobatics. Each time one zoomed by me it came so close it almost touched me, missing by a millimeter. Tim and I kept looking from the sea lions to each other and giggling like little kids. If I'd been quick enough, I might have reached out to pat one, but I was too mesmerized to move. Twice, one of the swimmers stopped a couple feet from me and poked its head out of the water, giving me a good look at a face like an adorable puppy. A *giant* puppy. Galápagos sea lions are the smallest sea lion species, but a mature male can still grow to eight feet long and weigh over five hundred pounds. If it wanted to, any full-grown sea lion could take out even the biggest, sturdiest human in the water. But these animals were clearly not malicious. Once, a snout bumped my leg. On another pass, the sea lion . . . bit me? It could have shredded my leg, but instead it gave me a tap with an open jaw. This was play, pure and simple. It was a magical experience, especially because this extremely intelligent wild animal *chose* to interact with us. There were no treats or rewards involved, and force was definitely not an option. It reminded me that humans are not the only inquisitive species; animals can take an interest in us, too.

As far as Tim and I were concerned, there was nothing to do but enjoy the sea lion show. I would have given anything for a camera in that moment, but as I watched them, I realized that taking it in was enough. We waited until these guys had finished literally swimming circles around us. When they left the cave, we paddled out behind them and back to our boat. We were the last snorkelers to return that day, but also the ones with the best story.

Full-on Jungle

We have beautiful forests and amazing wildlife in the Midwest. But the jungle? The jungle is the jam, the ultimate habitat. I'd idealized it for as long as I could remember, and the name that occupied my childhood imagination and my grown-up travel dreams was *the Amazon*.

It took a flight, a bus, a ride in a truck bed, and finally a three-hour riverboat trip to get there. With each change of transportation mode, the landscape got more exotic. The Amazon is teeming with thousands of species on every acre, and even though you can't hear, smell, or see all of them, your senses can't ignore how incredibly *alive* the environment is. This was all the jungle fantasies of my childhood come to life. The lush green canopy nearly enclosing the road. The sounds of birds and insects buzzing all around me. Craning around the side of the truck, I saw a tamarin race across the road in front of the vehicle and then stop to stare, his wizened face surrounded by a shock of red fur that made him look like a tiny monkey Einstein. He hurried on into the jungle before I could even snap a picture. I had arrived.

The next amazing creature wasn't elusive at all. Above the road, a sloth lazed in a tree. I asked the driver to stop and got my camera out to document my first encounter with this amazing animal.

Sloths have a lot of trophies on the shelf: Slowest-Moving Mammal on the Planet. Lowest Metabolic Rate. Slowest Digestive Process. Lowest Body Temperature. They also have a highly unusual ability to let their body temperature rise and fall with their surroundings—like reptiles. Whether it's too hot or too cold, a sloth's temperature can shift several degrees with the weather, and the animal can remain alert (though not active) while riding out either extreme. Of course, to the casual observer, absolutely nothing changes when this happens, because either way the sloth barely moves.

This was a three-toed sloth—an even slower species than his two-toed cousin. His fur was tinged with green, courtesy of the algae that grows there and helps camouflage him in the canopy. His body hung motionless, but his head slowly swiveled almost all the way around so he could look right at me. Sloths can't move their eyes much, but they can rotate their heads nearly 270 degrees—like owls. It was all I could do to sit still and not start climbing up the tree for a closer look. Sloths like the one I was studying make their homes in the relative safety of the canopy (often a single tree), inching along, eating a diet of mostly leaves, and watching the world go by. Unless they're mating or raising babies, they're mostly loners, content to go about their business at a pace that looks like slow-motion capture.

Once a week, the sloth gets surprisingly fastidious (for a creature with algae growing on it) and makes a long and dangerous trek—all the way to the ground.

Under its tree, the sloth digs a hole, poops in it, and covers it over with dirt or leaves. The adage about not shitting where you eat weighs heavily on sloth life—because while most spend only a tiny fraction of their lives on the ground relieving themselves, an estimated half of them die there. They're too vulnerable, too slow, and too predictable for predators to resist. Jaguars, ocelots, foxes, eagles, and wild dogs all help themselves to the easy prey.

A lot of people wonder why the sloth is so slow, and the answer is a perfect example of the evolutionary process. The sloth's diet is composed almost entirely of a few kinds of leaves, all of which are nutritionally limited. Technically sloths are omnivores, but they're not hunters, so they generally fill up (literally—the body weight of a well-fed sloth at any given time is almost half partially digested food) on leaves alone. When your fuel is minimally nutritious in the extreme, your body has a choice to make: find a better diet or limit your expenditure of energy. Guess which way the sloth went?

I put my camera away and nodded to the guide, and we were on the road again.

When the road met the river, we transitioned to a twenty-foot flat-bottomed boat with a motor in the back and five rows of benches, each big enough for two people, three if you squeezed. From the dock we set out on a wide swath of the Amazon—the actual Amazon River! For the first hour, we cruised along quickly, taking in the scenery, grateful for the breeze, which cut the heat. After that, though, we turned, gliding into a tributary where the river narrowed by half, and soon by half again. We were fully in the jungle, with gorgeous greenery surrounding us on all sides. I thought, *This is my happy place.*

As we cruised along the river, our guide pointed out some of the spectacular wildlife: a family of tiny squirrel monkeys in a tree; a caiman partially submerged in the water. We heard a hair-raising screech and the guide spun around, following the sound, then pointed high in the canopy where a pair of bright blue-and-gold macaws perched above us.

As the water narrowed, he turned off the engine and pointed to the base of a tree abutting the river's edge. The entire thing was alive with giant ants, each nearly as long as my thumbnail. Sometimes Mother Nature is tricky when she makes things outsized. An extra-large creature might be a gentle giant, or it might be a danger to everything that passes its way. These ants belong in the second group—not just big but fierce. Besides being the biggest ants I'd ever seen in person, they were also the most dangerous. They're called bullet ants, and they earned their name because of the way it makes a person feel to get stung—like you've been shot. I started filming the ants, filling in a little info about one indigenous Amazon tribe where the initiation for a boy to become a man involves packing two gloves with these SOBs, putting them on, and letting the ants sting you.

Our guide was amused by my enthusiasm. "The jungle is full of surprises," he said. "Listen to this." He made a few loud claps, then looked at me and smiled.

What happened next remains one of the coolest things I've experienced in the wild, especially courtesy of an insect. Within a few seconds, we heard a loud, rhythmic pounding along the water's edge. Everyone on the boat started glancing around from the shore to each other and back. Something was coming.

"It is the warrior wasp," the guide said.

Eh? All eyes rolled in disbelief. What we were hearing was *big*, stomping through the undergrowth, and coming toward us. But the guide explained that somewhere along the way in its evolution, this particular species had learned that size equals might, and they'd decided to get in on it. When a warrior wasp perceives a threat, it pounds its abdomen, and all the wasps around it start to pound their abdomens too. *In sync.* The effect sounds remarkably like heavy footsteps in the jungle. *Stomp. Stomp. Stomp. Stomp.* It boggles the mind to try to figure out how that masterful adaptation happened. Even after you know where the noise is coming from, it's impossible not to worry that you're about to be attacked.

Constrictors Big and Bigger

A big part of the lure of Central and South American travel for me is the snakes, and this was never more true than during that first trip into the Amazon. I scanned every inch of land and water I passed over in Ecuador looking for them. Every branch, every ripple, every unexpected color or movement in the canopy, on the ground, or in the water caught my eye, and my mind jumped to *Snake?!*

The jungle didn't disappoint. On our first day, Tim and I went out in kayaks and spotted an Amazon boa in a tree above the water, three feet of neatly coiled predator draped over a single branch. I paddled close, stood up, and pulled him down with both hands, falling out of my boat in the process. He was snappy at first—opening his jaw wide and giving me an unobstructed view of his gnarly recurved fangs. Cautiously gripping him behind the head, I waited for the tantrum to play out. After a few seconds passed with no harm to him, he calmed down and let me wrap him around my arm. Tim filmed while I explained that an arboreal snake like the one I was holding spends its whole life in the trees. When it gets hungry, it lies in wait for a bird, lizard, or small mammal, strikes, and bites it with those inward-curving teeth; then the boa rolls its prey up into a tight ball and squeezes the life out of it.

Most people assume that constrictors kill by asphyxiation, but the snake I was holding was capable of squeezing its prey so tightly it could stop the flow of blood through the animal's veins. The cause of death is typically circulatory arrest. This may sound like a potato/potahto comparison, but it doesn't feel that way if you're the prey animal. The upside, if you can call it that, is that circulatory failure is a faster and less painful way to die. Suffocation takes more time and causes more suffering. To be honest, if I *had* to be killed by any predator in nature, I think a large constrictor would be my choice. Most other predators—including "cuddly" ones like sea lions, who use their razor teeth to shred prey they can't swallow whole (and alive) into large chunks—kill in a much more violent way. By comparison, being squeezed until you pass out (which will happen in a hurry) doesn't seem quite as bad.

Despite their deadly power, their impressive fangs, and the way they've been made symbols of danger in cultures around the world, these snakes pose very little threat to humans. Constrictors aren't venomous. Even if you piss one off and get bitten (which generally takes some serious and intentional provocation, since they don't seek out human interaction), that bite won't kill you, or even land you in the hospital. Unless you're small enough to be constricted and digested, you don't qualify as prey and are basically out of harm's way, even with one of these sitting on your lap. By the time I'd stopped talking, the boa on my arm wasn't interested in biting anymore. He was just hanging out, completely mellow. After we finished filming, I took him back to the base of the tree I'd pulled him from, and he glided straight back to the same branch to retake his position.

Handling a boa in the Amazon was a dream come true, but

the next day out on the river with a guide I spotted the *ultimate* South American constrictor: the mighty green anaconda. Scotland has the Loch Ness Monster, central Asia has the Yeti, and South America has the so-called giant anaconda. That snake is supposedly somewhere between 50 and 150 feet long, and sightings of it have been part of South American lore for hundreds of years. After seeing a green anaconda, a truly magnificently proportioned creature, I can understand how a casual observer might think he or she was encountering something mythical. They're almost too big to mentally process. To this day, I've never faced a bigger snake in the wild than the one that was draped over a clump of bushes along the edge of the water, part of her hanging so low it was submerged. Her coloring was a mottled green, and she was easily thirteen feet long, possibly more because she was loosely coiled in a couple places. She was at least nine inches in diameter and looked thicker in the middle. These snakes can grow to over 400 pounds, but this one looked to be somewhere between 180 and 200 pounds. Middling for an anaconda; gigantic for any other snake.

I asked the guide to get us closer, trusting it would take more than a couple passing boaters to startle the beast from her basking place. I wanted to put my hands on her, but decided to film her first in case she took off. Pulling out my video camera, I zoomed in on her head, explaining that I was just a few feet away from one of the largest snakes on the planet, and that based on the size, this was probably a female. In this species, the girls dwarf the boys, with females growing to twenty to thirty feet long and weighing as much as 550 pounds. Males rarely exceed ten feet—XS in anaconda sizes.

As we watched her soaking up the sun, it was hard to believe that a creature with so much heft could be a stealth predator, but when an anaconda gets hungry, she slips down into the water, submerging her whole body except her eyes and her nostrils, which are on the top of her head. There she lies in wait until something worth her trouble comes along. Mice and lizards won't fill up a snake this size. She'll eat small prey like fish and birds if they pass her way, but her preferred game includes bigger animals like wild pigs, capybaras, deer, caimans, and sometimes even jaguars. Yep, jaguars. Anacondas are their only natural enemies. Do you know how fast you have to move to strike a jaguar before it can get away? It basically has to happen in such a short span that the cat is already hit before it knows it's being attacked. It seemed impossible that a snake that size could pull this off, but I knew she had a secret weapon (beside the obvious ones of her teeth and her massiveness). A snake's body has more than ten times as many muscles as a human body, and a significant portion of those muscles are used to create mind-blowing strike speed. This is a new area of study (because it takes some seriously high-tech equipment to measure), but research shows a snake strike happens so fast it can occur *four times* in the blink of a human eye. One blink, four strikes. Step aside, jaguar. There's a faster predator in town.

Once a snake like the anaconda I was watching makes her move, she's all business. After she's killed her prey, the super-flexible ligaments around her jaw allow her to open wide and swallow it whole. (Snakes are not nibblers—they *always* consume their prey fully intact.) Following a big meal, she may not eat again for weeks. She can just soak up the sun and digest.

Tim and I spent a week in the Ecuadorian Amazon, and by the end of it I was convinced that even my wildest childhood dreams had sold the place short. I love Kansas, Colorado, and California; woods, mountains, and beaches. But ever since that first time exploring in Ecuador, I've known that there's something about the jungle that puts me in my element. I can feel it in the way the air fills my lungs, the way my ears buzz with the sounds of all the teeming life, how the environment simultaneously puts me at ease and heightens my attention. I've since found that this holds true in jungles all over the world, but that was the first time, the first jungle, and my first realization that even when you've traveled thousands of miles by plane, bus, truck, boat, and on foot, sometimes you still find yourself in a place that feels so right it must be home.

4

Panama

The Pan-American Highway is a thirty-thousand-mile network of roads that can take you the length of the American continents, from northernmost Alaska to southernmost Argentina. If
you have the time, money, energy, and nerve to navigate some of
the most treacherous highways on the planet, you can drive the
entire way—*except* for a single sixtyish-mile stretch that encompasses the mountainous rain forests of southern Panama and the
swamplands of its Colombian border. That place, known as the
Darién Gap (the name also corresponds to the gap in the road),
is a largely roadless and not coincidentally lawless jungle where
both the land and the people have been resisting efforts to connect
the great highway for as long as cars have been driving it.

Due to a perfect storm of geographic, economic, political, and
criminal elements, the Darién region is one of the most dangerous places in the world. It's also a wild, unspoiled, mind-blowing
wildlife habitat that's home to only a few indigenous tribes, with
no major population centers. When I was a kid, I'd seen Jeff Cor-
win visit and rave about how many snakes lived there, and his TV
show was enough to make me decide to overlook the fact that

this wildlife hot spot is riddled with drug lords, human traffickers, guerrilla forces, and Panamanian and Colombian soldiers, all
trying to either contain or capitalize on its unique circumstances.

With so much crime and conflict, the Darién is a notoriously
unfriendly place to be a tourist—or a missionary, or a journalist.
Enough members of all three groups have been kidnapped or
killed there to keep it off most travel schedules. It's definitely
not the kind of place you want your mom reading up on while
you're visiting, so I left it out when I told my parents, girlfriend,
and friends about my South American itinerary. I figured I'd let
them know when it was over. The only one in on the secret was
my friend Tim.

I flew to Panama City and started hitting up tour compa-
nies for a guide—and getting no help. One after another they
declined, saying, *You don't want to go there. How about seeing
the canal? Or the San Blas Islands? Or surfing in Santa Catalina?*
Finally a company said they had a guide who'd grown up in the
area who might be able to help me navigate the human and natural obstacles. I told them to book him.

I met Eduardo the next day. He was older than I'd expected—
at least sixty-five, maybe seventy. He was small (about five foot
one) and lean (maybe 110), and he quickly proved he was mentally and physically nimble, sizing up hurdles and strangers
in seconds and figuring out the best way to get over or around
them.

Eduardo spoke no English, but through a combination of my
high school Spanish and charades, we came to an understanding that I should hide my passport. Then he looked through my
things and buried the few traveling tools I had that might be
perceived as threatening—snake hooks, a croc snare, and a couple knives—deep in his own duffel bag. As a local, he could get
away with carrying them. As a foreigner, I needed to keep a low,
nonthreatening profile.

Once we'd packed up our gear (much of mine was photo and

video equipment), we hit the road. None of the passage to the Darién is easy. Neither country wants you to go (nor do the drug cartels), so along the way, we were stopped at one checkpoint after another, flagged for questioning at every single one. Soldiers and border police, most armed with automatic rifles and many with machete scars on their faces and arms, inevitably wanted to know, *Quien es el gringo?* They also took particular interest in rifling through my stuff. After the first checkpoint, I knew what to do, stammering out, *"Yo español muy mal"* ("I Spanish very bad"), as if I could barely string the words together, all the while trying to look helpless and mildly confused. My guide kept his answers short, but when pressed he'd roll his eyes and gesture toward me as he explained that I was a student, studying snakes, and that I wanted to see the wildlife. More than once, he took out the snake hook, demonstrated how it worked, and passed it around. He seemed to know some of the military guys, and he pulled us through again and again.

Once the soldiers at each station were convinced I had no drugs, no weapons, and no money, they mostly wanted to know when I'd be leaving. I sensed they didn't think I'd last long in the inhospitable environment I was on the verge of reaching.

We took a bus to the first checkpoint, then a van to the next. From there we rented a motorbike and rode it to a dock (and another checkpoint). After a short trip in a johnboat and half a day in a truck that was either rented or borrowed (I definitely never saw a rental counter), we reached the last town, literally the end of the road: Yaviza. As soon as we were out of the truck, I realized, *This is happening.* I was in a place tourists do not go. I was the only white person, the only person wearing a backpack, the only one, I was pretty sure, there by choice rather than birth or necessity.

I'd been standing at the side of the road for only a matter of seconds, still trying to orient myself, when a wild-eyed man came rushing up with a crate, gesturing to me and clearly trying to sell me what was inside. I bent down and squinted into the box to see what he could possibly think I needed. A dirty, sad-looking baby armadillo.

There were so many things wrong with that scene: the man lying in wait to sell a baby armadillo, his rapid approach, the idea that this poor, sickly wild animal could be a pet. Not to mention the fact that armadillos are the only creatures other than humans that can carry leprosy. It's been estimated that half of armadillos in some regions of the Amazon carry it, and numerous modern cases of what we often think of as this Middle Ages disease have been traced directly to contact with them. I was in possession of none of the multiple antibiotics I would have to take for months if I contracted leprosy during the jaunt to the Darién, which I was already expecting to be harrowing.

So . . . was I interested in buying a little armadillo to take along on my jungle trek as a pocket pet? For the record, I am the last person anyone could accuse of being a germophobe; and I'm usually eager to get to know any wild animal better. But that whole interaction felt like a weird, bad omen. Besides, I knew that buying that poor doomed armadillo would encourage the guy to nab another one to sell as a "pet." I didn't want any part in perpetuating what he was doing.

"*No!*" I shouted, taking a couple giant steps away from the dude and the crate, then throwing in a couple more *no*s for good measure as I walked away. Just no.

My guide sized up the situation and said nothing, and the armadillo man cleared out. Eduardo pointed me toward a tiny wooden building with a sign on the door that read POSADA and told me I'd sleep there. We'd be leaving in the morning. Then he said, "*Mañana,*" and walked away.

My room in this tiny inn was barely big enough to lie down in, made of worn wooden boards that left me exposed to the elements (and anyone who might have wanted to look in at me). I spent my night watching rats skitter along the perimeter, passing just inches from my toes. I was too excited to sleep, and a little nervous about how far I'd ventured into a place where I clearly didn't belong.

In the morning Eduardo and I crossed a footbridge, hit our last checkpoint, and found ourselves on the far side of civilization with nothing but jungle ahead. The exploring was about to get real.

Frog Heaven

I had been to the Ecuadorian Amazon and seen the jungle, but the Darién Gap was a new kind of wild. There were no signs, and we seldom saw so much as a trail, often having to hack our way through the undergrowth with machetes. The foliage was so dense and the land so infrequently traveled that almost any path we cleared would grow over again in a matter of days. While it would be possible for someone to clear wider trails in some places, and to mark them, the most frequent travelers in the Darién are also the least likely folks to blaze the way. Drug smugglers and human traffickers thrive under the cover of anonymity the jungle provides.

To say that it was hot was an understatement, and the humidity stayed pegged near 100 percent. None of that bothered me, even carrying sixty pounds of gear and food. The jungle was my home away from home, and this might just be the wildest one on earth. I'd found my way in, and nothing was going to stop me from seeing my way through.

The farther we hiked, the more impressed I was with my guide. I'd spent a year working as a personal trainer before leaving for this trip, saving money to travel. I was seriously fit. But this guy could have out-hiked me any day, on any mountain, in his bare feet. The terrain was crazy steep in some places, precipitous enough that I had to use hands, feet, knees, and elbows to climb it. Nevertheless, Eduardo pushed on as if it were a path he walked every day.

Next to him I was one big, slow gringo. It was remarkably humbling.

The Panamanian portion of the Darién is almost entirely national park (though likely one of the least-traveled national parks in the world), and Eduardo had made arrangements for us to stay at a ranger station. The accommodations were basic—a couple bunks and running water I could sterilize. The two young rangers there were welcoming, if a little confused as to why I was there. For the few days we had there we followed a simple routine: get up, eat something from the rations we'd carried with us (peanut butter is heavy as hell in a backpack but worth it), hike all day looking for wildlife and taking turns carrying my equipment, rinse off in a creek, eat beans and rice, then sleep like a rock.

I was in heaven.

One of the first creatures you notice when you hike in the Darién is a particular species of poison dart frog. They congregate everywhere—near the edges of rivers, in creek beds, and even in puddles. I never found anything in the creek near the house in Kansas where I grew up that could hold a candle to these little gems. Their coloring is glowing green and jet black, swirled into a gorgeous marbled pattern. Their skin sparkles, and the sun glints off it. It would be tempting, seeing one of these little amphibians in the wild, to scoop it up because it's so pretty you want a closer look. Just keep in mind that this kind of frog comes equipped with enough poison in the skin covering its tiny body to stop a human heart. Indigenous people in Central and South America once coated the tips of their arrows and spears with this poison to make them more deadly—that's where these guys get their name. Despite their deadly history, if you handle these frogs gently and respectfully and don't have any open wounds, they generally won't hurt you.

Honestly, my big concern in Panama wasn't whether one of these beautiful little creatures might harm me; it was whether I might crush one of them—or an entire family—under my boots. They were *everywhere*. In some areas the ground was teeming with them. This is a species I'd hoped to see in the jungle, but not one I'd ever imagined I would encounter by the thousands.

If you're a frog fan, you probably know that most species lay large quantities of eggs, then leave them to mature into tadpoles and adults on their own. The way poison dart frogs raise their young is completely different. These frogs lay only a few eggs at a time, then guard them until they hatch. Once the tadpoles emerge, one of their parents carries them on its back for days, bringing them into the trees and to water until they start to mature. Which parent is the carrier depends on the particular species of poison dart frog—but in the case of the green-and-black frogs I was seeing, it's the dad who hangs around, waits for the little buggers to climb on, and then totes them around to ensure they get what they need.

One more fascinating fact about the poison dart frog is that when they are bred in captivity—or even kept in captivity over long periods of time—they're no longer poisonous. Turns out their bodies are able to generate and maintain their toxins only when they can get certain chemicals from the insects they eat in the wild.

At the end of every day in the Darién, the name of the game was getting some of the jungle grime off me and trying to cool down enough to sleep. In the evenings I trekked to a creek close to camp for a quick rinse. On the second night, while I was still at the shore, I spotted a river otter about seventy feet downstream. I had come up cautiously, watching for snakes, trying not to step on any poison frogs, eyes peeled for any wildlife—or any dangers—I might miss if I rushed. The otter didn't seem to have a care in the world. He was flipping around, splashing and playing, a blur of sleek brown fur in the water. Unlike some of their relatives who live in close-knit families—and completely unlike the comparably carefree sea lions I'd met in the Galápagos—neotropical river otters in Central and South America live mostly solitary lives. It's actually pretty rare to spot one, and as I stood there, completely still, I knew I was lucky to have the chance.

These otters are extremely self-sufficient and highly effective predators. In fact, they're one of only a few species of animals who feed themselves largely through the unlikely skill of *outswimming fish.* It's true. These guys choose their prey, then stalk it through the water, eventually picking up the pace until they overtake it. Most fish can swim fast in the short term but can't maintain their speed for long. These river otters, on the other hand, are such accomplished swimmers and have such a fast metabolism (typically 50 percent higher than an active and comparably sized land mammal) that they can keep up almost indefinitely, even while taking quick sips of air.

Once they catch their prey, otters like the one I was watching waste nothing, eating most species skin, bones, and all, to derive as much nutrition as possible from their conquests.

I started to creep down the shoreline, hoping to get a closer look, but the otter heard me coming, dove under the water, and ghosted me before I could even travel a few feet.

I couldn't help but wonder if the local river otters, who supplement their pescatarian diets with reptiles and amphibians, ever accidentally ingest the poison frogs. After all, there were hundreds of the little toxic bombs near the creek the otter and I were enjoying, just hanging around and looking an awful lot like free food.

The answer, I learned, is a fun one. Even though river otters don't typically eat poison dart frogs, research has found that when food is scarce, otters do consume even poisonous amphibians without suffering any harm. How do they get away with it?

They skin them.

Mother Nature never ceases to blow my mind.

Once Bitten

I can't really share any more of my adventures with the snakes of Panama or anywhere else without confessing that when I was a teenager, I took a serious bite. I was seventeen and still living at home in Kansas when I caught my first venomous snake, a copperhead. She was all the colors of the autumn leaves around her, with a wide, diamond-shaped head defined by the deep heat-sensing pits behind her nostrils. I knew this snake was venomous, but that just made me more fascinated. I wrangled her with a "custom" snake hook I'd built out of a copper pipe epoxied to a rubber-coated bicycle hanger, gently hooking under her belly, then moving her to an open space where I could snap away with my camera.

When the photo shoot was finished, I should have walked away and been grateful for the encounter. But I wasn't that smart or considerate yet, so I popped that beautiful copperhead into the duffel bag I usually used for my lacrosse gear and took her home.

It was a bad idea on so many levels. This was a venomous wild snake. Strike 1.

A snake that did not belong to me (or anyone). Strike 2.

I knew I couldn't keep her, but I was having a hard time saying good-bye, so I set up a "habitat" in a terrarium next to my bed and watched my new pet until I fell asleep. The minute daylight broke through the window, I was back in caretaker mode. Over the next couple days, the snake was my main focus. When I fed her, she ate pretty well, and that quieted the voice in my head that kept telling me she deserved a lot better than a glass box in my bedroom.

After a week, it looked like she might shed soon, so I moved "my" copperhead to the bathroom sink to soak her scales and facilitate the process. Up until that point she'd been mellow—so mellow that for a moment I let my guard down. I was just admiring her, hands off. I leaned in close, my hook not even in play.

And that's when she sprang up and bit my nose. Strike 3.

For a split second I hoped it had been a dry bite—one that

doesn't inject venom—but almost instantly I realized that I hadn't been that lucky. I felt my nose inflating like a balloon, getting harder and fuller by the second. From there the pressure spread toward my mouth, cheeks, and eyes.

This was a moment I would replay in my head a thousand times, wishing I'd been smarter or more careful or both, but right then, I went straight into fight-or-flight mode, placing the snake back in the enclosure, racing through the house, jumping into the car, and speeding to the hospital. I drove so fast that what should have been a fifteen-minute drive took about six. I was lucky I didn't get a ticket on my newly minted driver's license.

I careened into the parking lot, abandoned the car in a loading zone, raced through the sliding doors of the ER, and rushed the attendant at the counter. "I've been bit by a copperhead," I stammered. Then—just in case there was any question about what had to happen next: "I need anti-venom right now. Immediately."

To the hospital's credit, nobody asked me to take a seat or a number or to wait my turn. The ER team swung into action—and quickly determined that they didn't have the anti-venom I needed. I was freaking out, but the staff stayed cool, loading me into an ambulance to transfer me to a second hospital while they called ahead to make sure I got treatment ASAP on arrival.

Luckily, when it comes to potency, copperheads are one of the least "hot" of all pit vipers. If I'd been bitten by a coral snake or a rattlesnake, it might have killed me or permanently wrecked my face. Copperhead venom is a little less potent, and that bought me enough time to get treatment.

Of course, I still had a different kind of reckoning coming. After the hospital dosed me with four vials of anti-venom through fast-acting IV push injections, they admitted me—and called my mom.

I was coming off the adrenaline surge that had gotten me from bite to treatment and realizing my panic had been masking a world of pain when she arrived. My face was swollen and hard, burning deep beneath the skin. It must have looked as bad as it felt, because my mother's face contorted in horror with her first glimpse of my poor disfigured head. Every few minutes a doctor or nurse had been coming in to check my breathing, and soon I heard one of them explaining to my mom that they were doing it because I wasn't in the clear yet. The inflammatory reaction to the venom could still close my throat. I know now they could have managed that with a tracheotomy, but in that moment as I was lying there, in excruciating pain, I thought, *If I can't breathe, I can't live!*

It was the last straw. After more than two hours in full-on fight-or-flight mode, I was done. First I puked. Then I passed out.

Not my finest hour.

I woke up much later, still traumatized but no longer in pain, thanks to the miracle of morphine.

Although I had loved and been fascinated by snakes ever since I was a little kid, that's the day I learned that if I really wanted to continue to engage with these magnificent and quietly powerful creatures, I'd better start giving them their due respect.

In a messed-up way, the entire incident was probably a blessing. I had found out the hard way that wild animals are *always* wild. Since that day, I've put myself in many situations where I'm at the mercy of a wild animal (many of them far deadlier than a North American copperhead), but I never forget what they're capable of, and I never allow myself to be complacent.

Sometimes I think someone was looking over me that day— luck hardly seems like enough to explain how I walked away from such a nasty bite with just a little warp on the left side of my nose and a wounded ego.

Hot, Hot Herp

I tell you the story about how I got bit by that copperhead to provide a little context for what happened next in the Darién Gap.

Eduardo and I were carving our way through the jungle, looking in, on, and under the trees for creatures I could photograph and film, when we spotted possibly the most gorgeous snake in the world stretched out right in the middle of a rare open spot. The sun was reflecting off its bright orangey-red skin like a neon sign flashing, EVAN, OVER HERE! It was a coral snake, and a spectacular one.

Coral snakes have what's known as aposematic coloring— bright, bold colors that are meant to serve as a warning to other wildlife. Predators tend to take a beat before engaging with anything that looks exotic, bright, or different from their usual meal. Even in the animal kingdom there are unspoken rules about some things being just too weird to eat.

Of course to me, the coloring wasn't off-putting at all. It was gorgeous. So much of what you see in the jungle is green and brown, and here was a creature so shiny it looked like its gleaming bright red and yellow bands had just been polished. This one was slithering across the trail in front of us—three feet long, slender, shimmering, beautiful.

If you're like me, you grew up hearing an easy-to-remember adage meant to keep you from picking up a coral snake that might kill you. "Red on black, friend of Jack," maybe, or "Red on yellow kills a fellow." In Central and South America, following that guideline is a good way to get killed. Nature does not like to be overly predictable, and the snake in my path in one of the wildest jungles in the world had wide red and black stripe pairings (in addition to the narrow bands of yellow) but was definitely no friend of Jack. It was actually a textbook example of the most venomous snake in that part of the world. It was also, at that point, the single most potentially lethal snake I'd ever seen in the wild.

It was not, however, the most dangerous. Just because a snake *can* kill you doesn't mean it'll be in the mood to. Coral snakes can be nasty if they want to, but generally speaking that's not their nature. It's rare for even wild specimens to strike. This snake was remarkably chill as I hooked him under his body and grasped his tail. I would not be wrapping this beauty around my arm, the way I often do with nonvenomous species. If you have a snake anchored around your arm and it gets pissed, you can't *immediately* let go. Anytime a venomous snake is involved, you don't want to put yourself in a position where you could find yourself trying to get it off you.

Holding this snake at all was surprisingly challenging. If you need to control a viper, you can grip it at the base behind that great big head. It's like a handle, wide and curving out from the back of the head, keeping your hand out of reach of the fangs. Coral snakes, which are not vipers, tend to be skinny, with narrow heads that rarely exceed their body width. There's nothing to hold there. If a viper wants to back out on you, it can't slip back past your hand. If a coral snake wants to slide back, it's much tougher to control. To make matters worse, the coral snake has thin, smooth scales—so smooth they feel slippery just from the oils of your hands. Vipers have rougher, keeled scales that provide some friction and traction for your grip.

So standing there holding the coral snake, I was incredibly excited, but also terrified. This moment was a high point in my trek across the Darién. There I was, on a steep jungle mountain, dozens of miles from the nearest town and even farther from a hospital. It was just my guide and me, and since I was easily a foot taller than him and outweighed him by at least eighty pounds, it was a safe bet he wouldn't be carrying me to safety. If I got bitten, I wouldn't have a chance. I knew it would go quickly—the neurotoxin in coral snake venom makes you feel super-wasted, super-fast. First you're nauseous, then you faint, then you're unconscious. What actually kills you is when it stops your diaphragm from contracting. Once again, no breath means no life.

But I was twenty-five, and I felt invincible. This trip was my last hurrah before hunkering down with my books for vet school. I was so hungry for the moment that there was no way fear was going to stop me. I was committed to having the experience, and equally committed to documenting it so that my holding this snake might contribute to a better understanding of it. I knew the footage would not be nearly as compelling if I were just standing next to the snake in the shot.

My heartbeat might have been pounding out, *Don't bite, don't bite, don't bite,* but my conscious thoughts were on something that seemed even more urgent: teaching my guide how to use my damn cameras.

I have no idea why I hadn't given him a lesson ahead of time, why I hadn't taken the time to teach him what to do when a big moment comes along. But I hadn't. So I was standing there holding a snake that could kill me at any second, with both of my hands decidedly occupied as I tried to coach Eduardo through setting up a tripod and camera, using a half click to focus and a full click to shoot ("half click" is not one of the handy phrases in my Spanish arsenal), how to look through the view window, how to make sure the snake and I were both in the shot. Eduardo kept glancing from me to the snake, and as cool as he'd been talking his way past armed soldiers, he was *not cool* in that moment. He was kind of freaking out. When I leaned in to show him how to adjust the camera, his eyes went wide. He leaned back as far as a man can without falling over, maintaining a steady distance between himself and the snake. He was hesitant to touch the cameras, and the confidence he'd shown the whole time we'd been together faltered when he had them in his hands. Suddenly the guy who could walk through the jungle like he owned it was unsure.

It was terrible timing, but the snake was remarkably tolerant, waiting for us to settle down and figure out how to do this together.

Finally we had a couple still photos and the camera running, and the mellow, deadly fellow and I stepped in front of it to record a short video. I explained that there are more than a dozen different types of coral snakes and their impersonators in Central and South America, and that the one in my hands was the real deal. There are a few guidelines for determining whether a snake that looks kinda sorta like a coral snake might actually be venomous, I said—for instance, the pattern on its skin, the length of its tail (for most people an entire snake may look like a tail, but in this case it's the distance from the vent on an animal's abdomen to the end of its body), and the size of its eyes (big eyes usually mean nonvenomous, whereas small eyes more often indicate that a snake is venomous). The thing is, though, you really don't want to get close enough to look deep into the eyes of a snake if it even *might be* a coral. Generally speaking, I concluded (while starting to wonder if I should be taking my own advice as the snake got restless), it's best to admire these beautiful creatures from a distance.

And with that I gently lowered the coral snake to the ground and stepped back to admire his departure. I was torn between relief at being out of danger and regret that our encounter—something I felt like I'd waited my whole life for—was over.

After the Gap

Eduardo and I emerged from the Darién seven days after beginning the trek. I was dirty, hungry, and exhausted, both mentally and physically—but also as elated as I'd ever felt in my life. Few places on earth are that completely wild, and I knew that if I hadn't gone into that jungle with the most wily, rugged, kick-ass guide ever, I might not have made it out. Eduardo was my savior, and as I paid him and shook his hand (and tipped him as generously as a broke pre-vet student possibly could), there were not enough rounds of *Muchas gracias* in the world to thank him for the experience I'd just had.

I headed back toward Panama City in search of a shower, a milkshake, and a room with a mattress. Eduardo stayed behind in Yaviza. I don't think there's any way he could have known how the adventure we'd taken had changed my life.

Rescue (Cleaning) Mission

From Panama City, I traveled to Panama's mountain highlands to the town of Boquete. In many ways, this area is the anti-Darién. It's popular with tourists and expats, offering golf courses, resorts, and restaurants, and its miles of coffee plantations keep the land tame and organized. The city sits at a high altitude—not quite a mile high, like Denver, but close. I wasn't there to take advantage of any of the high-end amenities, however; I couldn't have afforded any of them, anyway. Instead, I'd read about a place called Paradise Gardens Wildlife Rescue in a *Lonely Planet* guide, and I wanted to see if they'd let me volunteer for a few days.

I'd tried to e-mail the organization ahead of time, but I hadn't received an answer. So after riding two buses a total of about twelve hours from Panama City, I just showed up. The director was very nice and pretty and American, but I could tell she wasn't new to Panama. Very tan, with blond streaks in her hair, she seemed to be living the dream here at the rescue. She looked me over and asked how I felt about cleaning enclosures.

I didn't hesitate—I figured nothing would get me closer to the wildlife in the preserve than mucking around in their habitats.

I stowed my gear at a hostel in town and got to work that afternoon. My first encounter was with a creature completely new to me: a northern tamandua. These arboreal anteaters have white arms and legs, then dark brown fur on their bodies, so it looks like they're wearing little fur vests. Crazy cute. These playful, active creatures don't pose any harm to people, so I let the little female who lived in the enclosure stay to "help" me while I cleaned. This girl had been orphaned after her mother was electrocuted on a power line, then brought to the rescue facility, so she was used to people. And she was friendly. As soon as I stepped into her enclosure, she skittered off her tree and came right over to me, crawling up my leg and perching on my shoulders.

For an hour I was her jungle gym, and in between bouts of cleaning I held still or moved depending on what she seemed to want from me. She ran up and down me at will, nuzzled my head, and hung off my back while I was doing the actual work of cleaning up her enclosure. I was soaking it all up, and in my excitement I was mostly focused on her adorable pinched face and her little furry-vested body. It wasn't until after I stepped out of the enclosure and saw how the director looked me over that I glanced down at myself.

My T-shirt was a patchwork stretched between hundreds of tiny holes. My arms and hands were covered with scratches. A lot of them were trickling blood. I'd observed that my new friend had long, sharp claws, but in my excitement to play with her, I hadn't even noticed that I was getting the pointy end of them. I lost a good shirt that day, but I gained a friend of a new species—a trade I'll make anytime.

The T-shirt wasn't the only part of my wardrobe I lost in Boquete. The next day I worked in the enclosure of a tayra, also a new animal to me. Despite his small size, if this guy had made a direct run at me on arrival, I probably would've scooted out of his territory in a hurry. A tayra looks like a little badger, with a narrow head and a muscular body that could rival the physique of a pit bull. It's a bit intimidating. As they age, their heads turn gray but their bodies stay black, and I'm guessing that's how they got the nickname locals sometimes use for them: *cabeza del viejo*—"old man's head." I can't imagine that anybody ever called a *cabeza del viejo* Snuggles or Muffin. The one I was meeting was a non-releasable juvenile who'd been hand-raised since he was a baby. He weighed around twelve pounds, and his name was Tony. When I stepped into his enclosure, Tony's body language was anything but the aggression or even ferociousness I thought I might encounter. His ears perked up, he tilted his head to look at me from one angle and then another, and then he jumped out of his tree and ran right for me, planting himself at my feet and wiggling, like a little kid who's about to get an ice cream cone.

Everything about this guy was saying, *Play with me!*

He raced back to the trunk of his tree to watch my reaction. When I smiled and said, "Hey, Tony" in my best I'm-no-threat-to-you-pal voice, he rushed me again, this time bumping my leg with his head.

That's pretty much how our time together went. Tony would rush me, touch me like he was doing it on a dare, then run away. After a few passes, which he was clearly enjoying, he started nipping at me before he took off again. Little bites, clearly for fun and not to do damage. I was doubled over laughing at how cute all this pseudo-aggression was when on one "attack" he took a bite of my boot—a bite *out of* the good leather hiking boot that had carried me through dozens of miles of hikes and into and out of the Amazon and the Darién Gap. I inspected the damage and studied the tayra for any sign of actual hostility, but all I could see was playfulness. One of the other volunteers explained later that Tony had a few rubber toys and had probably just gotten confused when he'd tested the sole of my boot with his teeth; still, it gave me a new regard for the big bite force of such a small animal. And it left me with a damaged boot I'd continue to wear for the remaining weeks of my trip, yet another trade I was happy to make for the experience.

It was at Paradise Gardens that I discovered a weird truth that still belongs on my Ten Things You Don't Know About Me list: primates like me. Not all of them, but more than I could reasonably expect from a class of creatures who tend to be choosy about who they take to and who they don't.

One of the habitats at the preserve was for a pair of young capuchins who'd been orphaned and were being raised together. I went into their enclosure to move around some of their toys and equipment, trying to help ensure that they had plenty of mental stimulation. There is nothing cuter than a baby capuchin. They have these sweet, open faces—big eyes, big ears—on tiny bodies that weigh no more than a couple pounds. They are naturally curious, and since these two had known human contact all their short lives, there was nothing guarded about them. It took them all of a couple minutes to decide they liked me, and for the next hour or so they used their dexterous little hands and feet to climb up and down me, wrestle and roll around with each other, poke my ears and nose, pull my hair, and, when they got tired, rest their little heads against me.

When I'd decided to volunteer at a rescue, I'd understood that I couldn't expect—or even reasonably hope—to have the kind of interaction I wound up having with each of these species. And yet there I was, in my holey T-shirt and bitten-through boots, capuchins climbing all over me, camera in hand, having the time of my life.

That was my first significant amount of hands-on primate time. When I looked back at the footage I'd shot, it was obvious that I'd been so distracted by how cute the monkeys were that I'd failed to do a good job of narrating and educating. It was mostly video of the monkeys paired with audio of me laughing and oohing over their antics.

Sometimes you've just gotta be in the moment, and that was a moment I'll never forget.

Turtle Trance

I was so hooked on the stunning landscapes and incredible wild-life experiences I had in Panama, I went back the very next year, trying to recapture what I'd seen and felt and learned. But that's not the way nature or travel (or life) works. That second summer, I ended up in a small coastal town on the island of Bastimentos in the Bocas del Toro Archipelago, on my own, walking the beach for miles at night by the moonlight.

One evening, I spotted something big on the beach. It turned out to be a turtle, and I hoped she was just resting and not injured. As I got closer, I realized that I was looking at a massive leatherback who was nesting. She'd cleared a pit around herself by digging in with her back flippers—kind of like making a snow angel in the sand. Then she rested in the middle of it and set about the work of laying dozens and dozens of eggs. Scientists don't really understand exactly what happens in the minds of these turtles when they're nesting, but observation tells us that they go into a kind of trance. Once that happens, they rarely notice any outside disturbances. They do their work with total focus.

For this reason, I felt it was safe both for me and for this leatherback mama if I approached her to quietly observe. I lay down a few feet from her on the sand. I took a couple pictures, but mostly I stayed still and silent, watching her lay her eggs. Her big eyes were open, but she looked past me and out into the night as if I weren't even there.

After about an hour and a half, she finished, gently covered the clutch of eggs with sand, and slowly made her way into the ocean.

The moment had none of the danger of my trip to the Darién, none of the fun of my time at the rescue preserve. It was a different kind of magic, peaceful and almost surreal. Yet another unforgettable experience I could carry home from Panama.

5

Costa Rica

Costa Rica might be small (just about an eighth of the size of California), but it's a giant when it comes to wildlife. It's arguably the most biodiverse country in the world, home to an estimated 4 percent of all species on the planet. Unlike so many nations with amazing wildlife to share, Costa Rica recognizes the value of its incredible natural resources and looks out for them. More than a quarter of the country is designated as national parks, forest preserves, or protected lands, and the government tries to make it possible for people to see all of it. This country has been ahead of its time in recognizing that it has a vested interest in protecting and sharing its natural beauty.

Because of Costa Rica's small size and diverse landscapes, it's possible to visit tons of different ecosystems in a short time. In a week you can experience volcanoes, mountains, waterfalls, beaches, deciduous forests, cloud forests, and—my personal favorite!—epic jungles. The amazing variety of landscapes and environments lends itself to equally amazing opportunities to encounter native wildlife. And that's what was on my mind when I arrived for the final leg of my two-month sojourn through

Central and South America the summer before starting veterinary school.

The birds alone were enough to take my breath away. In a lot of destinations, it's easy for me to overlook the animals in the air because I am so intently focused on the reptiles and mammals on the ground. In Costa Rica, though, birds don't take a back seat to anything, and there is *zero chance* of overlooking them. This is a place where the scarlet macaw, the toucan, and an otherworldly-looking green-and-blue beauty called the resplendent quetzal roam free, perching in the trees, flying overhead.

The first time I watched a pair of scarlet macaws pass right above me and land in a treetop fifty feet away, I just stood there, eyes wide and mouth open. It was like seeing a rainbow flapping its wings. Or fire flying. Seeing a bird like that makes you rethink color in the natural world, especially for someone who, like me, grew up thinking that cardinals and blue jays are colorful, and that a robin's breast is "red."

Nothing but Noise

I snapped awake at five a.m. my first morning at the Costa Rican shore and jumped out of bed, still half asleep, taking a minute to place the source of the earsplitting sound I was hearing. It sounded the way I imagine an actual hellhound sounds: gruff, bellowing, tooth-rattling. I looked around my room, then out the window, and finally outside the door, expecting the culprit to be right there, shouting into the keyhole.

Turns out, that noise is just part of daily life when your neighbors are a troop of howler monkeys. They weren't right outside my door. In fact, they were about two hundred feet up in a tree about three hundred yards away. The amount of noise these guys can put out is mind-blowing. They can be in the trees a quarter mile away, and when they get going it sounds like they're screaming straight into your ear. They are the loudest land animal in the world, capable of howling at levels that exceed 140 decibels. For reference, that's louder than a chain saw. Louder than a gunshot. Louder than a foghorn. It's loud enough that if you were close and had prolonged exposure, you would suffer hearing loss.

The secret to a howler monkey being able to generate such a ridiculous amount of sound is in its anatomy. Humans and primates have what's called a hyoid bone in our throats. In people, its main function is just to anchor the tongue. For the howler monkey, though, the bone and the air-filled structure around it work as an amplifier. A howler's hyoid is more than twenty times larger than other, similar-sized primates', and it's curved to help make his every grunt, growl, and howl resonate far and wide.

Years later, when I actually got to lay hands on one of these creatures as a veterinary student working with zoo animals, I was amazed at how huge his larynx was. Picture a pug with a softball tucked under his chin and you'll get the idea. That one feature was out of all proportion to the size of the monkey's body. At first glance, I thought it was some kind of massive, rock-hard thyroid tumor, but then the vet I was working with reminded me that we don't call these monkeys "howlers" for nothing. I instantly flashed back to being rattled out of bed that first morning in Costa Rica. No doubt some distant cousin of the little guy on that exam table in Peru was at that very moment shocking the eardrums of a new visitor to his territory along the coast of Costa Rica.

The Devil in the Boat

One of the things I most wanted to do while in Costa Rica was witness a sea turtle release. I got my chance by volunteering at Tortuguero National Park, on the Caribbean coast. Tortuguero gets its name from the thousands of sea turtles who return there every year to nest. (In Spanish, *tortuga* means "tortoise.") It's the largest nesting site in the Western Hemisphere for green sea turtles, and also a destination for leatherbacks and loggerheads.

Historically, a local nickname for the people who've been protecting these turtles for decades is *los celadores*—"the watchmen." I took a boat ride out to join the volunteers who dress in dark colors and walk the black beach at night, watching over the turtles, helping tag them, measuring them, and counting their eggs. As a group, the conservation teams and volunteers don't just do research—they also create a presence that deters the poachers who are the single biggest threat to the turtles' survival as a species. I felt cool and purposeful and even important at the thought of being, even for a single night, one of these guardians.

The Sea Turtle Conservancy has been working for the protection of Costa Rica's turtles for more than fifty years. In that time, its members have helped produce a 500 percent increase in the nesting population.

In the world of sea turtle conservation, the only thing more exciting than seeing a massive mama haul herself up on the sand to dig a hole and lay her eggs is witnessing a hatching. I was lucky enough to be there to see it happen. One minute you're standing on a quiet beach. But under the sand, dozens of tiny babies are starting to wake up after close to two months in the ground. Mother Nature equips them with a tiny temporary tooth they use to break through their shells. Once they're free, these little creatures (a few centimeters long and less than an ounce heavy) dig up through the sand to the surface, poking themselves out flippers first, then heads, followed by their back halves and rear legs. They orient themselves toward the moon's reflection on the water, start madly swinging those flippers like wind-up toys, and waddle across the sand and into the sea. To help ensure their success, we even had some volunteers standing in the ocean with big spotlights to mimic the moon and guide these babies to the water. Light pollution can seriously confuse creatures driven solely by instinct—just like it confuses the insects who swarm helplessly around outdoor lightbulbs.

Because green sea turtles lay around a hundred eggs at a time, once this process starts it snowballs, with one turtle becoming two becoming ten becoming a hundred or more, all racing toward the water. I stood on that sand completely in awe of the entire process—a witness to the world's smallest, cutest parade, entirely conducted on pure instinct.

Watching the turtles go, I hated to think about how few would survive. From every clutch of eggs, some hatchlings never make it out of the sand. Others get disoriented and don't find their way to the sea. If the weather isn't warm enough, some die of exposure. And the list of animals that prey on sea turtle hatchlings even once they do reach the water is about a mile long: crabs, raccoons, lizards, crocodiles, snakes, wild cats of all sizes, boars . . . you name it. For a species that has just a small club of powerful predators as adults—sharks, killer whales, jaguars, and humans— the hatchlings are shockingly vulnerable until they grow several times larger. Only about one in a thousand of the hatchlings that start their lives on Tortuguero or other beaches around the world will survive to full adulthood, reached at around age twenty. The rest never have the opportunity to mature and reproduce, making it no wonder this species is endangered. Those that do, however, become quiet masters of the sea, living as long as one hundred years or more, as part of the cycle that brings these turtles back to the same stretch of Costa Rican sand year after year to mate and leave their eggs under the protection of the *celadores*.

When my ferry from the park arrived back at the town dock the next morning, a small crowd was gathered around one of the tied-up boats. A fisherman, apparently the owner, stood at the edge of the water, cursing and waving his arms at something in the bottom of his boat. He leaned in, then leaped back, shouting again. I climbed onto the dock and peered down to see what the fuss was about, hoping this was an animal I could help out.

A huge green iguana stared back at me. He'd backed himself into the corner by the motor and was puffing up and whipping his tail, clearly and completely freaked out. I have no doubt he was at least as upset as the fisherman, who appeared afraid to get any closer.

Sure as the sun was shining and baby sea turtles crawl to the sea at night, this was a job for . . . me.

"*Necesitas ayuda?*" I asked. You need help?

The fisherman nodded.

The iguana was about two feet long from snout to vent (not counting his tail). He had three potential weapons at his disposal: his fine-pointed claws (the better to climb trees with), his small, razor-sharp teeth (designed for shredding vegetation), and the fast-swinging, spiked tail he'd use as a whip if he decided to mix it up with a fellow iguana. As if he knew I was measuring him up, he fanned out his dewlap—the broad flap of skin between his chin and neck—seven or eight inches, trying to look bigger.

I took a step closer, speaking calmly: "It's okay, man. I'm not gonna hurt you, but you can't stay here." I had a pet iguana named Pete when I was growing up, so I had a soft spot for this frustrated and defensive big guy; even so, there was no way I could explain to him that I wasn't going to hurt him, or that I was positive he'd be happier out of the boat than in it.

I stepped down into the rocking hull and waited for it to stop swaying from the distribution of my weight. Not-Pete didn't like that much, looking right at me, opening his mouth, and letting out a hiss. *I wouldn't if I were you!*

By that time there were a dozen people around the dock, waiting to watch this iguana bite the hell out of me. I'd been handling lizards all my life, but I didn't usually have an audience or a rocking boat to up the stakes. The biggest challenge of this job, though, was the fact that the animal was trapped. Cornering animals makes them significantly more stressed and aggressive. It's not their fault. When they only have one direction to go—toward you—there are not a lot of peaceful options at their disposal.

Standing in that boat, I felt protective of the roaming iguana who'd found himself in such a crappy situation and eager to show the small crowd watching that it could be handled peaceably. It seemed like an excellent opportunity to do what I'd been trying to do with my videos for years: educate a group of people about the nature of a wild animal. I saw myself as something of an aspiring Steve Irwin out there—one who had a dozen-strong live audience instead of millions of people glued to their TVs. The whole thing was exhilarating, a reaffirmation of why I'd chosen this path of wildlife education in the first place.

It was time to help my angry green friend out of his crisis. I made my move, covering the distance between me and the panicked iguana in one long stride and waving my left hand directly in his face. His head followed the hand, and while he was watching it, I used my right arm to reach around, grasp him behind the neck, and scoop him up. He landed a couple good scratches before I got him under control, but it was a pretty quick, clean grab.

As I hopped up onto the dock, the crowd erupted in a cheer. I couldn't resist the opportunity to talk about the species for a minute. I'd been doing this with every creature I encountered across Central and South America in front of a camera, and now I had a live audience. In my broken Spanish I basically said something like "Behold the green iguana. He doesn't want to hurt you. He likes fruit." It was, perhaps, not my finest narration, but the crowd smiled politely and even took pictures. As soon as my impromptu pro-iguana PSA was finished, I set my snippy new pal on the sand away from the dock, close to the trees. He was quick to scrabble away from the loitering crowd and find a new, less-contested place to hang out.

I still have a picture of me holding him, a huge grin on my face and blood trickling down my arms.

It was a good day all around.

Christmas in July

Costa Rica is home to an amazing variety of snake species, and I was able to get up close and personal with what I considered the ultimate quartet of South American species: the fer-de-lance, the eyelash viper, the bushmaster, and the jumping pit viper, whose video would become my calling card with snake wranglers all over the world.

In general, pit vipers are ambush predators, able to stay motionless for as long as it takes for prey to come to them. Not all snakes are like this. Cobras and mambas, for example, are "roving" predators—meaning they actively move to seek out potential prey. If you don't have good jungle vision, you can walk by the same ambush-predator snake a dozen times without seeing it. Your eyes just scroll on past. So everywhere I went, I scoured the ground and the trees, looking for a telltale difference in shape or a pop of color that didn't belong. Each time my eye detected an anomaly, my heart started pounding. *Is that it?*

And then one afternoon as I wandered through an area of heavy rain forest, it *was*. The fer-de-lance. It was camouflaged in a pile of leaves and dirt, but the X pattern down its back snagged my eye. Normally I'd go straight after a snake I was so excited to meet, but this species has a serious reputation. The fer-de-lance is a predator with attitude. Even when it's young and small (long before reaching a mature length of over seven feet), it's known for being one angry little dude with a fiercely hot venom. Nearly half of all venomous snake bites in Costa Rica are delivered by this species, and those bites can be devastating—causing permanent damage, amputation, or even death.

So even though I wanted very much to touch the snake in front of me, I knew doing so would be a calculated risk.

The more menacing and angry something looks, the more it fascinates me, and this badass little two-foot snake had all the markers. First and foremost, she had a diamond-shaped head—the better to accommodate her venom glands. Up close, I knew her eyes would look fearsome, with narrow vertical-slit pupils—a telltale sign of a predator who hunts at night. And one of the features I love most about pit vipers is their prominent upper eyelid ridge. It's a beautiful structure, and it's also a statement because it makes them look pissed off twenty-four/seven.

Deadly or not, the snake was a beauty, and I was going to film her. Nobody was going to tell me no. This would be my first wild-caught pit viper in Central America.

But I didn't have enough light to shoot. In order to make this happen, I was going to have to move an extremely dangerous snake to a better location (and then bring her back to her home). I looked at the few supplies I had and hatched a plan.

Moving as stealthily as I could, I got out my snake hook and eased close. I slipped it under the snake and received a halfhearted snap of the jaw in return. Once she was on the hook, I dropped my rain jacket to the ground and propped open the pocket. Then I swung the hook to the jacket and directed her into the cave of the pocket. Knowing that the next moment was the one in which I was mostly likely to get bit—and that I'd be mortified if I had to tell people for the rest of my life that I got bit by a deadly snake *while I was putting it in my pocket*—I laid the hook across the seam on the same side of the pocket's zipper, and my hiking boot (which I was still wearing) alongside that. I tilted the thick rubber sole of the boot toward the snake, giving her a big, safe target if she decided to strike. This step was absolutely critical, because these snakes are basically built to strike in exactly the conditions I'd created—her coiled up in a dark, safe place; me putting my hand (which she would effortlessly detect and locate with the heat-sensing pit organs in her face) up to it. The material of my jacket would never stop a strike, so the boot was my insurance. Finally, I reached out and closed the zipper. The jacket material was light enough for me to make out the snake's silhouette, and she immediately curled up and lay still. I lifted the jacket by the collar and started walking out of the shadows and into the fading daylight.

It was now or never. I set up my camera and then reversed the whole process, blocking the pocket with my hook and boot, unzipping, coaxing the snake out with the hook. As soon as she was fully visible, I gently pinned her with the hook. (Yes, gently! Like many snakes, this one was almost as delicate as she was lethal, and she required appropriately careful handling.) I reached down and gripped her behind the head with one hand and at her tail with the other. Finally I lifted her high enough to get both of us in the shot. At first, I was so excited to be holding this snake, I kind of forgot to say anything for the camera. I wanted to see her eyes, her mouth, feel the rough scales on her head. This was a big moment for me, and the snake was doing all I could hope for: tolerating it.

Finally I remembered to narrate, explaining that we want to regard any pit viper with lots of respect. Even as I was saying the words, the snake opened her mouth nearly 180 degrees and snapped it shut. The bulk of her body was lax, but the jaws were working and the tip of the tail was twitching fast, a reminder to not get complacent. I pointed out the small pits in her face and explained that this amazing adaptation allows the snake to sense infrared radiation coming off warm bodies, even from a few feet away. So when this snake is lying in wait for her next meal, she can calibrate the size and distance of the prey—a creature that usually never even sees the strike coming.

As soon as I was finished taping, I transferred the fer-de-lance back into my jacket pocket again for safekeeping, then returned her to exactly where I'd found her.

I spent a couple days near the town of Limón, and one morning a young Scandinavian tourist asked my guide if she could come scouting for snakes with us. The three of us headed out, walking through a protected section of jungle. The two of them were out in front, with me lagging behind, when my eye jumped to a color combination on a low gray-brown tree branch. Red and green, bright and bold. I leaned closer and felt all the joy of a kid at Christmas—it was an eyelash viper. This was the most colorful venomous snake I'd ever seen in the wild. And not only was it colorful, it was wildly unusual. These distinctive snakes have a modification that makes them stand out even among the weirdest and most wonderful wildlife: they have two or three scales above their eyes that have evolved to spike up. From a distance, it looks like they have huge winking eyelashes. It's not hair, but the effect is the same: *Is this snake flirting with me?*

I knew I had to move fast—I did *not* want to miss my chance to interact with this beauty. She was only about eighteen inches long, and as my companions realized that I had stopped and came back to watch, I extended my snake hook her way, easing it under her so that she slowly transitioned her weight from tree to hook. As long as she felt securely supported, she didn't seem to care if the "branch" beneath her was wood or metal.

Since she was staying with me by choice and I didn't have any grip on her, I wanted to get a couple pics right away. Balancing the snake hook in one hand and not breaking my focus on the snake, I pulled my digital camera up and took a few shots. Then I placed her on the ground, gently pinned her head, and lifted her up for a short video. I was careful not to keep her for very long or manipulate her more than the minimum necessary. The way I saw it then (and still do) is that if I could respectfully handle this wild animal long enough to capture something educational about her, the low level of stress she experienced could potentially help protect the rest of her species in the wild. By coping with a small amount of hassle, this snake helped me explain and promote her kind. While my guide filmed us, she never showed an ounce of temper or hostility. She was a beauty inside and out.

Mutual Respect

My guide took me to a serpentarium in Limón where he knew the owner, so that I could get an up-close look at several species of indigenous snakes that I was unlikely to find in the wild. The owner was captivating to talk to, telling us about his animals, how he'd come to have them (many brought to the facility after being confiscated from the illegal pet trade), and tidbits about their personalities and behaviors. He had the most amazing jumping pit viper. These are really thick-bodied snakes with slow locomotion but a crazy-fast strike—so fast and so enthusiastic that they sometimes lift themselves right off the ground, thereby earning their name. They're über ambush predators.

I wanted to hold that snake in the worst way, but the owner wasn't about to just hand me a hook and say, "Go for it, kid." You can't just let some tourist come in off the street and handle a potentially lethal venomous snake because he asks for it.

I decided to make my case, starting with showing him that I was traveling with my own snake hook. He nodded. *"Sí, sí."* Then I pulled out a picture of me working with a rattlesnake in Colorado. His eyes widened a bit, and he nodded again. *"Bueno."* Then I told him about the fer-de-lance and pulled up a picture on my camera. *"Esta semana,"* I said. This week. I could tell he was softening up. He looked from me to the enclosures and seemed to have an idea.

"Try this," he said, leading me to a yellow rat snake coiled on a pile of brush. Rat snakes aren't venomous, so they're harmless, but they're also aggressive. As I accepted the challenge and moved in the snake's direction, he reared up and bobbed his head at me to let me know he wasn't in the mood. I said, "Easy, big guy," gently hooked him, and lifted him with both hands. He wrapped around my arm nicely enough, but then he whipped around and bit me on the hand. Depending on who was judging, that moment might have been interpreted as an indication that I didn't know what the hell I was doing. After all, I got bit.

The serpentarium owner saw it differently. He knew that this was an especially grumpy snake; he hadn't wanted to see if it would bite so much as how I would handle it if it did.

The strike didn't hurt. Most bites from small, nonvenomous snakes aren't very painful, but they can come as a shock to people who aren't comfortable or experienced handlers. If you want to work with snakes, though, you have to be able to stay calm, even when things are going a little haywire. Panic breeds carelessness—and sometimes it's catching. The fact that I didn't spaz out—or even flinch—seemed to win the owner over. He actually shook my hand, a sign of mutual respect. Then this guy who was probably thirty years older than me, a true expert and the keeper of a stunning collection of snakes, patted me on the back and told me I could go ahead and interact with any of the snakes I wanted.

I knew *exactly* which one I wanted. I went straight to the jumping pit viper. This snake was about two and a half feet long, not much longer than the fer-de-lance—but his body was about twenty times as thick. Actually, it was thicker than my wrist. Just. Huge. He had a head to match, ridiculously wide, indicating XXL venom glands. If this snake were a man, he'd be about five feet tall and 250 pounds, solid muscle from head to toe. He'd have a Mohawk and he'd be wearing a spiked collar, and every single thing about his appearance would say, *Do Not Cross Me.*

Man, I could not wait to get my hands on him. The video we were about to make together remains one of my all-time favorites. Given the green light (and knowing this guy was well fed and looking a little sedentary), I used the hook to stabilize the snake. Unlike the fer-de-lance, this was a snake of significant strength. I had to hold him with a strong hand or I could end up getting bit. His body felt heavy in my grasp, and his lethargy disappeared as I gripped him behind his head. He opened his *massive* jaw— nearly as big as my palm—and exposed a mouthful of some of the largest fangs I'd ever seen in my hands up to that point. These were giant, curved, monster fangs, wide as a fingernail, capable of puncturing anything and—like massive hypodermic needles— injecting it full of deadly venom.

With the camera rolling, I gripped that head with one hand and brought the long handle of my snake hook close to him, on the hunch that he was pissed off enough to bite into nearly anything. His mouth snapped closed over the handle and—while I watched and the camera kept recording—his fangs *poured venom*.

Just. Freaking. Awesome. Even as an enthusiast, even as a guy with pet snakes, even as a veterinarian, I might have gone my whole life without seeing venom flowing freely like that. It was magic.

Back in my room, I put together a handful of short videos and a few photo highlights of my trip so far and e-mailed them to a producer, a friend of a friend. Until that day, I'd been recording to have a catalog of experiences I could share on Facebook and YouTube. In the back of my mind, though, I was always thinking they might one day find a bigger audience, maybe catch the eye of a producer or a network that would provide me with a support system to go more places and see more animals. I didn't know if my e-mail would lead to anything, but every time I got in front of a camera with a new animal, I felt like I might be doing something valuable, encouraging a little more understanding and a little more respect for the amazing creatures I was meeting.

An Irresistible Croc

My girlfriend flew out to meet me in Costa Rica, and we spent one of our first days hiking and then taking a three-hour drive along the Pacific coast to our hotel. When we arrived in the early evening, she decided to grab a nap, but I wanted to scope out the area while there was still some daylight. That night I was planning to look for crocs, and I needed to know where I'd have the best odds of seeing them without a crowd hanging around.

If you travel in Costa Rica and want to take your best shot at a guaranteed croc sighting, you don't have to look any farther than the main bridge over the Tárcoles River. Locals call it *puente de cocodrilo*—crocodile bridge. The muddy shoreline underneath has become a popular gathering place for crocs, and on any given day you're likely to see at least a few—and sometimes dozens—of these behemoths lazing in the water. Why the migration to that one spot? Mostly because people feed them there. It's become such a sure thing that vendors sometimes set up stands to sell souvenirs.

The American crocodiles in Costa Rica are massive—often measuring fifteen feet long and weighing in at over five hundred pounds. They're bigger and toothier (some teeth show even when their mouths are closed) than their alligator cousins. They're also meaner, going after anything and anyone who encroaches on their territory. These are apex predators with no natural enemies, and they will attempt to eat anything they damn well want—including large livestock, sharks, and even humans. There have been a bunch of documented cases of these crocs attacking people. Unlike alligators, which usually stick to fresh and brackish water, crocs are totally at home in salt water, and they occasionally meander up among waders and bathers at popular beaches and stop a few hearts.

We'd driven right by the crocodile bridge, but I wanted to find a spot on my own, away from the tourists, so I jumped back into the rental car and drove down the coast, looking for promising locations. As dusk was coming on, I stopped at a sheltered, quiet lagoon, hopped out, and shined my flashlight out into the water. A pair of huge, bright, orangey eyes stared back. *Oh my God, there he is!* This was the closest I'd ever come to an American croc in the wild, and I was suddenly panic-stricken at the possibility of letting him get away. I was looking right at him. The water was clear, so I could see that it was shallow beneath him. He was a manageable size—probably a juvenile, between five and six feet long. If he'd been a snake, I would've been in the water in a heartbeat, knowing I'd have to grab him quick and that I'd have an advantage in the water if I could keep him in sight.

Not so much with a croc. They're far faster in water than on land, so if I dove in, he'd be long gone. I crept silently toward the water, wading in an inch at a time, keeping my light near his eyes so I could see him better than he could see me. The water reached my knees, then my thighs, but I was totally focused on being *this close* to making contact. When I got within ten feet, he submerged to the bottom, but he didn't otherwise move. After a few minutes of stealth, I was directly over him—and he, amazingly, was still there.

It was now or never. I put my flashlight in my mouth (do not try this at home while you restrain your own croc, because it's a great way to break a few teeth) and lunged for him, getting a grip right in front of his shoulders. The croc flipped out, swinging his tail and clasping and unclasping his jaw angrily. I knew I had to wait him out, that he'd settle down if I could briefly keep him still. I focused on not hurting him and not getting bit.

After about twenty seconds, the croc relaxed—and that's when I realized I'd been so focused on getting him, I hadn't thought about what would happen next. Here I was with the first croc I'd ever caught in the wild in my hands, and I didn't even have a camera. I might never get the chance to document a moment like that again. I stood there by the lagoon, my clothes soaked, my arms full of crocodile, thinking, *What the hell?*

Call it ingenuity or stupidity, but the only idea that came to me was to make an equipment run back to the hotel. It made sense in the moment, nearly ten years ago. For the record, this is something I would never do now. But that night, I carried the croc to the rental car, tied my belt around his snout, and put him on the floor in front of the back seat. Before I could think hard enough about this plan to reconsider, I was driving up the coast road, minding the speed limit with exceptional care so I wouldn't get pulled over.

At the hotel I parked far away from any other cars, checked on the croc (who was completely mellow), and hurried to my room. I figured I'd grab my cameras and my girlfriend and we'd head out together to film.

Not so fast. I walked in, and she looked up at me in midsentence, phone in her hand, her eyes red and wide. Her voice dropped instantly from pitched panic to a lower, more even tone. "Oh my God, he's here," she said, sizing me up, clearly noting the wet clothes and the muddy forearms and hands. "He looks fine."

I glanced at the clock and realized I'd lost track of time and been gone a lot longer than I'd said I'd be. I opened my mouth to say I was sorry just as she started to cry. "What the hell, Evan? Where have you been?"

I felt terrible. I wrapped her in a big, wet hug, told her everything was fine, and said I was very, truly sorry.

Then I waited, like, three whole minutes to make sure we were okay before fessing up to what I'd done.

By the way, I have a live croc in the car. I'd love for you to help me get some pictures with it?

To her eternal credit, after telling me I was out of my flipping mind, she put on her boots, slung a camera bag over her shoulder, and headed for the door. In a matter of minutes she'd gone from ready to alert the embassy to toting a camera and helping me out.

As we were walking toward the car, all the feelings I should have had *before* I put the croc in there hit me. Panic. Fear. Worry about getting arrested in a foreign country. Worry about mutilating yet another rental car.

The croc was still where I'd left him, awake and calm. I knew I owed him a proper return trip. We hopped into the car and took him back to the exact place where I'd found him. I popped him out of the back of the car, took the belt off, and held him for five more minutes so I could talk about his habitat, his diet, and his predatory habits while my girlfriend gamely manned the camera and a light. When the five minutes were up, I carried him to the edge of the water, exactly where I'd taken him out, lowered him to the ground, and jumped back toward the shore. He swam away immediately.

If I met that croc tomorrow under the same circumstances, I am positive I'd be happy just to see him in his environment, living his life. A lot of years have passed, and I have had so many amazing adventures and interactions with wildlife all around the world that I no longer feel the need to put my hands on every single interesting creature I see. But back then, I was incredibly hungry for that experience; the idea of just letting the first crocodile I'd ever encountered in the wild keep going about his business without getting up close and personal never even crossed my mind.

Looks Like This Is the End

Our next stop was an ecotourism lodge, and that was where the tenor of the entire trip changed. While we were checking in, somebody broke into my car and stole everything in it. In monetary terms, it wasn't much: some dirty clothes and my spare shoes, a snake hook and a machete, a backpack with a hammock. My fer-de-lance rain jacket. A video camera.

But in personal terms, it was nothing less than devastating. Along with my travel gear, the thief had taken the box that contained hundreds of hours of video footage on mini DVs and my still camera with all my digital photos from the entire trip. That footage included the Galápagos tortoise and pink iguanas and sea lions lounging on the sand between sunbathers. It had my first sloth encounter and my first anaconda sighting. My arduous and breathtaking trek into the Darién Gap and the guide who saw me through it. The coral snake that could have killed me; the little tamandua who played so hard she left puncture marks all over my arms and chest and back; the tiny capuchins who put their fingers in my ears and my nose; the sea turtles; and the great and powerful crocodile who had ridden in the back of my car.

I am not an angry person. I don't have a nasty temper. I believe that most people basically have good intentions and that the same things are important to all of us. And so it surprised me how freaking livid I felt after my stuff was stolen. Now those documented memories and experiences would exist only in my head. For days I stomped around and lay in wait for somebody to say or do something offensive enough for me to destroy them. (Luckily, this didn't happen.) I'd saved and planned for a year to take that trip, to have those experiences, and to create the AV catalog of them that I considered to be my life's work up until that point. I was seething inside.

I'd started my trip at a fit and muscular 225 pounds. After hiking, climbing, hitchhiking, going hungry, and sacrificing in every way necessary to get to the places I wanted to see, meet the animals I wanted to meet, and document my experiences, I'd be going home 34 pounds lighter and basically empty-handed.

It took me a while to settle down and realize that even if my photos and videos had been stolen, nothing could rob me of the experiences I'd had over those two months. And I did have a small, critical cache of mementos—the handpicked photos and videos I'd e-mailed to the producer. It wasn't much, but it was something.

Back in the States, I used those precious few remaining records and a few I'd made before my trip to create my first full-length reel. My girlfriend came up with the hook *Beast Charmer*, insisting I needed to "brand" myself. I figured it could only help me. The reel opened with this disclaimer: "Do not attempt any of the activities you see here. Evan is trained, skilled, and very experienced. All caution must be taken with wild animals."

Confidentially, it's true that I was experienced. And sometimes I was skilled. But trained? To wrestle crocodiles? To hook snakes? To play with orphaned mammals? To extract venom from deadly vipers? To hack my way through the jungle with a machete?

Not so much.

I was learning all of that as I went, one wild experience at a time.

✧

PART THREE

Southeast Asian Quest

6

Thailand and Cambodia

In the summer of 2011 I made my way to Thailand and Cambodia for forty days and nights of hot, sweaty jungle travel. It was just what I needed to clear my head and get my blood flowing again after months of studying like a madman in veterinary school. I liked the classroom and the fast pace of learning, and I loved the hands-on labs and experiences even more, but by the summer I was way overdue for an *outdoor* kind of adventure.

My trip started in Khao Yai National Park, the oldest national park in Thailand, a couple hours and a whole world away from the bright lights and urban pace of Bangkok. The park is geographically unique, especially because over 80 percent of it remains forest while the rest of the wilderness in southern Thailand is rapidly disappearing, thanks to logging, road building, and spreading population centers.

You'd never know that's a problem within the park. It feels like you're in the endless wild out there. The first day I hiked to the Pha Diew Die viewpoint to take in the scenery. At over three thousand feet above sea level, flat rocks on the cliffside offer views out over Thailand's answer to the Grand Canyon—vast, heavily forested, with one mountain ridge after another as far as you can see.

Trekking through the forest jungle, I kept my head on a swivel, looking for any (or all) of the fantastic creatures that live within the park. Khao Yai is home to more than seven hundred animal species—and those are just the ones we know about. There are lots of endangered animals among them, including Siamese crocodiles, Asian elephants, tigers, and hornbills. There are also bears, pythons, leopards, wild pigs, multiple types of primates, and some seriously badass scorpions.

The scorpions were among the critters I most wanted to see, and I made slow progress through the jungle because I kept stopping to peek under logs and poke through leaf debris in hopes of finding one. Finally, at the base of a decomposing stump, I hit the jackpot—a five-inch scorpion with a deep bluish-black hue.

I *love* scorpions—everything about them. The big snappers. The fact that they look like they're wearing armor (and they kind of are). The stinging tails! Those tails are some of the nastiest weapons in the arachnid world. This blue guy was a pincher, digging in much harder than I expected when I picked him up to take a closer look. I held him by the last segment of his tail—the business end of any scorpion. Whatever he can do with his snappers is nothing compared to the damage he can inflict if he holds on long enough to sling that tail forward and shoot its hook into you. The venom generally won't kill you (unless you happen to be allergic), but it will for sure hurt. The whole time I was holding my new blue friend for the camera and admiring his incredibly powerful grip, he was dripping venom all over me. It was running down my hands—which, to be honest, were way too scratched up from hiking and herping for that to be wise.

I made quick work getting my video, explaining that scorpions live in all types of climates and landscapes. They are one of nature's hardiest creatures, capable even of slowing their metabolism to a near stop in bad weather or when food is scarce—and then fully recovering afterward. These guys are built to last.

After a few minutes of bonding, I set Big Blue back in the leaves, where he could find quick camouflage. Then I washed my hands the best I could with my drinking water, scrubbing them on the hem of my T-shirt. I couldn't afford to lose a single day in the park to the pain and suffering of scorpion envenomation.

Nature's Big Top

In Khao Yai, every morning brings the sound of gibbons calling each other in the jungle. The sound is so remarkable—one part whoop, one part birdcall, one part slide whistle. It starts with one individual, but it often becomes a duet between a pair of these romantics—who couple up for life. For all the noise they make, gibbons are surprisingly elusive and difficult to *see*. They live almost exclusively in the trees, and they move wickedly fast (they are the fastest non-flying arboreal mammal), so while you may glimpse the shadow of one or hear it swinging around in the treetops while you're in the forest, chances are by the time you focus your eyes it'll be gone.

I met a PhD student named Jackie who was researching gibbons and convinced her to let me tag along on her telemetry treks. Telemetry is the most common method used for tracking wildlife in remote areas because it's a harmless way to allow scientists to follow an animal's movements and periodically check in to see what they're up to. Since gibbons are most active in the morning, we set out from our campsite before dawn to find the troop.

Jackie had been observing one family for a few months, so she knew where to find them, even without her tracking equipment. I followed her as she walked quickly and quietly, first along a worn path and then through thick lowland grass surrounded by walls of jungle. Even as we got close and the sounds of the calls got louder, all I could see was a dense barrier of green, gray, and brown vegetation and shadows.

Just when I was starting to think our search would be fruitless, Jackie stopped at the edge of a small clearing and ducked down to peek into the opening. I copied her, and suddenly I could see the creatures I'd been hearing, live and in color. It was like stumbling onto a Cirque du Soleil rehearsal in the middle of the Thai jungle. Beautiful little gibbons launched themselves from tree to tree, spinning with grace and athleticism to cover as much as forty feet in a *single* swing. They looked like they were flying as they zipped across the canopy, creating momentum with nothing but some magical combination of their body weight, their musculature, and the flexibility of the branches. Their long, powerful arms propelled them, and they gripped each landing with the furry white hands that make them look like they're always wearing mittens.

The mechanics that allow gibbons to travel so effectively make them unique among primates. They are lesser apes, not monkeys. The major differences between the two categories lie in the presence (or lack) of a tail (monkeys have them; apes do not), the animals' size (apes are generally bigger), and the size of their brains (apes have larger brains and often exhibit great intelligence). Despite their classification, gibbons are among the smallest of the apes—up to twenty-five inches tall and usually well under thirty pounds. If they were bigger, they wouldn't be able to swing and soar so gracefully or so high because the branches wouldn't hold them. If they were smaller, they wouldn't be able to generate the kind of force that powers them through the jungle. Of course, nobody's perfect, and there is definitely a learning curve in mastering that kind of acrobatics. Every once in a while a gibbon takes a dive, and research suggests that it's very common for these fabulous little trapeze artists to break bones and somehow survive to "fly" again.

Even now, sometimes that moment at the edge of the clearing replays in my mind, taking me back to that perfect morning and the opportunity I had to witness nature's circus as half of an audience of two.

Tangled Up in Green

Jackie wasn't the only fellow wildlife admirer I met in Khao Yai. At the beginning of my stay, I'd told a ranger I was especially interested in seeing local snakes. As my visit had gone on, I'd figured he didn't care or had maybe forgotten, but on my last, rainiest morning in the park he found me near the station and waved me closer. We crept around the corner of the building, and he pointed up into the eaves. There, sheltered from the rain, were two snakes, two *different* species of green tree vipers, completely entwined with each other like some incredibly cool snakey braid. I'd never seen anything like it. There was no indication that they were copulating (after all, they were different species); it looked more like they were just snuggling up on a wet day.

That was the first ranger I met who was fully aware that a venomous snake was in his area and was fine with it. He wasn't afraid—he seemed just as fascinated as I was. I got some incredible pictures of those two snakes, and despite my almost constant desire to be a hands-on explorer, I never attempted to touch them. I didn't know what had driven them to braid themselves together, but I wasn't going to be the one to ruin it.

Don't Cage the Elephant

In Chiang Mai Province in northern Thailand, Elephant Nature Park is a haven for abused elephants rescued from the tourism and illegal logging industries. This place will always hold a special place in my heart—although when I picked it as a destination, I had no idea what I was in for. All I knew was that the park was a legit rescue center and not a tourist trap, so I signed up to volunteer for a few days in hopes of getting firsthand experience with the elephants.

The park itself is an oasis, with a raised walkway under a thatched roof that offers visitors views over the property's 250 acres and its elephant residents. Rule Number One was made clear at the gate: The park belongs to the elephants. Since most of them arrived after spending years or even decades in wretched lives of servitude, ensuring their comfort and happiness is everyone's priority. The elephants do what they want, when they want, and if you're a volunteer on the property, you're there to serve them.

Sounded great to me.

The park relies on a volunteer workforce, and each week brings a new group of people who want to help. The first morning of our stay, my group gathered for a short orientation session. I knew we'd learn about the history of the park and what kinds of jobs we'd be doing, but I was unprepared for the other component of the program: a video about the dark circumstances that had led many of the park's elephants to their old lives. Yes, I knew that the elephants came from abusive backgrounds, and that over half of the estimated three thousand elephants in the country had been domesticated for industry, but that day I learned that in many cases, "domestication" is achieved by a practice called *phajaan*. That term means "mentally break," and the sole purpose of the process is to crush the spirit and independent will of an animal through intimidation and corporal punishment.

Elephants are by nature strong, intelligent, emotionally complex creatures. Because of all those things, they also tend to be resilient. They can reason. They can put things in perspective. It takes an almost unthinkable level of abuse to break them. As I sat through the volunteer orientation watching secretly filmed footage of *phajaan*, the word *unthinkable* rolled around in my head, and I realized how barbaric this process is. A baby elephant was taken from its family, confined to a cage so small it was unable to turn around or lie down, then forced to watch its mother's murder. After that trauma, the captors turned their focus to ensuring that the baby would become a fearful and compliant adult. This infant was starved, denied water, screamed at, beaten with bull hooks, and whipped with ropes and chains.

Look, I was not a naïve traveler. I'd been enough places to know that people do what they have to do to survive, especially in places that are overwhelmingly poor. It doesn't make it right, but a poacher, for example, may just be trying to feed his family. Even so, as I sat there watching that movie, swiping at tears and trying to tamp down a growing, seething rage at what I was seeing, I understood that this was something else. Beating a baby. Murdering a mother. Trying to kill the soul but not the body of a creature as majestic and intelligent and powerful as a five- or six-ton Asian elephant through a depraved process that works only *because* elephants have such good memories and are such thoughtful animals. *Unthinkable.* I lost a lot of innocence that day about how far a member of my own species might go to make a profit.

After the orientation, I walked out into the park and met the elephants with my eyes wide open to what they'd endured before finally finding refuge, and I started seeing things I'd missed on my first impression. Scars, limps, torn ears, battered and mutilated trunks. At every turn I thought, *What the hell? How is this even possible?*

I got to see the park's founder, Lek Chailert, interact with the elephants that day. Lek is five feet tall and bustling with energy, and it is obvious that the elephants adore her. They like to be near her, huddling close when they can and gently nuzzling up to her. I don't know how they can tell that she is the person who found them, who rescued them—often by purchasing them from their captors.

Under Lek's guidance, rescued elephants are brought to the park and gradually become reacquainted with nature and freedom. They have fields and mountains to roam, streams to drink from, and ample grazing land. One mahout, or caretaker, is assigned to each elephant, and that person is charged with making sure his or her elephant is rehabilitated and can resume something of a normal life. With a little luck and a lot of patience, the elephants learn to find free will again, and they may even build relationships with other elephants.

During my stay I helped with feedings, bathing, and cleanup—there is a *lot* of cleanup with so many elephants roaming around. I also got to work with a veterinarian, treating one elephant with a large abscess on his foot and another who had a nasty eye infection. As we worked, he showed me the scars of some of the injuries his patients had arrived with—including lacerations and the sites of poorly mended broken bones. Can you imagine the force it takes to break an elephant's bones? Either by beating it or by giving it a task so monumental one of its limbs breaks from the strain? The idea is mind-boggling.

Watching the elephants interact with one another was one of the most moving parts of the experience. One afternoon I sat watching a pair of elephants who seemed to keep close together. They were both females—both obviously old, one slow-moving and tentative, the other more confident. When they came near enough for me to see them more clearly, I realized that what was happening between them was more than friendship. Another volunteer came over to tell me their story. The elder elephant, Jokia, was born in 1960 and lived the first decades of her life as a slave to the logging industry. She had suffered a miscarriage while working on a logging road and had not been allowed to stop or to check on her baby. After that she wouldn't eat—and she wouldn't work. In response, the loggers beat her so badly she was blinded in both eyes.

I looked at this elephant, with her wrinkled and sagging skin, her graying lashes, and her eyes white and blank where her pupils should be. Another in a long line of soul-shattering moments.

When Jokia arrived at the park, in 1999, nobody knew how

well she might—or might not—be able to adapt to her new life. It didn't take long for the staff to see that she would be fine. Another elephant rescued from logging, Mae Perm, came and stood beside the newcomer when she arrived. Within days Mae Perm was gently leading her new friend to her meals and her baths. They slept side by side at night. When I visited the park, their partnership had been going on for more than a decade. I heard Jokia moan and saw Mae Perm touch her trunk to the inside of her friend's ear, letting her know she wasn't alone. I watched them eat together, walk together, and splash side by side in the river, trumpeting away as if they didn't have a care in the world. I've been present for some amazing moments of kindness between animals, but to this day I've never seen anything as touching as the relationship between these two elephants.

I shot a lot of video at the nature park, hoping to help bring attention to the elephants' abuse and the devotion this organization dedicates to their care. Even now, whenever I have the chance, I make sure to tell anyone traveling to Asia that every dollar given to any organization that lets you ride an elephant or watch an elephant do tricks (like painting or pulling a carriage) contributes to another generation of juveniles being subjected to *phajaan* and living tortured lives.

On my last day at the park, I hiked up to a high point on the grounds to look out over the mountains. There, taking in the same view, was a slowly lumbering elephant. I'd noticed her before because her gait was so distinctive. As a logging elephant she'd suffered a broken ankle, a dislocated hip, and a fractured femur. Her hips are crooked, and her gait is awkward. Even without a veterinary degree, I could tell from a glance at her lopsidedly angular stance that walking must cause her pain. I paused and waited for her to pass, not wanting to crowd her, but that's not what happened. Instead she came and stood beside me, so that we were side by side gazing out over the park. She leaned a little toward me, and I instinctively put my hand up, waiting to see if she wanted to be touched. She pressed against it, and I stroked her side.

I left Elephant Nature Park feeling a little wiser and more world-weary than I'd been when I arrived, but also deeply grateful to have played a tiny part in helping such an amazing place fulfill its mission.

A Bite and a Climb

My next Thai adventure took me to Khao Sok National Park, where I was—*surprise!*—looking for snakes. I wanted to see primates and monitors and whatever else fate had in store, too, but most of all I wanted to see snakes. The park is home to the oldest evergreen rain forest in the world, and it has the most gorgeous wild rivers, with steep, jagged limestone formations jutting out of the water. The landscape wasn't like anything I'd ever seen in Kansas or Colorado or even in South America. I hired a guide to show me this region, and the first day he took me floating down the beautiful Khao Sok River. I was drifting along in my tube, minding my own business, blissed out by the landscape, when a fish bit a chunk of flesh out of my ass. I never even saw the little prick coming (I guess maybe he thought I was the prick, since it was his river). He bit right through my shorts and startled me so much I jumped out of my tube, looking around to see what the hell was going on behind me. The fish swam away, but I still have the scar today.

The next day the guide and I took a hike along the river, scanning the shoreline and the trees, looking for lizards, crocodiles, and, of course, snakes. This was my first time in Thailand, and there were plenty of species out there that I'd never yet seen in the wild. Cobras, kraits, and reticulated pythons—not to mention civets, sun bears, and clouded leopards. I was looking for any of them (or, more accurately, all of them) when I spotted a big mangrove snake. These snakes are in the Colubridae family, the largest family, but their genus separates them from many of the others in that category. While most of the colubrids—including garter snakes, king snakes, and pine snakes—are nonvenomous, these guys are an exception. The mangrove snake I was looking at was jet black with thin, horizontal yellow bands going all the way down her body—beautiful, dramatic coloring. She was at least six feet long, coiled on a branch about twenty feet over the water. She had big bulgy eyes that were out of proportion to her narrow head. And, of course, big eyes almost always equals cute. This mangrove was no exception—a pretty, adorable snake. She was not as dangerous as even a copperhead, and I was fascinated with her rear-fanged venom-delivery system and wanted to get closer.

No question as to what should happen next. I started climbing, hoisting myself up the tree until I was level with the snake. I straddled the same branch where she was lazing above the river and started *ever so slowly* scooting forward, snake hook clutched in one hand. To be honest, I didn't have the capture quite figured out, even as I got close. The logistics of how I'd cling to the branch, hook the venomous snake, and position both of us to make an educational video would have to work themselves out. I was winging it, with a capital *W*.

As it turned out, a tree-based capture was not in the cards. When I got about eight feet from the snake, she looked up at me with those big, pretty eyes and just poured herself off the branch and down into the water below. *Sayonara.*

She probably thought she was done with me, but I can be pretty persistent when I want to make a new friend. I lurched back toward the tree's trunk and scrambled down as fast as I could without breaking my neck. The time for stealth was over.

The water was clear and slow-moving, and the mangrove snake was far too big to be inconspicuous, so I could see her hiding beside a ledge. Locking onto her location, I jumped into the chest-deep river. A distance of about thirty feet separated me from her, and I half-swam, half-waded as fast as I could to close the gap. When I finally reached her, I got a grip on her tail and used the hook to steady her. The languid, lounging creature from the tree was not amused. As soon as she hit the air, she lunged for me. I blocked with the hook. She lunged again, and I blocked again. It takes a special kind of hook—eye coordination to hold a six-foot snake's tail over your head while simultaneously blocking her lunges for your face. My hook game was exceptionally good that day as I redirected every shot, careful not to hit or hurt the snake in any way. And all the while, I was wading back toward my camcorder and my guide, who was filming.

By the time I reached the shore, the snake, true to form for a reptile, had settled down, and a few tourists had gathered on the bank, taking in the show. They hung around to watch while we filmed a video, the snake calmly tolerating my handling. The pictures we got that day are among my favorites from my time in Thailand. When we were done filming, I put the mangrove snake back at the base of the tree where I'd spotted her, and she casually made her way back down the bank to the water.

Come to Cambodia

Heading across the Thai border and into Cambodia, I had two major destinations in mind: the ancient Buddhist temples at Angkor Wat and the unspoiled rain forests in the Cardamom Mountains.

Besides being in the same country, the two attractions have almost nothing in common; each offers its own totally unique adventure.

I'd seen pictures of Angkor Wat and its temples that made the place look too exotic to be real. My mission was very straightforward: get there; have an Indiana Jones moment of being one with ancient archaeological history; and experience one of the great bucket-list man-made sights of the Old World.

My first realization when I arrived on the back of a motorbike with the guide I'd hired for the day was that calling the temples man-made is really not fair. There are very few monuments that can hold my attention for long, but the Ta Prohm temple—straight out of *Tomb Raider*—casts an indelible impression. Not only is this temple a seven-hundred-year-old marvel of artistry and architecture, but for much of that time it has been in the process of slowly, gradually, and almost completely being overtaken by the jungle around it. Massive, eerily white tree roots snake their way down from roof to ground, creating cave-like entrances into the once-formal galleries of the temple. Nature is slowly, gracefully winning a battle of longevity here, reclaiming these sacred structures for her own jungle.

Now, I can appreciate a great temple, but in almost any outdoor environment, snakes are always in the back of my mind . . . or maybe at the forefront. As I walked among the ruins, I pushed farther into the shadows and peered harder into the corners and crevices than most tourists, looking for the kind of creature that would belong—a hooded cobra or a viper, maybe. But the only animals I "found" at Angkor Wat were the macaques—and to be fair, it was more a case of them finding me than the other way around.

The temple monkeys are so habituated to people, they think nothing of climbing on you or even poking inside your pockets to look for food. True to my history of meeting primates who seem to like me, the monkeys made quick work of getting to know me, even though I didn't invite them or feed them. A trio of juveniles spotted me in the crowd, scrabbled up my legs, and started jumping on my shoulders and picking through my hair. I don't know if they chose me because I was the tallest, because I was wearing a backpack that might contain food, or for some other reason, but I walked around for a long time with those monkeys on my back, feeling a little like Curious George's beloved man in the yellow hat.

A Beautiful, Brutal Jungle Week

The Cardamom Mountains, in southwestern Cambodia (and eastern Thailand), are the site of one of the largest rain forests in Southeast Asia. They are as remote as they are rugged—so much so that even now, large swaths of them remain unexplored. Such an untamed environment makes the mountains an ideal habitat for tons of rare and alluring species, among them tigers, bears, leopards, elephants, wild dogs, gibbons, and a huge wild cattle species called the gaur. They were all on my must-see list, right up there with the region's reptiles, its unique varieties of turtles and monitors, Siamese crocodiles, and *so many snakes*—vine snakes, pythons, kraits, pit vipers, and one of the species I'd been dying to see in the wild since childhood: the king cobra.

I had a week to spend in the mountains, and I wanted to get out and experience the real, unspoiled environment. This, though, more than most places on earth, is not a destination to go it alone. One of the reasons so much of the region is left untrekked is that it was once heavily laced with anti-personnel land mines left over from when the Khmer Rouge retreated there in the late 1970s. That kind of thing tends to cut way down on tourist interest.

After scouring a bunch of websites, I found an ecotourism company that could provide a guide and a cook to take small groups out into a protected area of marshes, rivers, and mountains.

I tried to set things up by e-mail, but between limited Internet access on both ends of the arrangements and the language barrier, I didn't get very far. I was hoping to get word to a park ranger who only checked e-mail sporadically, and after a long wait he finally got back to me and explained that even though they had never hosted a tourist into the region I wanted to explore, they were willing to make it happen.

I started in Thailand and took a bus across the border into Phnom Penh, Cambodia's capital city. Lots of times when I tell people about my travels, they presume that the sorts of foreign capitals I move through are small cities, but this one, at the juncture of three major rivers, is huge and home to more than two million people. From there I took a smaller bus to a smaller town, then a van to a tiny village. After that, I hitched a ride on the back of a motorbike to a dock and boarded a boat that took me to a hut on the riverbank—the tour company's headquarters.

When I arrived, I again explained where I wanted to go. I couldn't believe it when the young man in the hut told me that another American tourist was on his way to visit the same area. They asked if I could wait two days to see if he showed up, because they'd prefer to take us together. I figured it would be safer and maybe easier to go with another person who spoke my language, so I agreed. There was plenty I could do during day trips until the guy got there.

Two days later, that guy still hadn't shown, and I was done waiting. The guides and I agreed to set out first thing in the morning. I was a little bummed that I wouldn't get to meet the other tourist; I rarely run into people who are as crazy as I am about wildlife—especially wildlife it takes a flight, three buses, a bike, and a boat to reach.

It's a good thing we didn't spend any more time waiting around for that guy, because when I finally got a look at one of the e-mails from the other traveler, I realized that the man we were waiting for who was as crazy as me was . . . me. The communication between me and my hosts was so rudimentary that they hadn't realized that *both* Americans were named Evan Antin.

The guides and I packed our supplies, all of which we had to carry on our backs. I had all the essentials I needed to survive, look for animals, and document the trip, plus a few medications—most importantly, steroids. I'm exceptionally sensitive to poison ivy and poison oak, and I never know what sorts of similar allergens I'll come across in distant jungles on the other side of the world.

Interestingly, nothing I've encountered in the developing world rivals the potency of the poison ivy in the backyard of my childhood home. One touch of that plant and I'm a rashy, itchy mess.

So three guys go into the jungle and two of them speak Khmer and not a word of English or Spanish. One (me) speaks only English and *un pequeño* Spanish. This is something I was starting to get used to in my travels, but it takes patience and goodwill on both sides of any exchange to make it work. We communicated with hand signals and facial gestures and occasional full-body charades, but we figured it out.

To reach the starting point of our trek, we rode for twenty minutes in a truck, which dropped us off in the middle of nowhere. The three of us then rode on the backs of motorbikes for another hour, into the heart of the bush. From there we were on foot. It felt like the farthest I had ever been from civilization—and that's saying something for a guy who had been to Ecuador's Amazon and Panama's Darién Gap.

Each day we hiked ten to fifteen miles, using hand signals as we went. The trails were limited and not well maintained, so we spent a lot of time bushwhacking our way through with machetes.

The Cardamom Mountains have a classic tropical rain-forest climate—which means high humidity and blistering heat—and this trip brought new meaning to my idea of living off the land. Luckily for me, I was traveling with two men who had wildlife skills to rival Bear Grylls's. I consider myself a good hiker, probably better than most Westerners. I rarely slip and fall in rough terrain; I can trek all day without complaint. But these guys made me look like a rank amateur. They moved effortlessly through the jungle, making their way across some of the most rugged terrain I'd ever seen. I straggled behind, getting stuck in the mud, being whacked and scratched by the brush, and sweating so much I teetered on the verge of major dehydration. All the while, I was wearing quality hiking boots and my compadres were wearing jelly sandals. At one point I offered to send them boots when I got back to the States. They both laughed—as if anything *I* had to offer could possibly make them more adept out in the jungle. I'm pretty sure the last thing they wanted was a pair of big clunky boots to slow them down. I guess it's all a matter of perspective.

Every day we had to ford water in one place or another, and each time we emerged from a stream or river or swamp, the upshot was the same: leeches clinging to our legs and feet. They easily made their way into my hiking boots, even plastering themselves between my toes.

With that in mind, the end of each day went something like this: An hour before sundown, we'd reach our camping spot and I would sit on a log or a stone and start scraping hundreds of leeches off my legs and feet. In the time it took me to complete that one simple task, the two guides would remove their own leeches, hang hammocks, dig a fire pit, get a flame going, and build a shelter for our provisions. By the time I looked up from my last leech each night, there were ramen noodles boiling in water and a little pocket of order in whatever nook of the jungle they'd chosen for us. These guys were the real deal, and I have zero doubt they could have survived in that jungle indefinitely on nothing but their resourcefulness and their wits.

On one stifling afternoon, we were hiking in an open grassland area adjacent to a thick wall of forest. One of the guides spotted a vine snake and hissed my name to get my attention. These things are gorgeous. They're tree-dwelling snakes, bright green with elongated faces. They distinguish themselves by always sticking their tongues out, as if to say, "Stay away from me." This one was five feet long and very slender. From side to side, it wasn't even an inch wide—like a great green slithering ribbon.

Technically, vine snakes have a mild venom, although it doesn't do much more than subdue their prey. Generally it won't adversely affect a human unless you're allergic to it. Fortunately for me, I wasn't.

I was admiring this beautiful snake, taking pictures and shooting video, talking about it to the camera. I was also continually trying to teach the guides—so incredibly adept at managing in the jungle but woefully lost in handling my equipment—how to film me. Our interaction would have looked like a comedy routine to anyone watching as we pantomimed taking pictures, shooting video, holding the snake, and capturing the right angle to make the best use of the light.

Just after I finished recording and set the snake free, the guides started talking to each other really fast, in lower voices than usual. I could sense that something wasn't right, that they were concerned. Their eyes were wide, and it was clear that they were nervous.

As I glanced from one to the other, I finally heard what they'd already detected: the crackle of sticks and branches snapping in the distance. It sounded like somebody was hacking their way through the forest. Given that we were basically in no-man's-land, I wondered what or who it could be. Was it developers scoping out the area?

The commotion had been faint at first, but it became more pronounced as its source grew closer. The guides crouched down behind two large bushes. One of them motioned for me to take cover, too, so I ducked behind a tangle of foliage. I was starting to get worried. From what I'd seen so far, these guys weren't afraid of *anything*.

The three of us stayed crouched down as the ruckus got louder. The cracking of branches was getting more aggressive, as if whole trees were being knocked down. I was starting to think maybe we should make a run for it, rather than hunkering down to wait for whatever was coming our way.

Of course, it was already too late. The ground was shaking, and we had obviously run out of time to clear out. And then, *BOOM!* A massive bull elephant burst into the open about fifty yards from us. This guy was in full rampage mode, crushing everything in his path at an all-out charge. I don't scare easily, but I think my heart may actually have missed a beat in that moment. The big fern-like plant I was squatting behind quaked. I watched in total fascination, paralyzed by awe and fear, knowing beyond any doubt that if that elephant turned my way, I was a dead man.

The magnificent beast was moving at about thirty miles per hour, and he mercifully kept going in a straight line, obliterating everything in his path—which we weren't on. Even though their vision isn't the sharpest, elephants have a great sense of smell. If he'd been interested in us, the bull could likely have picked up our scent from as far as a mile away. Luckily for us, he had something else on his mind that day.

When the elephant was gone, I glanced over at the guides. They looked like they'd seen a ghost—a six-ton, mad-as-hell powerhouse of a freaking ghost. Neither of them moved, so I didn't, either. We stayed in our hiding places for another ten minutes, until the sound of the elephant had completely faded away.

No other experience in Cambodia could hold a candle to that heart-stopping encounter with the bull elephant, but when I think of that trek, there is one more indelible memory I carry with me and have vowed not to repeat.

As it turned out, we didn't boil enough water to get us home on the last day of our hike. Every previous day had been partly overcast, but this one was full sun. I hope I will never be as dehydrated again as I was late that afternoon as we made our way back to civilization on a different route from the one we'd taken on the way out. The return trip took us across long stretches of farmland. I knew I was in trouble when I stopped and longingly contemplated the filthy water in a man-made ditch in a cattle field. I knew I couldn't drink it, but a cow-water enema was not off the table. The colon is such a bacterial cesspool anyway that it can handle a little filthy water and hydrate the body from the back end up. I mimed to one of the guides, asking how much longer while pointing to the water and then to the sun. He shook his head. No. Maybe he was just telling me not to drink it, but I took his advice on faith. The two of them had kept me safe through a week in the mine-ridden mountains, and so it seemed a safe bet to trust him a little longer.

An hour later, I was sitting in a chair with a fresh cup of water, both the adventure and the dehydration coming to an end. I thanked my guides, repacked my gear, and got ready for the boat/bus/plane trip back to Colorado, where another year of veterinary school was waiting.

7

Indonesia

Quick litmus test to see if you're packing for leisure or adventure:

Will you need your spitting cobra eye protection?

As I scanned the gear piled on my bed in the fall of 2013, I knew I was getting ready for an epic adventure. It started with the everyday stuff: daypack and backpack (no suitcases), cargo shorts and boots (wear 'em together), swim trunks, cameras, camping air mattress, palm-sized sleeping bag, flashlights, headlamp, batteries. Check, check, check.

And then the good stuff: telescoping snake hook, homemade telescoping croc snare, bush knife, machete, rope, pillowcase (for snake relocation, not for a pillow), antibiotics, passport, vaccination record.

Venom-repelling eyewear.

The gear was in piles, organized alongside half a dozen purple Crown Royal bags. I'm not sure when I realized they were the perfect size for adventure packing, but ever since then I've been adding to my collection. I worked hard in college, but I wasn't a saint.

The last item I laid out was something I'd never packed

before: a stethoscope. After four years of keeping my head down, working my buns off, and getting through more and harder academic work than I'd ever thought I was capable of, I was about to take my first trip as a bona fide veterinarian. I intended to find opportunities to proudly use that stethoscope. I wanted to have fun and get dirty and explore, but I also felt that this time I had something new to offer.

I'd wanted my first trip after vet school to be far away and exotic, somewhere with jungle and amazing animals, somewhere I could spend the entire ten weeks off I'd negotiated when I got my first DVM job and experience something new every day.

For someone spinning a globe with all that in mind, it's impossible to find a more fitting destination than Southeast Asia in general, and Indonesia in particular. The country is vast, complex, and packed with wildlife. It's composed of more than seventeen thousand islands and is home to over 260 million people, who manage to communicate with one another even though they speak hundreds of different languages. The Indonesian Archipelago is part of the Pacific Ring of Fire—a dynamic geographic belt that boasts three-quarters of the world's volcanoes and a staggering 90 percent of its earthquakes. It's got mountains; it's got beaches; it's got forests and swamps and plains. Most importantly to me, it's got the biggest expanse of rain forest in Asia.

So. Much. Jungle.

Indonesia's wildlife is just as exotic and untamed as much of its geography, and it's home to several rare species, among them tigers, pygmy elephants, orangutans, and tree kangaroos. It has some of the world's most endangered crocodiles, countless gorgeous and highly venomous snakes, and massive marine and freshwater turtles. It also has the world's largest and deadliest lizard: the Komodo dragon. Meeting one of these beauties face-to-face had been a dream of mine ever since I was a reptile-and-dinosaur-obsessed little kid. I mean, *dragons.* Does it get any better than that?

It seemed fitting that Tim, the friend who went with me for much of my last-hurrah-before-vet-school trip, should attend the I-survived-vet-school bash, and we were both able to clear our schedules for another adventure. Every year this becomes more of a challenge, and I realize how lucky we've been to have times in our lives when we could go out and see the world together.

Komodo Island Life

Komodo Island is a relatively closed ecosystem, meaning its unique combination of wildlife is different from that found anywhere else in the world—even on the surrounding islands. That ecosystem played heavily into the evolution of the Komodo dragon. These massive lizards have grown to be large (150-plus pounds) and in charge because there are no predators to compete against them. As a result, the island is one of the few places on earth where lizards have assumed the role of apex predator. They are masters of their domain. And their confidence helps make it easy for the dragons to become habituated to all kinds of other creatures, even humans. That's how it happened that a few were just sitting on the open sand, basking in the sun, when our boat arrived at the island.

Maybe it was the days of planes, buses, and boats it took to get there and the resulting straight-up exhaustion, but when I spotted the dragons, I actually got a little choked up. I'd waited twenty-five years and traveled nine thousand miles to have that experience, and it was *happening*. I tried to stay cool as we checked in at the ranger station, but inside I felt like a little kid who's wished and pined for something completely out of reach and finally, against all odds, gets it.

Most people spend only a day on the island, since there's not much in the way of overnight accommodations, but Tim and I had a different agenda. The only habitation on Komodo is for the rangers, who spend a week or two at a time maintaining the park and taking tourists on guided walks; however, through some combination of my veterinary credentials, wildlife experience, and unbridled enthusiasm, I'd worked out a deal with them to let us stay a few nights. Tim and I would pay to sleep in vacant employee housing and be included in the rangers' meals.

Our quarters were a wooden A-frame hut on stilts that had just one thing in it: an ancient, holey, full-sized mattress with foam and springs protruding from it, numerous stains, and the odor of decades of sweat baked in by the heat. It was just the kind of situation where that palm-sized sleeping bag comes in handy—it could never keep anybody warm, because it's basically just a silk sheet, but it creates a barrier between body and bed. In any case, the sleeping arrangements were irrelevant to me. I'd have slept on the floor of the latrine if it meant I could camp among the dragons. One mantra of the intrepid pursuer of rare and remote wildlife experiences: *I can shower later.*

The living conditions gave me a lot of respect for the hard-working locals who served as rangers. An assignment on Komodo Island is not a cushy job.

A note about the stilts: they're there to make sure no dragons wander in. These creatures wouldn't necessarily set out to kill a guy in his sleep, but food is food. Remember the apex-predator thing. To a Komodo dragon, every living creature gets assessed for suitability as a meal—and they're not terribly particular about what fits the bill when they're hungry.

Watching these lizards in their native territory was even better than I'd been imagining all my life. They mosey around with a wide, knuckle-dragging, swaying gait—one that's generally so slow and lumbering you'd think they'd never catch a meal. But pity the fool—deer, water buffalo, snake, or even man—who underestimates one of these creatures when it's hungry. The lumbering—and willingness to lie in wait—allow the dragon to get close enough that when it turns on the speed and *runs*—up to thirteen miles per hour—there's not a big gap to close. Seeing one take off with its big, chunky legs suddenly whirring is like watching a cat swim or a turkey fly—they can do it, but it's always kind of a surprise.

At its top pace, a dragon could potentially overpower some of its prey animals with its weight and strength, but that's not usually how they go about their business. That technique wouldn't play to their strengths, since they don't have the stamina or speed to chase their typical prey, like deer, over significant distances. Instead of aiming to conquer their victims at once, the dragons just try to get in at least one bite. The bacterial colonies in the mouths of these lizards are seriously dangerous, probably the most septic mouths of any animal, and so one bite—combined with the inevitable exposure to stagnant water and the other bacteria in any nonsterile environment—can almost guarantee sepsis and a slow, painful death.

The progression from bite to full-body lethal infection can take a few days. Where is the dragon during that time? Stalking. Waiting. The dragon knows the drill, and knows that it takes time. Once the prey is near death, the dragon will start feeding. And yeah, that's *near* death. It is the final insult of being killed by one of these formidable creatures that it may decide to eat you alive.

It may also invite its friends. Komodo dragons are unique among lizards in that they feed in groups. Most predatory lizards—even other monitor species—hunt and consume only food they can fit in their mouths whole. But the dragon's prey animals are often huge, like deer or buffalo, and as many as a dozen dragons sometimes share a single large-animal meal. This surprising cooperation within the species is yet another adaptation of evolving in an environment where there's no competition for the top of the food chain. That sense of community has its limits, though. When food is scarce, the dragons are not above turning to cannibalism to survive—and for better or worse, *that's* something they have in common with other monitor species.

The dragons are so habituated to the presence of rangers

and ecotourist visitors—and so confident in their roles as island kings—that they hardly flinch when approached at a respectful distance. Their fearlessness gave me the opportunity to capture some of my favorite wildlife photos to date. We followed them for hours, all over the island, me talking about them, trying to understand and mimic their movements, observing how they interact with one another—and Tim manning the camera.

That evening, after a meal of rice, canned sardines, and green beans with the rangers, we settled in our wooden hut. A big part of me wanted to explore the island at night, but for safety reasons that's frowned upon. We were exhausted anyway, so we curled up on the gnarly mattress, ready to call it a night.

Mother Nature had other plans. Minutes after I closed my eyes, I heard animals chattering outside—animals that sounded like monkeys. The bickering dialogue they were having got closer, until I was sure that whatever was out there was right on top of the hut. I crept toward the steps and peered out. A pair of mischievous macaques sat just outside the A-frame, holding our dinner plates up to their faces. One stayed hard at the task while the other gazed back at me with an apathetic expression that seemed to say, "Yeah, yeah. I'm licking your plate. You got a problem with that?"

Adorable, appalling, and an unforgettable lesson about taking better care to return our dishes to the secure food-prep building *immediately* after eating.

Sleep vs. Snake Is a No-Brainer

In a place like Komodo Island, any adventurer might meet something fascinating on a night walk—even just strolling to the kitchen. Before making the very short trek with the plates (after the macaques were done with them), I strapped on a headlamp (the best way to have both light and free hands). From the path, I swung my head back and forth along the ground and up and down in the trees, partly watching to make sure I didn't have an unexpected face-to-face with a dragon, partly looking for what else might be awake. My light skimmed over the slats of the rangers' quarters, which I knew might be prime perches for nocturnal animals, including snakes. I caught a glint of something unexpected and swung the light straight back to pinpoint the creature that had caught my eye. Jackpot!

Up on the roof, gazing back toward the light, was a gorgeous seven-foot Timor python. These thin, agile pythons have a stunning brown pattern on their tops and fronts, but not on their bellies or lower halves. They love to climb, and they're usually tolerant of handling. I knew this snake would be safe to hold, but I was equally confident that the rangers in the hut probably didn't want it directly above them, navigating the gaps in the roof, while they slept. They heard me muttering to myself as I calculated the angle to the roof and tried to figure out what I could grab to steady myself, and they good-naturedly came out to shine another light so I could capture and relocate the snake.

I tightened my laces and scaled the side of the hut till I was standing on the ledge of the roof's frame. Balancing on the narrow side of a decades-old two-by-four, I extended my stance to reach for the snake. I was two feet away, then one foot, and finally just inches. I was trying to stretch just a hair farther when SNAP—the board fractured under my boots. It plummeted, with me on it, ten feet to the floor of the hut.

I'd like to say I always land on my feet, but I'd be lying. This night, though, my first thought as I touched down was *How the hell am I still standing?* I was at the center of a huge pile of debris, and a cloud of fifty-year-old dust was raining down around me. But my body was upright. I tipped my head down to scan for damage by the light of the headlamp. No obvious fractures or puncture wounds. Two feet, two knees, two hands, and everything else seemingly still in its rightful place. I leaned back, craning my neck to see if the python was still there, only of course it had slipped off into the night.

Outside, Tim and the rangers hadn't been able to tell what was going on. They'd heard the snap, and then a thud. When I opened the door of the hut and walked out, half a dozen pairs of eyes blinked back at me. As soon as everyone saw that I was unharmed, they burst out laughing. Tim asked, "Dude, what *happened*?"

Yeah, I fell through the roof. An instant replay would have shown me with my eyes wide, mouth open, and arms whirring before the resounding *thump* of my landing. Steve Irwin meets Wile E. Coyote. I'd find a deep bruise on my inner left biceps the next day and an even bigger one on my left thigh—both so bad they looked like they might have been inflicted with a baseball bat. Those bruises were nothing, though, compared to the potential wounds I'd narrowly missed: a bone fracture or a body full of puncture wounds from rust-covered, tetanus-infected nails would have seriously compromised my Indonesia itinerary. I figured I'd take the bruises without complaint.

I should have headed straight to bed after that, only I was stewing about how close I'd been to the python. Every time I get super close to catching something and it slips away at the last minute, I grow ten times as motivated to find a new creature. I get obsessed. I can't think of anything else. I was wide awake, wired, frustrated, excited—anything but tired.

Mother Nature must have taken pity on me, because in the couple hundred steps between the site of the crash and my own hut, my headlamp caught a second glint of something unusual a few feet above eye level. I leaned in and spied—a green tree pit viper! It was like the answer to a prayer.

I've always had a huge crush on Southeast Asia's vibrant green vipers, so I had yet another reptile fit on the spot. Bruised ego, dusty face, and blackened knees aside, I was not going to let another chance pass me by.

Yet again some of the rangers gathered as audience and light crew. Tim manned a camera, determined to catch my next disaster if it came to that. The rangers were considerably less amused that I was going after this snake—knowing that it was far more dangerous than the beautiful python on the roof. The viper was less than ten feet from the ground, coiled over a branch. Grimacing a little at the soreness starting in my legs, I made my way up the tree—and it held. I reached out with my snake hook and gently eased the viper to the ground, following quickly so I could grab her for relocation rather than risk her taking up residence in one of the huts. She was a little snappy for a minute or two, but she quickly mellowed.

What followed was documented in videos and pictures, a session I will never forget. The rangers started out guarded and afraid for me, but by the end of the encounter, I was teaching an impromptu snake-hooking lesson, showing them how to safely (for both person and viper) capture a snake without touching it with their hands. It was a skill they seemed to appreciate, as they often needed to relocate snakes for tourists' safety.

After relocating the viper away from the huts, I was definitely content to call it a night. Despite the heat, the tiny size and offputting odor of the mattress, and the excitement of the day, in the end it was yet another native creature that had kept me awake a little longer.

The last thing I remember that night was the pitter-patter of little rat feet—Right. Across. My. Back. For a minute my mind zoomed, trying to formulate a plan to bring this invasion to a stop. But in the end, I knew there was zero chance of sealing up that structure, and I was too tired to let a few rats keep me awake. I fell asleep thinking of dragons and snakes, jungles and tree climbing.

A Spitter

After a couple days of tracking dragons and getting to know the rangers, there was only one creature left on my Komodo Island wish list: the spitting cobra. The species on Komodo is the

Javan spitting cobra, and like all spitters, it aims to propel its deadly venom directly into the eyes of its targets. To improve their lethality, these cobras have evolved with a small opening at the front of the fang rather than at the bottom. So when the snake contracts the muscles surrounding its venom glands, venom is forced forward, onto potential threats, instead of downward (typically into soft tissue when we're talking about snakebites). Of course, spitting cobras can still bite and readily inject venom the "old-fashioned" way, but why bite when you can cause the same amount of damage from a safe distance? The venom has an immediate effect on the cornea, resulting in intense pain and possible blindness. That's why it's absolutely necessary to wear protective eyewear when working with spitting cobras. I prefer a transparent pair of woodworking glasses because they have good coverage over my eyes but don't impair my vision with any tinting.

One man's luck is another's misfortune, and when the rangers found a mature, three-foot spitter close to the kitchen, I had a hard time tamping down my enthusiasm. *Somebody* was going to have to relocate that snake away from one of the most heavily trafficked locations on the island.

I was the first (and only) volunteer. I wanted to do it for a lot of reasons, starting with the fact that everything about this snake fascinated me: its fierce attitude, its unique cocktail of venom, its highly adapted delivery system, its quiet power (even when it was just curled up in a quiet corner). I've always jumped at every opportunity to interact with intimidating animals, and as I've gotten older, I've learned to see those moments not just for the satisfaction they give me but also for the chances they create to share information. Maybe it was too much to hope that somebody would come around to admiring the spitting cobra as much as I did; although if I could foster even a little respect and understanding, I was on the job.

After our shared adventure with the tree viper, the rangers

didn't hesitate to guide me to the site: a five-foot hollowed-out log. Hollow logs are common havens for cobras because they offer protection, some temperature moderation, and even occasional food opportunities when rodents live inside or nearby. I was excited, but respectful. I cautiously picked up the log from one end (using the tip of my snake hook just in case the adorable little cobra head was waiting to strike), slowly turned it sideways, and gently shook it in hopes that the snake would show itself. It was like winning the lottery when a gorgeous, slim, deadly cobra answered my knock and came slithering out.

He cut right to the chase, immediately posturing up, hood out, ready to spit or strike. *You rang?*

He was magnificent, a flat-out stunning snake, the perfect combination of beauty and grace, aggression and confidence. I shifted a bit to one side and his head followed, the hood angled toward me, his look imperious—like a king disturbed from his nap.

I set the log aside, checked that my glasses were positioned securely, and gripped my snake hook. I was about to wrangle my first cobra. I'd been dying just to see one, but this guy needed to be moved, so I would have the chance to touch him and to make an educational video about this amazing species—one I put on YouTube shortly after my trip.

Tim was firing away on my camera and at the ready with the camcorder. I created some distance from the cobra by steadying it at the end of the hook, all the while explaining to the camera some of my favorite cobra adaptations and features—most of all, the way their teeth are perfectly designed to spit venom, hard and fast and accurate, into the eyes of their prey. Just as I was going into detail on how cobra venom essentially paralyzes the nervous system and inhibits your ability to breathe . . . *splat!* The little bugger spat right onto my face. I could feel droplets of venom along my upper lip and nose. Holy crap.

I set both hook and cobra on the ground and backed off a little. I knew that technically I had nothing to fear—the venom was harmless on my skin, where it couldn't be absorbed. That said, the deadly compound on my face was centimeters from my eyes. On the inside, I was freaking out—not because I was scared, but because I was stoked. A cobra had just spit on *me*. I flashed back to seeing Steve Irwin blocking his eyes with a backpack when he was working with these cobras. I'm aware that getting fired up at the idea of having cobra venom on your face is absurd; nevertheless, I felt like I'd been initiated into some exclusive club for obsessive reptile enthusiasts.

No matter what I was feeling, I knew I needed to settle down. The rangers were watching, and I'd been giving them advice on how to handle the island's venomous species. I couldn't show fear *or* excitement in that moment. So I slowly wiped the venom off my nose and upper lip with the front of my shirt. Then I rinsed my face with water, all the while thinking, *Just stay cool.*

Trying to project calm, I stepped back toward the hook and glanced up at Tim and the rangers. They looked back at me in horror. Like I'd taken that shot straight in the eye. Like I might fall down and die.

I cleared my throat and reached for my hook, and that's when Tim had had enough. He shook his head and leveled a loud, clear warning my way: "Dude! We are *done*."

This from my most loyal and least complaining accomplice and cameraman, my best friend since childhood, the guy who'd spent two days filming me running alongside Komodo dragons without complaint.

I respected his comfort level, so I bagged the snake without further narration and moved it to a remote area of the island. The cobra had had enough, too, or he wouldn't have spit at me in the first place.

For the record, relocating that snake—and the dozens of others I've moved in my life—was done in his best interest. The truth is, a snake like that near a tourist footpath and building in a national park was a potential danger and also a potential target. The short-term stress he endured while I relocated him was a small price to pay for his continued freedom. Relocation can have risks of its own, but in this case, I was confident it was the best option for the circumstances.

I left Komodo Island feeling a unique sense of accomplishment. There are few places in the world where any combination of planning and luck could have handed me so many incredibly close, personal experiences in such a short time. I've spent days— even weeks—trekking scores of miles through jungle and come away empty-handed. But Komodo is so rich in wildlife, it turned out to be a can't-miss trip.

People of the Forest

Getting around Indonesia involves significant geographic, logistic, and linguistic barriers as you make your way between islands, so Tim and I frequently had to choose between sacrificing money or time to get from one point to the next. We decided to splurge on a flight rather than take the long bus-then-boat trek to the island of Borneo.

We started in northeast Borneo's Wehea Forest, a gorgeous protected landscape and one of the best clouded leopard research areas in the world. Tourists rarely make their way to this area because it's so inaccessible, but Tim and I didn't mind the hardship. We hitchhiked rides with semi-trucks heading to a local coal excavation (one of the biggest in Southeast Asia). The wildlife was rich at Wehea, including a mother-son orangutan family that fed in the fig tree above our wooden bungalow. The forest was pristine, too, but we could stay for only a few days. We wanted to see more orangutans, and we were across the island from what's probably the best place in the world to watch them close-up: Tan-

jung Puting National Park. The park is home to proboscis monkeys, long-tailed macaques, gibbons, and, at a place called Camp
Leakey, the epicenter of the world of orangutan protection.

The camp was founded in 1971 and is home to the longest con-
tinuous study of a wild mammal by one principal investigator in
history. Dr. Birute Galdikas has been working there for the past
forty years to help the world understand and protect orangutans.
She is a legend in wildlife conservation, and I had my fingers
crossed that I might even meet her during my visit.

The orangutans are desperately in need of her protection.
More than half of the planet's orangutan population has been
wiped out in the last hundred years, killed for bushmeat, in
service of the illegal pet trade (killing mothers to take babies),
and most of all by logging operations for the palm oil industry.
Orangutans are considered nothing more than agricultural pests
by workers as they move into territories the apes have lived in for
hundreds of years. Most of the world's orangutans live in Borneo
(the rest live in Sumatra), and without protection they could one
day be a species we only remember, not one that exists.

The word *orangutan* means "person of the forest" in Malay,
and if you spend any time observing them, it's easy to see how
these highly intelligent and sensitive animals earned their name
through their similarity to humans.

For decades, Dr. Galdikas and her team have been rescuing and
relocating orangutans from the pet trade and rehabbing them.
After a quarantine period, these animals are released into vast
tracts of protected lands, where they are free to roam (or leave) as
they please. Most, especially the females, choose to hang around
and even raise their babies close to this place they consider home.
Since many of them have lived as captives, camp staff members
and volunteers regularly stock feeding stations to make sure they
won't go hungry in the wild. The feeding stations are what I came

to see—the orangutans are semi-habituated to people and will come out of the trees and in from the forest to help themselves to fresh fruit (just bananas when I was there) and milk on their own terms.

As Tim and I set out with a guide to visit the feeding stations, we weren't sure what to expect. It's one thing to read about a magical orangutan forest somewhere in Borneo, but it's something else to be there, peering up into the trees, waiting for a sighting. The first thing we learned is that the preserve is huge and the feeding stations are distant from one another, so it often takes a boat ride and a long hike to get from one to the next. Our plan was to visit one each day. We slept on our guide's boat at night to make sure we could hit the ground running each morning.

The first feeding station didn't disappoint. Just a few yards in front of us, a large female sat perched in a tree beside the station, looking everywhere but at us. I tossed a banana in her direction, hoping to get her attention, and this girl *caught* it in her palm without ever once looking at me. It was an astoundingly impressive demonstration of superior peripheral vision, not to mention eye-hand coordination.

When it was time to trek back to our boat, we stepped onto the wooden walkway we'd followed to get to the feeding station. Vegetation grew high and thick on both sides. As we walked back the way we'd come, I looked up to see a burly male orangutan peering onto the walkway ahead. There was no mistaking his gender—he had the wide cheek pads (flanges) males develop as they mature and was far larger than the female we'd just encountered at the feeding station. Our guide put up a hand to halt us, saying, "We wait."

So we did. When the big guy moved away from the path, we continued. Minutes later we heard a rustling behind us and turned around to see him again, clearly watching us.

I was a little freaked out by this apparent stalking. Of all the animals I've worked with and species I've gotten to know, few intimidate me the way primates can. Despite all our similarities, they seem the least predictable creatures. Orangutans have a reputation for quiet intelligence, for calm, for a lack of aggression. That said, they are wild animals who will fight with effective brutality when they feel the need to defend, and the average orangutan is easily several times stronger than the average man.

Did this macho male perceive us as a threat? We wanted nothing more than to stay out of his way. My heart was pounding as we picked up the pace, continuing along the walkway, moving away from the orangutan. Five minutes passed. Then we rounded a bend and there he was, burly as hell, completely blocking our path. He had his left arm stretched out to grip a high branch on a tree, and his left leg was lifted and braced against the tree as well. You know how a guy who's looking for a fight takes a wide, tall stance? This was that times ten. He held his head high and stared down at us, as if to say, "'S up? Don't you know this is mine?"

And then he started walking toward us.

My mind started madly replaying a story a zookeeper had told me about an orangutan who lived in an enclosure with a wide-slatted walkway above it, to give zoo employees access. The keeper instructed a new employee to stay off the walkway, explaining that it was too easy for the female orangutan below to reach through. The new guy walked across anyway. Curious, the orangutan moved closer. Then she stretched her long arm through the slats and grabbed the guy's foot. He screamed, and when he did, she screamed too, releasing her grip and racing to the corner of her enclosure. It was obvious that she hadn't meant the poor guy any harm. It didn't matter, though; every bone in his foot was broken. The doctor told him he was lucky his foot had stayed attached to his leg.

How much of that story was accurate? I had no idea. But it seemed very real in the moment as I glanced down at my own body and my own vulnerabilities. I wondered if orangutans would rip off men's genitals the way chimps have been known to do; I figured I didn't want to take any chances, given how closely related we all are. So I crossed my hands over my loins and said a silent prayer to get out of there with no bones broken and all my parts intact.

When I glanced over at our guide, he was slipping a few steps back. Tim, behind me on the walkway, froze. We couldn't run, because there was no way we could have outraced the great ape if our fleeing provoked a chase response. We couldn't keep going, because that might be mistaken for aggression. Our best bet was to get small. We gingerly stepped off the path, crouching as we did so, turning slightly away from the walkway and averting our eyes from the orangutan. Then we waited. His move.

Macho lowered his leg from the tree and took one step our way. Then another. In my mind I was screaming at my 210-pound, six-foot-two self to shrink, to blend in, look passive, be one with the forest.

Ask almost anyone who spends time working with primates in general and orangutans in particular and they'll tell you this species is known for their thoughtful, solitary nature. They are thinkers, philosophers even. But this was my first day among these magnificent creatures, and what I was seeing was unmistakably aggression.

In the end, Macho seemed satisfied with our stand-down. While we held our breath, he ambled up the walkway toward us, and then mercifully eased right by—so close he actually grazed my daypack as he went. I suspect I've never been so happy to see a magnificent wild animal walk away.

Since we were already off the path, I got to thinking that I might spot a native snake if I ventured out a bit. Maybe a python, or a coral snake, or even a flying snake. I pushed into the jungle a short distance, focused on spotting a distinctive curve or hint of movement in a tree or on the ground ahead. When I reached a small clearing, I glanced up at the unexpected brightness, looked across the small patch of sunshine, and saw a middle-aged woman with a round face and shoulder-length gray hair. She wore glasses and a wide-brimmed hat, and I recognized her instantly: Dr. Galdikas!

I raised my hand in a wave, thinking I would introduce myself.

Dr. Galdikas looked me up and down, unsmiling.

I grinned, tongue-tied.

"*What* are you doing in this area?" she asked sternly.

I peered around myself, confused but still smiling. Had I wandered out of the visitor-friendly area? Had I offended the great doctor in some way?

I turned back to where she stood waiting for an answer, clearly not feeling the overwhelming surge of warmth and affection that I was experiencing.

"I'm sorry," I stammered. "I didn't realize this area is restricted."

She kept her gaze level.

"Um, I'll head back now."

She nodded and waited for me to go.

Call it what you want, but as far as I'm concerned, that interaction totaling seven curt words from the doctor and a few eager replies from me counts as meeting one of the great primate researchers of all time. Dr. Galdikas was a student of the famed anthropologist and archeologist Louis Leakey, along with Jane Goodall and Dian Fossey. The three of them set out to virtually untraveled corners of the world to raise the level of primate studies, and succeeded. Had it not been for her, my trip to this remote spot in Indonesia might never have happened, and I would surely not be coming off a heart-stopping and mind-altering personal interaction with an orangutan in his natural habitat.

My only regret was that I hadn't thought to introduce myself as *Dr.* Evan Antin. Maybe asked an intelligent question. Maybe shaken her hand.

Ah, well. I bounded back toward the jungle path, turning the moment over in my head, happy enough with what I'd gotten. Dr. Galdikas had spoken to me. I really didn't mind that all she'd done was politely tell me to beat it.

Each day in Borneo was a new orangutan adventure. It's impossible to observe these creatures and not be fascinated by how similar they are to humans—and yet how different. This is always the primate conundrum: one minute it's like looking in a mirror or seeing your own mannerisms aped back for you (pun intended); the next you are clearly seeing a completely wild creature. One area where you can almost recognize the similarities, though, is when you watch a mother with her kiddos.

The final station we visited was the most spectacular. It was bigger than the others, constructed so that the jungle leads your eyes to it, almost like a natural amphitheater in the forest. Rangers put out food on a set schedule, so if you arrive there before a day's meal is delivered you have a great chance of getting a glimpse of the orangutans coming to eat. For nearly two hours we sat a few yards from the feeding platform, mesmerized by the show.

When the orangutans finally left the platform, we reluctantly headed back toward our boat, but our encounter wasn't over yet. On a narrow footbridge we encountered a juvenile male and his mother. The young orangutan was not a baby, though he was still small and immature, and naturally curious about the strangers in his habitat. He came up close to us, checking us out, then eased back a little without looking away. It was nothing bold, just a little bit of engagement. He was the cutest thing, big wide eyes in his bald brown head, pudgy belly, long arms and legs, with a quizzical look on his face, like he just wanted to figure things out. At one point he decided it might be okay to touch me, and he reached out his hand and brushed mine.

And that was when Mama, who'd been watching from a cautious distance, decided she wasn't having it anymore. She put herself between me and her son, squared off, and then started marching toward me, chiding away in a steady barrage of vocalizations that it took zero imagination to interpret as a mother telling a stranger to get away from her kid. I'd heard that tone before—from my own mom, from my grandma. The international, interspecies tenor of mothers who are not taking any more crap from you right now, so cut it out, thank you very much.

I respected the mother's wishes and retreated, ready to hike back out of the forest. At no time did her tone or body language seem hostile, like that of the male orangutan who had blocked our path the first day. She was issuing a friendly warning, one I accepted and respected. The last thing I wanted to do was upset her or the peace in her precious family of people of the forest.

Surgery in Sulawesi

North Sulawesi is a thousand miles from Camp Leakey. It's a critical location for the illegal wildlife trade because it is the closest Indonesian island to the Philippines and an export point for animals and animal products bound for China, Taiwan, and Japan. Authorities here have confiscated everything from orangutans to sun bears, pangolins to cockatoos on their way out of the country. Without a safe, capable wildlife rescue center to care for these animals, though, those confiscations wouldn't lead to any kind of positive outcome for the animals.

That's where Tasikoki Wildlife Rescue Centre comes in. The sanctuary cares for, rehabilitates, and, when possible, releases a wide variety of rescued species, and it does it with a team of local experts and volunteers who come from all over the globe to participate in their mission.

I wanted to be a part of this, but I'd tried to contact the organization through its website a couple times without success. I'd read that the facility only takes veterinarian volunteers who can stay for a month, something I couldn't do, but I still hoped I'd be able to pitch in and work with this team, even if for only a few days.

So with no invitation or reservation, Tim and I made our way to Tasikoki and were greeted at the gate by a volunteer who seemed distinctly stressed-out. Was it something we'd said? I told her I was a veterinarian, and she said just that morning over breakfast, the staff members had been talking about how much they needed a vet to help out, but all their usual resources were unavailable.

As far as I was concerned, that was fate. I told her we could stay for four or five days and that I was at the facility's disposal to help in any way I could while I was there.

That's when we realized that her distress had nothing to do with unexpected company. A totally unexpected drama had been unfolding just as we'd arrived. The volunteer had left her fanny pack sitting too close to the enclosure of a male orangutan, and he'd snatched it and picked through it. To her horror, the one thing in it that had interested him was a pill bottle. It had taken him a few seconds to figure out the childproof cap, but once he had, he had proceeded to take all the Ritalin pills inside. The poor young woman was devastated, telling us the story through tears.

It seemed I was the closest thing to an expert who was going to show up that day, so I asked how many pills she'd had in the bottle. The answer was reassuring: no more than five. There was an active discussion going on among the staff about whether this orangutan needed to be sedated so he could have his stomach pumped, but I was fairly certain that such a step would pose a greater danger than the pills. Humans and orangutans have similar physiology, and given the animal's weight and the relatively low amount of the overdose, we decided to monitor the pill pilferer rather than go overboard and dart him. Remarkably, over the course of the next twenty-four hours, there was *no* observable difference in his behavior. People who take too much Ritalin may find themselves wanting to clean their homes, and when I heard about this orangutan I immediately thought of that scene in *There's Something About Mary* where someone accidentally takes an upper and then aggressively cleans her house. I wasn't anticipating behavior like this in a greater ape, but I would've kept my eyes open for apparent restlessness—acting jumpy or excitable, hyperactive, more vocal (just like people on drugs like this)—or a loss of appetite, increased urination and/or defecation, or, worst case, cardiac arrest/coma/death. Unfortunately, it would be too dangerous to try to do a physical exam on an orangutan, but it would've been nice to monitor his heart rate, body temperature, and blood pressure. In the end, though, the medicine didn't seem to affect him at all.

With the crisis averted, we could get to more urgent issues. First on the list was a crested black macaque with a nasty tooth abscess. This was not a species I knew. I'd encountered other macaque species in my travels, but this particular kind—also called a Celebes macaque—is rare and critically endangered, not an animal I would have met without going out of my way to find one. I watched the troop that morning in awe of how beautiful they were. They look like small-scale black baboons, with sleek fur, expressive amber-brown eyes, and hairless black faces whose long shape makes them seem permanently concerned. I love to watch these guys in action, because they're 100 percent sleek black, like little monkey ninjas in the forest. The staff pointed out one monkey who was staying to the sidelines, especially at mealtimes. An infection in his canine (fang) tooth had spread to his maxilla (a.k.a. upper jaw) and was hurting every time he tried to eat. He'd lost weight, and the staff was worried about him. This is a common issue in large-fanged monkeys, so I wasn't surprised to see the tooth-root abscess.

I'd never done dental work on a monkey, but I'd done plenty on dogs and cats, and I'd taken enough exotic animals classes to know that one of the most common refrains in exotics is that a lot of what we do in the field is extrapolating from what we *do* know.

Dogs and cats are our basics, where we have the most experience and knowledge. And they help us learn how to approach other mammal species. I knew I was capable of the job. The facility had an anesthesia protocol they'd used successfully before, so I helped prepare the little OR while they darted the macaque.

As I operated on the monkey, I was outwardly cool. Inside, though, I was nearly overwhelmed by two different trains of thought. The first was just about successfully completing the task at hand. The upper incisor I was working on was more prominent than any animal tooth I'd encountered in my training, with deep roots. I focused on a just-another-dog mind-set, but the fact is, these teeth were unlike anything I'd ever touched before.

The second train of thought was more unnerving. When you are working on a dog or a cat, you understand that your patient is someone's family member. You are painstakingly careful because you know that pet is treasured. When you work in an environment like a wildlife rescue, the stakes are different, and for different reasons. The monkey on my operating table was a critically endangered primate who could die if I made a mistake, and who could also die if I failed to stop the spread of his infection. There might have been only a few hundred of this rare species left in the world, and if I contributed to the loss of the beautiful, sleek black monkey under my hands, that loss would have a toll for the overall population of his species, bringing them one step closer to extinction.

In the moment, I knew the best I could do was to push all those feelings down and focus on the surgery. Extract the tooth, clear the infection from the socket, flush the wound, suture, and administer antibiotics while my patient was unconscious. Through it all I kept thinking, *Stay calm, Evan. This is what you came for.*

Some of the scariest moments of my career have happened in the operating room. Most veterinarians who do surgery will tell you the same. But that day my hands were steady, my eyes were sharp, and I was confident that I was fulfilling my purpose, putting four years of veterinary studies to good use.

Over the course of the next few days I performed examinations, cleaned and stitched a laceration on another crested black macaque, repaired a wound on a moor macaque, and helped manage a chronic wound on a massive Bornean river turtle—probably the largest freshwater turtle in that part of the world—but no moment stands out more vividly in my memories than one from our last day in Sulawesi, when Tim and I lingered outside an enclosure and watched the crested black macaque who now had only one large upper canine tooth in his jaw feast on his dinner along with his troop. He had recovered beautifully. It was huge for me. I swear that this one moment, not to mention the thousands that would follow, was worth the four years I'd invested in vet school—all the studying, all the exams and practicums and lectures.

I stowed my stethoscope in my bag as we headed for the airport and the long trek home, completely satisfied with the ten weeks we'd spent in Indonesia and with the life choices that had brought me to this place.

PART FOUR

Critical

My fave warning sign in all of my travels, further encouraging me to find a wild cobra. This was in Wehea Forest in Kalimantan (Borneo). I never found that cobra there, but I found a bunch of other snakes and monitors, and I saw my first fully wild orangutans. One of the most gorgeous jungles I've ever visited.

My pet iguana "Pete," which my uncle gifted me. I'm ten years old here.

My Maasai homestay experience in Tanzania. My homestay brother, the chief's son, is standing to my left, his best friend to my right, and another friend and that friend's little brother on my far left.

At the Elephant Nature Park in Thailand. I've seen some amazing moments of kindness between animals, but to this day I've never seen anything as touching as the relationship between these two elephants, named Jokia and Mapong.

Sharing the water with tiger sharks in the Bahamas made my life!

[OPPOSITE] A wild Philippine crocodile in the Sierra Madres Natural Park, Northern Luzon, Philippines. Joey and I pumped her stomach for his crocodile diet study. I didn't expect freshwater snails to make up such a significant portion of their diets!

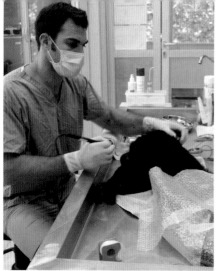

Dental procedure on the crested black macaque, also known as a Celebes macaque, at the Tasikoki Wildlife Rehabilitation Center. Besides my clinical work near Los Angeles, this was my first wildlife veterinary procedure after graduating vet school.

Komodo National Park in Indonesia is home to the world's largest and deadliest lizard: the Komodo dragon. Meeting one of these beauties face-to-face had been a dream of mine ever since I was a little kid. I mean, *dragons*. Does it get any better than that?

Also on Komodo Island is the Javan spitting cobra, and like all spitters, it aims to propel its deadly venom directly into the eyes of its targets. Pack your goggles. This is the first cobra I ever encountered in the wild.

Two different species of green tree viper intertwined in Khao Yai National Park, Thailand.

Making a new friend in a subadult male orangutan in Tajung Puting National Park, Kalimantan (Borneo).

An adult male orangutan in Tanjung Puting National Park. This was the male that scared the bejesus out of us on the trail.

A baby slender loris checking out my hand while I'm checking out him. Those eyes are cute, but his bite is venomous. This kiddo was an orphaned rescue and being cared for by a wildlife zoo and educational center in Sri Lanka.

During my 2019 visit to the Lwiro Primate Rehabilitation Center in the Democratic Republic of the Congo, I was able to hold this new friend: a freshly rescued baby red-tailed monkey.

Gorillas are native only to Africa, and the two species (eastern and western) are separated by about six hundred miles of Congo basin forest in the center of the continent. Eastern gorillas, seen here, are divided into two subspecies, and the critically endangered mountain gorilla was the species I was able to witness here in Rwanda. There are only around a thousand of these gorillas left in the wild. I later saw eastern lowland gorillas in the Democratic Republic of the Congo.

Here with the indigenous Palawan water monitor on the island of Palawan, Philippines.

Is it a mustache? Is it a bear? Is it a cat? It's a bearcat. This is a baby, but adults grow into massive sixty-plus-pound tree-dwelling mammals with faces like little bears, cat eyes and whiskers, a prehensile tail like a howler monkey, and long, sharp claws like a wolverine.

Baby rhinos are the best selfie companions. Here I am with an eight-week-old female orphan in South Africa at the Hoedspruit Endangered Species Centre.

In the fall of 2019, while helping relocate a small seed population of giraffes from Murchison Falls National Park to Uganda's Pian Upe Wildlife Reserve.

8

Fiji and Tahiti

I'll start with a happy memory from the Kansas City suburbs. It's 1999. I'm fourteen years old, hanging out with a bunch of friends in one of their basements. We're watching a movie, trying to find girls to invite over, sneaking a couple beers, and laughing our asses off.

Among the boys in that basement is my new friend Joey Brown. I met him early in freshman year, and he and I had a lot in common: both (pretty) good students, both athletes, both born with a wild streak that made us quick to sign on for any out-of-the-ordinary adventure. Joey had a huge, disarming grin that gave him an air of total innocence, but it didn't fool his close friends.

Flash forward to 2017. I walk out of Nadi International Airport in Fiji, seven thousand miles from Kansas City, and there's that big grin. My longtime bro is now a highly respected wildlife expert, a herpetologist, a conservation biology scholar, a wildlife consultant on *Survivor*, and my host as I assist for a week with his research on the critically endangered Fijian crested iguana.

I've always had a good imagination, but if someone had told

me that night in 1999 that one day the two of us would be working together on a tropical island halfway around the world from
where we started—trying to help save a reptile species from
extinction—I'm pretty sure I would have laughed hard enough
to choke on my beer.

Super-Sleepy Iguanas

Joey was headquartered on Mana Island, where there are plenty
of creature comforts, but his research was on nearby Monuriki
Island, which is uninhabited. When he was in research mode,
he'd pack up his tent, gear, and food, then boat over for a few days
at a stretch to work. The entire island is less than a square mile,
surrounded by coral reef on all sides. It's visually stunning, a tiny
mass of jagged cliffs, gold sand, and lush vegetation jutting up in
the middle of the Pacific. It's so much the definitive island setting
that with the whole world to scout, the producers of the movie
Cast Away chose to film on Monuriki.

It was a fittingly beautiful environment in which to catch one
of the most colorful lizards I've ever seen. The Fijian crested is
so bright it almost seems unreal. A typical specimen is vibrant
emerald green with white and black stripes. His legs are blue,
his toes green, his eyes bright amber, and his mouth and nostrils
marked by tiny yellow streaks. Altogether, those features add up
to a creature that looks more like it just walked out of *Alice in
Wonderland* than one that has evolved in nature.

With most of the research happening at night, Joey and I
spent the days catching up and hiking to the edges of the island.
Monuriki's peaks are pretty high, considering how small the total
expanse of land is, but you can still reach its tallest peak from the
beach in less than two hours. Back at camp, we ate canned food
and sat in the little lagoon near where we'd pitched our tents.
The water was warm and crystal clear—a big, spectacular bath-
tub courtesy of Mother Nature. I travel to a lot of places where

the process of making my way there and the accommodations are things I have to endure for the privilege of getting close to the animals. This was the opposite: we may have been sleeping on the ground and eating out of cans, but it was the most gorgeous, isolated tropical beachfront camping a traveler could ever desire.

Each night around eight, after a big dinner, we'd set out to go trekking—rested and ready to spend the next six to eight hours straight looking for iguanas.

At night we could see all the stars, which provided just enough natural light to help us scout. Joey was familiar with locations where he'd seen individuals in the past, and he'd also fitted some of the iguanas with radio telemetry trackers. These systems are often used in wildlife research; each device puts out its own unique radio wave frequency—almost like its own radio station. Joey and I carried an antenna designed to pick up these signals and tell us if we were getting close. It's kind of like a seeking game where if the signal gets stronger you're "getting warmer" and if it gets weaker you're "getting colder." When it gets loud you're downright hot, and chances are if you shine a flashlight up into the trees you're standing under, the iguanas' fluorescent coloring will glow back at you. You can't miss them once you get close enough to spot that reflection.

Of course, if you want to measure and tag the iguanas, you've got to climb up into the canopy and catch them. When it comes to most arboreal lizards, if they're that far up, you might as well not waste your time. They'll have way too much of a head start. But *these* iguanas live a chill island life. They have very few predators, and they are remarkably deep sleepers—like Ambien deep. We were climbing these trees, edging onto branches, reaching out for these guys, and it wasn't until we were within a foot or two of them—grabbing distance—that they'd wake up and go from sound asleep to bright-eyed and confused. The key is to get your hands on them right before that happens so they don't have time to flee. These are wild lizards, and they can be aggressive, biting and turning your forearms into bloody scratching posts.

To reduce the stress on the iguanas, whenever possible we'd place a little cloth mask around their faces that covered their eyes. Limiting their sensory input worked like a dream to calm them down, and that's when we'd weigh them. Joey had rigged up a hanging scale with a little leather harness, and he'd slip each iguana's front legs over the strap and then lift them up to get an accurate weight. You'd think that process might piss the little buggers off, but no. Without exception they just hung there in the harness, legs loose, bellies pooched out, occasionally giving us a little side-eye if the mask slipped, but otherwise content.

Each time we caught an iguana we'd weigh and measure it, clip a tail scale for a DNA sample, get a cloacal culture to test for bacterial colonies, and microchip it if it wasn't already tagged. In some cases, we placed radio transmitters, so that Joey could track the individual and its habits. More of the iguanas had already been tagged by Joey than not, so when we encountered one already in his database we'd just record a few quick measurements and let it go. We took turns filming, both of us happy to have an experienced cameraman on hand. We'd both had to learn every trick about making your own videos through years of trial and error, so having an accomplice was a nice change of pace and took a lot of the pressure off.

Joey had been doing this for months, so his tree-climbing skills were at almost spider-monkey level. He'd scramble up and down as if it were nothing. As for me, I love to climb, but I'm a little big for it and definitely not as practiced as the reptile whisperer I was working with. I spotted one specimen in a tree with a few dead branches and decided to chance it. Just as I grasped the iguana, the branch I was standing on gave way, dropping me, the iguana, and a ton of leaf litter and wood dust to the sand. I wasn't too surprised that I'd fallen, but I was not expecting to look up and find Joey actively filming, narrating my crash landing. He zoomed in on my hands and nodded his approval as he announced for the camera, "Evan! . . . And he's still got the iguana."

Even after the fall, this colorful little lizard was relaxed. She had managed to wrap the long toes of her front feet around my thumb, but if she was experiencing any fear, any tension at all, any concern whatsoever about the dive we'd just taken, she was hiding it like a pro.

Working with these sleepy little iguanas, I felt like I'd gone down a rabbit hole and landed in a herper's wonderland, replete with days on the beach, nights spent climbing trees (which I enjoy even when there are no reptiles involved), and interactions with these crazy-colorful lizards. The experience had so little in common with my experiences trying to catch wild arboreal lizards anywhere else in the world that it felt more like playing a video game than like research.

The only downside of this whole trip was that it was predicated on the fact that these iguanas are critically endangered. If "desperately endangered" were a category, they'd be in that one. Estimates put the remaining population of Monuriki's iguanas at only one to two hundred individuals. There are a few reasons for the decrease in their numbers, but three of them can be attributed to other species I love: goats, rats, and cats. More and more, forest that was once iguana territory has been made inhospitable to them by grazing goats. Rats steal their eggs; female iguanas mostly live in trees, but they nest on the ground. And on many of the islands where these guys used to be safe, one of nature's most efficient and deadly predators has been introduced: the cat. Honestly, the sedentary, trusting Fijian crested iguana is a poster child for easy prey.

Monuriki is an exceptionally safe place for the iguanas, not just by nature but also by design. In a 2011 initiative, Fijian federal nature authorities partnered with the U.S. Geological Survey and the San Diego Zoo to clear the island of goats and rats and then introduced a group of the "neon dragons" to repopulate.

For now, at least, the only predation iguanas on Monuriki have to contend with is occasional bird swoops, and thanks to Joey's research, the iguana's patterns and habits are better understood than ever. Understanding a creature—things like what it eats, how it travels, when and where it sleeps, and how it reproduces—helps conservationists do everything in our power to protect it.

After a few days of getting rugged on Monuriki, Joey and I headed back to Mana and the luxuries of beds, running water, and freshly prepared food. I had learned more than a man should be able to know about the diet (mostly leaves), breeding (mating happens in the spring, followed by a nine-month incubation period), habits (sound sleeping!), and conservation of the critically endangered Fijian crested iguana. As we hugged good-bye at the airport, Joey and I were almost twenty years older than when we first met, but it felt like both our careers were just starting to take off.

Magical Island

Roughly two thousand miles east of Fiji, the volcanic island of Tahiti rises up out of the Pacific. This figure-eight-shaped island is home to gorgeous black sand beaches, even prettier black pearls, and a diverse collection of tropical wildlife both in and out of the water. My objective was the nearby island of Mo'orea, which lives up to its nickname "Magical Island" with blue skies, clear water, a series of eight mountain peaks surrounding the island, and warm, friendly people who welcome tourists with open arms.

I arrived on Mo'orea hoping to get up close and personal with humpback whales, but on my way to dinner the first night, I found five tiny kittens by the side of the road. These poor munchkins still had their umbilical cords attached and their eyes closed. It was clear that they'd been abandoned, and that there was zero chance they were going to make it if left on their own. Unfortunately, this is something that happens all over the world—

domesticated animals wind up without anyone to take care of them.

I figured it was a "finders keepers" situation, and even though I knew there was no way I could pack five kittens in my carry-on back to the States, I wanted them to have a fighting chance. I took on the labor-intensive job of feeding them and stimulating them to pee and poop ("piddling" them) for the short term. Mo'orea doesn't have any major animal hospitals or rescue organizations, any place I could just drop the kittens into someone else's care, so I did the best I could to keep them alive until I could find them a home. Two days later, I took "my" kittens on their first boat ride, a ferry trip to French Polynesia's main island, Tahiti, and Papeete, its small capital city.

I'd found Dr. Olivier Betremieux on Instagram and told him about the kittens, and he had welcomed all of us to his veterinary office. Walking through the door and shaking his hand, I immediately thought that Olivier reminded me a little bit of somebody. He was a pretty big guy, young, fit, needing a shave, and totally dedicated to the animals in his care. We seemed to be wearing matching uniforms, too: faded jeans and worn T-shirts.

Dr. B's dog Hannah came straight over to check out the kittens. This sweetheart mixed breed was wearing a doggie backpack that said GIRL POWER, and she stood with her front legs on the exam table to give her new charges a sniff. She was super gentle, as if she'd been taking care of orphaned kittens all her life. I introduced the five: Brownie (who got his name because he kept pooping on me), Cheese, Napoleon, Sharky, and Bandit. The vet seemed a tiny bit surprised these three-day-old kittens already had names, but I suspect that being a fellow animal person, he understood that there was no way I could have carried them around for any length of time without naming them. I had already bonded with these babies, and I was hoping the good doctor could help them find homes.

Broken Bone

Dr. B agreed to shelter the kittens until homes could be found for them, and while I was there he asked if I'd take a look at a dog in his care. The stray looked like a scruffy, long-haired Jack Russell terrier. He had the sweetest face, with floppy brown ears and big brown eyes. It didn't take an expert to see that this poor puppy was in pain. It was etched in his expression, but he didn't let out a sound.

The stray's leg was totally busted—a compound fracture had left bone and blood exposed. Around the wound the affected tissue was septic and necrotic, badly infected and dying. Dr. B had rescued the dog off the street, even though he knew—just like I did after my first look at this wound—that an amputation was the only chance this poor guy had of recovering from the infection, which had already reached his leg bones.

If I'd encountered a patient that needed to have a limb amputated on one of my very first trips after vet school, I'm not sure I would have felt equal to the task. I would have done it, but I would have been scared. Back then, I could clean out wounds, extract teeth, and stitch up lacerations. I'd done a few abdominal surgeries. I knew the mechanics of lots of major surgeries, but I had limited experience with them. One of the things I've learned since then is that if you meet someone who walks out of veterinary school thinking he or she is already an awesome vet, you should call them Dr. Narcissist or Dr. Crazy. A more realistic attitude—just like in any other career where you hold lives in your hands—is one that's scared, hopeful, humble, and eager to learn. It takes experience and practice to get good at anything. Although vet school is an amazing start, any vet needs years of eyes-on and hands-on work in the field to even begin to reach their potential.

By the time I got to Tahiti, I'd been a veterinarian for five years—not an eternity, but long enough to have learned a lot. In that time I'd been working on animals every day, gaining the experience that makes it possible to handle complex surgeries with confidence. I'd performed amputations not only on dogs and cats but also on lizards and wildlife, including a coyote and an opossum. My hands were steady, and I was ready to help. Dr. B didn't have another veterinarian nearby who was available to assist, and besides wanting to help out any way I could, I was glad I could do something to aid the man who was taking in Brownie and Napoleon and the rest of "my" kittens.

Dr. Betremieux is one of the good guys, doing everything he can to serve the animals in his community, including this dog who'd come to him with big needs and no money.

We worked together to administer anesthesia, monitoring the dog's heart rate, oxygenation, blood pressure, and respirations, and then we moved on to removing his mangled and infected left front leg. For almost an hour, we worked on opposite sides of the operating table, making sure everything in our power was done to clear out the infection, perform a clean procedure, and give this dog a fighting chance.

When the surgery was over, we decided it was past time the stray with the shattered leg had a name. Olivier jokingly suggested "Evan." Even though it had a nice ring to it, in the end we agreed to name him Papi (short for Papeete, the city he lived in).

Post-surgery and wrapped in a blanket on his cot, Papi looked tiny. He'd been through two traumatic experiences: his injury and his surgery. There was no way I could explain to him that while the first of those had threatened his life, the second had likely saved it.

This story has a happy ending for pretty much everybody. Dr. Betremieux and his nurse fostered the kittens until they were old enough to be adopted—and all the kittens found homes. Papi made a full recovery from his surgery, figured out how to walk with three legs in no time, and, with a little help from social media, found a loving owner.

And as for me, I was glad to have been able to help with the dog and kittens—but I'd actually come to Tahiti see something a bit bigger.

A Big One for the Bucket List

My number one objective during my trip to French Polynesia was to achieve a lifelong goal: swimming with whales. Among whales, humpbacks are one of the species it's realistic to hope to get near in the water. Now that I was a veterinarian with a growing social media audience, I was finding it a little easier to get connected with wildlife experts. On this trip, I scored the invite of a lifetime: I was invited to go out on a research mission aboard a small boat with Dr. Michael Poole, a marine mammal researcher. Dr. Poole has been studying whales and dolphins for over forty years, and he basically knows everything mankind has gleaned about humpbacks and their movements and habits in the South Pacific. I had *so many* questions for him, but before I could begin a round of Ask the Expert or even start scouting for whales I had to find a way to close my mouth and take my eyes off the stunning scenery. This is a place that's really so beautiful it's hard to look away. The water is a crystal blue in the depths and bright aqua in the shallows. The shoreline is made of forested, jagged peaks that jut high around you. There are so many and they're so steep, they look like something out of a fairy tale.

Dr. Poole had made it clear when he'd invited me to join the expedition that there would probably be plenty of time to enjoy the scenery. The most important words in whale studies, he'd said, are *patience* and *fortitude*. I hate to admit it, but even though I've got plenty of fortitude, patience is not my biggest strength. For the first hour we floated in the ocean, still in sight of the shore, looking out at the open water. About forty minutes in, the part of me that desperately wanted to swim with whales started thinking, *No whales today. This isn't going to happen.* Not quite *Woe is me,* but I'd been dying to do this, and the possibility that it might not happen was killing me just a little bit. Since we had a cameraman filming the entire outing, I was trying hard to manage my expectations. As if I would be equally fine with *not* encountering humpback whales that day . . .

While I was trying to come to grips with the possibility of a fruitless trip, the captain (my man Captain Maui!) ran to the side of the hull and leaned over, pointing at what looked to me like more blue water. Within a minute, though, about a hundred feet off the port side of the boat, a mama humpback breached the surface. It was like she was rolling the whole ocean. Magnificent. Then her calf rolled up beside her—managing to look both massive and adorable.

A mother-and-baby pair was what we'd hoped to find, but seeing them live and loud and beautiful in the ocean was even better than I'd imagined. Their appearance was probably the only thing that could make Tahiti *more* beautiful.

As the female whale swept forward, her tail waved over the water. Aware that each whale's tail is divided into two flukes and is unique, almost like a fingerprint, I wondered how this one was different from every other one in the world.

On Dr. Poole's go, we slid into the water with snorkels and fins, trying not to splash, then swam as smoothly and peacefully as we could toward the pair of whales, hoping not to disturb them. I had come a long way since my first deep-sea encounter, with manta rays in Australia. That day, in my excitement to be near them, I'd scared them all away before any of my classmates could get close. By this trip I'd (mostly) learned to contain the impulse to completely freak out at first sight. On the inside I was screaming—*LOOK AT THAT!*—but on the outside I was tamping it down, keeping calm, thinking, *Don't scare the whales.*

It was so worth it. Within a few minutes we were swimming right alongside them. Magic. The calf was clinging so close to his mama it looked like he was perched on her nose. This position and one under the mom's flipper are common ways for calves to "ride" because they're hydrodynamic spots that help the calves conserve energy as they migrate through the ocean. It's called slipstreaming, basically hanging close enough to a larger moving object to reduce your own drag. To keep their strength up, these giant babies also nurse underwater, consuming around 150 gallons of milk each day for the first months of their lives.

We approached cautiously and kept a respectful distance, and the whales went about their business, clearly not stressed by our swimming nearby. All the while, a steady, semi-hysterical chatter ran through my mind: *This is CRAZY! I can't believe this is happening!* I mean, I could hear them vocalizing to each other. I could see the rippled pattern of the mother's throat pleats. I could feel the wake of the water when they moved.

Humpbacks are a global species—they live in every ocean. But they're divided into several different populations, based on their migration patterns. Even though they are geographically diverse, they are still an at-risk species. For hundreds of years they were hunted nearly to extinction. Finally, in the second half of the twentieth century, the world started taking action, passing increasingly restrictive laws to protect them. The fact that the numbers of these creatures are rebounding today is proof that conservation efforts can work and save a species. One population of humpbacks that had dwindled down to just a few hundred whales in the 1950s has now recovered to an estimated twenty-five thousand.

It's mind-blowing to think about what conservation can do while you're actually watching it in action. There I was treading water in the Pacific Ocean, watching a whale calf playing, rolling on his back, waving a flipper, and brushing up against his mother—totally casual and content. Every few minutes he'd surface for a sip of fresh air. The mother was calm and observant, nuzzling the "little" guy when he came close but not following him to the surface. Mature humpbacks can go nearly ten times as long as calves between breaths of air if they choose to.

When the calf got tired, he tucked himself under his mother's chin, another clever adaptation for a creature learning how to manage its giant body. Whales aren't born understanding how to control their buoyancy in the water, and until they get the hang of it they can rely on mama to hold them secure when they want to stay down by putting themselves under her.

Being in the water with these whales was a much bigger event than just seeing them—we were feeling and experiencing their presence. These creatures can grow to sixty feet long, can weigh up to forty tons, and can live as long as ninety years. They are a force of nature in every sense. And all the evidence we have available to us tells us that they are also highly intelligent, emotional creatures. They're indisputably mighty, but they can also be gentle, protective, playful, angry, and sad.

As a traveler, as a vet, and just as a person, I rarely encounter any species that inspires the kind of fascination I experienced getting close to these whales.

When the whales swam away, Dr. Poole and I changed gears, moving into research mode. By studying the shed skin the whales leave behind in the water, a university team can garner information from each individual's DNA and also track their migration patterns.

Surprisingly, this job required nothing more than one of the same tiny aquarium nets I use on fish tanks at home. We swam through the water, scooping up sloughed-off skin samples. Just like all mammals, the whales are constantly shedding skin, and it was surprisingly easy to pick them up in the water. The time we live in now is a whole new age in veterinary science, when just the capturing of those few samples can provide a wealth of knowledge about the whales we saw, their genetics, and even their diet and habits.

By the end of our day on the water, Dr. Poole, Captain Maui, and I had identified, swum with, and collected shed skin samples from *eleven* different whales. For me, the entire day was a dream come true.

9
South Africa

Nothing makes you feel that you've gone from the sidelines of animal conservation to the heart of it like being part of an operation designed to keep a critically endangered species alive for the next generation—especially when that operation involves a helicopter, colleagues armed with dart guns *and* real guns, a team of conservationists, and power tools.

Of all the species we need to worry won't be around for our children and grandchildren to see, one of the highest on the list is the rhinoceros. These animals are among the most iconic representatives of African wildlife, and at this writing the world is losing at least three to five of them every day in Africa, where the majority of their population lives. Their slow pace of reproduction can't begin to keep up, so the numbers in their herds are dwindling, with no end to the decline in sight. The reason for all this loss is a huge misconception about the powers and value of a single commodity: rhino horn. Misinformed patients buy it to treat a huge variety of ailments, and a clique of greedy collectors covet it as a status symbol, in showy forms like ornaments, jewelry, and cups.

As a veterinarian and as someone educated on this topic by

intensely personal experience, I can tell you with 100 percent certainty that a rhino horn is made almost entirely of keratin. It contains trace amounts of calcium and melatonin, but it's chiefly composed of the same basic protein structure your fingernails are made of, or a cow's hoof, or a bird's beak. Keratin is an inert substance, and nothing special. It absolutely cannot restore youth. It won't make you a sex machine. It won't set you right after a hard night's drinking. It can't bring down a fever, relieve gout, or cure cancer—not any more than powdering and ingesting your own toenails could.

Despite the facts about the medicinal properties of rhino horn, in some parts of the world (in Asia and particularly in Vietnam in recent years) crackpot "medicine" practitioners are still selling it as a miracle cure for almost every kind of ailment. True traditional Chinese medicine has officially disavowed this, but with a heritage that's over two thousand years old, nothing stops on a dime. Investigations have found rhino horn and other poached and illegally traded wildlife products readily available in China. Even if the denial by practitioners of traditional Chinese medicine were effective, every time one group turns away from an ancient "cure," it seems, another one rises up to embrace it. At the time of this writing, the poaching of rhinos in South Africa has been on the upswing for more than a decade, with the numbers of animals killed jumping from 83 in 2008 to a staggering 769 in 2018. The value of the horns has increased during that time as well, to the point where it's become so ridiculously inflated that the substance is worth more than its weight in gold and at times is the most expensive product on the black market. Rhinoceros horns have become such a commodity that even decades-dead specimens aren't exempt, and the 2010s saw more than twenty rhino horn heists from museums and auction houses in Europe alone.

As the price of rhino horn has exploded, so has the level of sophistication and commitment of the people who deal in it. I've traveled all over the world and encountered poachers on every continent and in dozens of countries. Most of them do what they do simply to feed their families for another day or week or month. That's a different kind of problem from having an entire criminal cartel committed to stealing, smuggling, and selling a single body part. And it doesn't begin to help us process the fact that every new supply means there's another dead rhino and the whole species has taken a huge hit so that some greedy dealer can get his hands on a few pounds of horn.

It was learning about all of this, especially the fact that it's a problem that is rapidly getting more dire, that led me to South Africa to meet with a group called Rhino 911. These guys are at the epicenter of what can only be described as a war to save the rhino from extinction.

The first step in achieving real change is just making people aware of the problem. By the time I learned about Rhino 911 and the work they do, I'd built up a decent following on social media—enough connections to allow me to effectively reach out and share some of the facts and falsehoods about the value of these animals with about a million people. That's how I got invited to come out and help with a horn trim—the painless removal of the part of the rhino greedy poachers find so irresistible. To this day, that event remains one of the most exciting and rewarding wildlife encounters of my life.

Have Saw, Will Travel

In the summer of 2017, I made the first of many trips to South Africa to help raise awareness about the growing threat to these giant, iconic mammals. My short stay was one of the most noteworthy of my time in wildlife conservation, and it started with a horn trim on day one.

In theory, trimming a horn should be a quick, easy procedure. I mean, I can trim a dog's nails or a bird's beak or even a pig's hooves in minutes. But trimming a rhino horn is an entirely different level of operation. Because of the size of the animals, their endangered status, the fact that the substance you're trimming is potentially worth hundreds of thousands of dollars, and the government oversight required, this is an *event*.

Although I knew the process was going to be a big deal, my first time assisting with one of these operations was still a shocker. First of all, there were a *lot* of people involved. Overhead we had a helicopter pilot and a veterinarian, Dr. Gerhardus Scheepers (who is an amazing shot with a dart gun). Our group on the ground included a veterinarian, a highly skilled vet tech, the owner of the land, several members of her private security and land-management teams, local and foreign veterinary students, and two representatives from the government, there to oversee the process and ensure that not so much as a sliver of the high-value horn disappeared in the process.

Waiting to get this operation underway, I was so eager I couldn't stand still. I kept pacing around the truck, ready to go and then some. We were all on radio comms, and the minute the helicopter team had pinpointed the rhinos (in this case, a female and her calf) and made their shots, they started tracking from above. We took off in trucks to follow. Once the darts hit, a rhino may continue to travel for miles before the drugs fully take effect, and there's nothing you can do during that time except follow and wait. If the pursuit goes on for more than seven or eight minutes and the rhino is still on the move, it means either the drugs in the first dart were insufficient, they didn't penetrate past the animal's thick skin, or the dart got stuck in bone or some other non-vascular structure. This day, the helicopter kept a visual on the rhinos, trying to gently "herd" them toward the road so the team could reach them quickly, meanwhile radioing coordinates for us on the ground.

When the mother started to slow, it was time for us to get to work. Watching her was a fascinating lesson in what a perfectly dosed sedative can do to a four-thousand-pound beast. This mama was weaving a little, not covering much ground, lifting her legs really high—like the bulkiest, least-graceful high-stepping show horse in history. Her balance started growing wobbly, and that was our cue to approach and get her eyes and ears covered. Anytime you dull the senses of a wild mammal, that simple act helps cut down on their stress. White rhinos aren't typically aggressive, but these were not typical circumstances, and we needed to take care approaching this mama, who was obviously running out of steam.

Running up from behind, we got a towel over her face and then positioned people on both sides of her to guide her to a safe place to ease her giant body to the ground.

So here was this huge, round, lumbering, stumbling rhino, with two pink darts poking out of her hindquarters and what looked like a handkerchief over her eyes. (It was a bath towel, but she dwarfed it.) I was on her right with another guy, and three more members of the team were on her left—all of us trying to steer her to a soft landing. The whole scene might have been hilarious if it weren't so deadly serious.

In my peripherals, I could see all of this playing out across the field with the second rhino, the baby. The little guy had no horn to trim, but having the kiddo awake while the mom is getting work done brings trouble and anxiety all around. The babies cry and grunt, they stomp their feet, they rush the human team, and more than anything they try to get close to their mother. It's not ideal to have that big and immediate a distraction while you're operating a saw in close proximity to an animal's face.

Even after these rhinos go down, typically they continue to hold their heads up, which makes it a little easier to do the job at hand. This one, though, flopped over on her left and lay there quietly. The keratin in a rhino's horn is highly dense, but more so than even a dog's nails, it has a quick where tissue and bones meet the structure. Doing a trim, you have to remove as much of the horn as possible without cutting into the living tissue, where things can get messy and painful for the rhino—and also where any exposure could leave the animal open to infection. As long as you stay on the horn, this process is completely painless and harmless to the rhino; nevertheless, it's important to get it right. We measured a short distance—about the width of four of my fingers—from the base of the horn and got started. Although some teams use chain saws, Rhino 911 prefers reciprocating saws because they're more accurate for fine cutting and avoid subjecting the rhino to fumes from a combustion engine, which can be caustic to their eyes.

While the vet tech monitored the rhino's breathing and heart rate, I started working as quickly and efficiently as I could with the saw to remove the bulk of the horn. This was heavy work, cutting through a material nearly as dense as stone. As I finished the clear cut, I lifted the horn away. It was heavy— between seven and eight pounds—and I found it impossible to look at it without thinking of its ridiculous value. The hunk of horn in my hand was worth a small fortune—to a smuggler who could get it to a final destination in Asia, around half a million dollars—for absolutely no proven medical reason or inherent value at all.

Once the horn is cut, what's left is a squared-off stump, and my next job was to smooth down its edges, first with the saw and then with an electric rotating sander with a tungsten plate. Tungsten is one of the few materials that can keep its form after grinding several rhino horns. The sanding was more delicate work, and I wore down the horn until I could just see a hint of the pink quick beneath. It's a sad fact that this job was necessary, because even the raised edges of horn that remained after the trim held too much value to be left behind; that small remnant of keratin would jeopardize her life. I went through the entire process with the large front horn and then repeated it with the smaller one behind it.

Typically, while the rhino is down, the team takes a few minutes to conduct a veterinary exam, give injectable medications (including anti-parasitics, antibiotics, anti-inflammatories, and a vitamin supplement), and check for wounds. This case was no exception, especially since this rhino had recently given birth. Rhinos are so huge, though, that lying on their sides can create enough pressure to damage their lungs or abdominal organs or even their muscles, if they're not in an ideal position or hold still for too long. There was no way this was going to happen on our watch, and so this experienced team moved in after about fifteen minutes to push this huge mama into a chest-up (sternal) position and then gently ease her onto her other side. It took all of us to make it happen. The rhino, bless her heart, slept right through it.

While I conducted an exam, the government officials documented the horn trimmings. This is a highly regulated process, with a lot of safeguards in place to ensure that no one steals an ounce of it. The entire event is recorded, including vital stats about the rhino and the precise weight of the horn trimmings. Then the horn is drilled into, microchipped on the inside, epoxied closed, and sealed in a box for transportation. To guarantee its long-term security, a small amount of it is also separated to serve as a DNA sample for any future potential identification.

As far as I was concerned, the best part of this process came after the work was done, after everyone except the veterinarians had taken a step back in anticipation. I crouched next to the rhino and injected her with the anesthetic reversal medication, then moved away to watch and wait. I could see the other vet doing the same thing with the baby.

Within a minute, the mama's head was up. She gave it a shake, clearing the cobwebs, and then clambered to her feet. Rhinos are very vocal and they don't have great vision, so as soon as this one had her wits about her, the first thing she did was call out for her baby. Across the field, the baby, also on his feet by then, called back. Their vocalizations sounded like someone forcing air into their mouth through their teeth—an innocent, low whinny, especially endearing coming from the calf. For a few seconds, they played this awkward, sweet savannah game of Marco Polo, until they finally found themselves facing each other. The mother's entire body language changed—relaxing and leaning toward her kiddo. The baby looked like he'd gotten a jolt of new energy, jumping toward his mom and coming running. He raced up to her, couldn't quite stop, and bumped her shoulder. Not wanting to move away, he leaned in and nuzzled her neck. The two of them stood together, snuggling, while the entire Rhino 911 team watched and smiled.

The mother's horn was gone, but its removal would never cause her a second of pain. And the simple act of removing it had made her a vastly less desirable target for poachers. As I watched these two rhinos trot off, calf in front of his mother, it brought happy tears to my eyes to know that we might have saved their lives with thirty minutes and a painless trim. I wanted to grab every member of that team in a great big bear hug. I was at a loss for words to express how much it had meant to me to be a part of their work.

Bearing Witness

After the extreme high of being involved in the horn-trim operation, I was unprepared for the devastating low that would follow. My host and Rhino 911's cofounder, Nico Jacobs, got a call from nearby Pilanesberg National Park, informing him of a possible poaching underway. Rhino 911's name isn't just lip service—it truly is the unit many private owners and government facilities turn to when there's a rhino emergency unfolding. We left immediately, knowing we were racing against the clock.

I wish I could say we got there in time to give an assist to the rangers, but that's not how it played out. We were too late. The poachers had been detected, and the park's anti-poaching unit had responded in force, but by the time the rangers and their dogs scared these criminals off, there were two victims lying along a park roadside.

It's part of my everyday job description to be immune to the sight of blood. It's part of the job to be able to stay strong in the face of an animal's emergency or suffering or tragedy so that I can render whatever treatment or assistance is available. It takes a lot to shake me. But the sight of the two rhinos that died that day is something I've carried with me. It depicted one of the most merciless acts I've ever seen. And it was all so completely pointless.

The two rhinos, mother and calf, were stretched out, side by side, along the edge of a dirt park road. From a distance, they looked like they might have been sleeping, with the mother spooned behind her baby, belly to back, her head tucked down protectively, her right front leg resting on the smaller rhino's shoulder. It looked like a cuddle, but it was so much more sinister.

Both rhinos had been shot, and as I neared the bodies, I could see shallow cut marks around the mother's horn, although it was still intact. The poachers must have thought they were minutes away from a huge score, only the area they'd chosen for their attack was wide open—no trees or high brush to duck into for cover—so the clock had been ticking for them, too. With an armed security team approaching, dogs circling the area, and the sound of a helicopter in the distance, the poachers had fled without getting what they'd come for. Since these poachers were expected to return home with horns and wouldn't, they were undoubtedly already plotting their next attack.

The aftermath, on that low, clear stretch of scrubby grassland, was that two innocent animals of an endangered species, who'd been living within the borders of a protected national park, had lost their lives for *absolutely nothing*. (We would later learn that the mother was pregnant with a female baby, meaning the world lost not two but potentially three southern white rhinos that morning.)

I was trying to maintain the demeanor of a professional, a veterinarian, a world traveler who has seen the devastating impacts of poaching more times than I can count. But inside I felt the way I might have if I'd faced this moment when I was about ten—an age when sadness and rage get all jumbled up and you can't decide if you want to scream or cry or strangle somebody. Standing over the bodies of those rhinos, I wanted to do all of that, and I could barely keep my emotions in check.

The only thing that made it possible for me to show restraint was looking around and seeing the members of the park's anti-poaching unit—the highly trained, deeply committed badass rangers who put their lives on the line every time they button up the uniform. While I was basically just passing through this place, this was their reality, the senseless destruction and depravity they have to deal with all the time. This team was working 365 days a year to keep their wildlife safe, and in that instance, their relentless efforts had come up short by a matter of minutes. Later that day, they'd be back in the war to protect the park's rhinos, but at that moment their faces were contorted with fury and grief. Admirably, they never showed those emotions in the field, and if they could keep it together, I had no choice but to swallow everything I was feeling, too. I decided to channel my anger and sorrow into something useful—like helping to let the rest of the world know, through my social media accounts, that two more of the last rhinos on the planet were dead and that the rest of them need our protection to survive.

Chubby Giant Unicorns

After witnessing that heartbreaking scene at Pilanesberg, I thought I'd encountered the full range of experience the fight to save South Africa's rhinos had to offer; I couldn't have been more wrong. Just when I thought I'd ridden that emotional wave as high and low and hard as it could go, the Rhino 911 team took me to meet the orphans.

One of the reasons Rhino 911 hustles to the scene of any new poaching, even if the rhino in question is already dead, is that if the victim is a female, there's a good chance there's a calf somewhere nearby, hiding in the brush, or lying on the ground, or, later, standing beside its mother's body trying to understand why she doesn't respond or why she's not letting down milk. If a juvenile interferes with the poachers, they will almost always kill it (or at least try to—I've seen plenty of orphans with machete wounds); but if it runs away (and if it doesn't have a horn), they won't waste their time chasing it. Mother rhinos are pregnant for about eighteen months, and when they give birth, they are typically doting, engaged moms. A calf will stay with its mom for up to three years, and during that time, she doesn't just feed her baby—she teaches it, plays with it, snuggles with it, and keeps in steady physical and emotional contact. The baby depends not only on its mother's milk but also on her protection and guidance. It's a surprisingly close and dynamic relationship, and it's the reason these babies need to be rescued and protected until they're old enough to make it on their own.

Cue the Rhino Pride Foundation's orphanage, where as many as forty rhino youngsters (and sometimes rhinos injured during attempted poachings) get the TLC they need. At the orphanage, volunteers start the rescue process by making sure these babies are nourished properly. To do that, they feed them a milk substitute initially formulated for one of the rhino's closest relatives: the horse. If you're wondering just how much milk these babies need to grow, the answer is So Much. Between six months and eighteen months of age, a typical rescued rhino orphan will be bottle-fed about four liters of milk per feeding—four or five times per day. That's a minimum of sixteen liters of hand-mixed, hand-fed formula every day for every animal. It says something about the devotion of the caregivers that they make this happen for these kiddos twenty-four/seven.

Orphanages also provide veterinary care, and one of the surprisingly common needs these juveniles have is antacid medication. They may seem too big to be vulnerable to minor ailments, but rhinos are prone to stress-related stomach issues, and since almost all the juveniles at the orphanage have lost their mothers—often having witnessed the murder and sometimes even having been injured during it—they carry a lot of anxiety; this can manifest itself in the form of gastrointestinal ulcers, which can easily be fatal. Just thinking about these giant, chubby unicorn babies suffering from bleeding ulcers infuriates me, but it is one of the realities their caretakers have to deal with.

Thankfully, when the babies are rescued, they quickly learn that they can find some of the contact they crave—getting their ears scratched or their bellies rubbed or their bottoms patted—from their loving keepers. And the next most effective stress-reducing "medication" for these animals is pairing them up with a friend. Although this is typically another rhino, over the last few years I've seen juvenile rhinos become besties with goats, sheep, horses, and even dogs.

At Rhino Pride, both black and white rhino babies are being raised together. These animals share more DNA with horses and tapirs than with other species, but if you spend any time observing them, you've got to wonder what other factor is part of the equation. Black rhinos can have a strong aggressive streak. You don't want to mess with them. White rhinos? Not so much. Of course, they'll defend themselves if cornered or protecting their young, but generally these are mellow, tolerant, forgiving animals. Even when they're intimidated, they're more likely to form a little group and back up butt to butt to create a defensive line than they are to charge. The only time you can expect these creatures to be aggressive is when two males are competing over something, especially a female. When that happens, all bets are off and things can get ugly—even deadly.

When they're juveniles, this trend toward gentleness makes the "little" rhinos offer up the kinds of behaviors you might expect from something *much* tamer, like a dog. One of the first rhinos I met at the orphanage leaned so heavily into my leg, he basically gave me no choice but to pet him. Another, who'd been injured in the slaughter that killed her mother, rubbed her head up and down against me, nuzzling in close. I fed a rhino named Tommy four big bottles—leaving me to wonder whether you're supposed to burp a rhino baby. When his belly was full, he flopped over on the ground, pushing his head against me and letting out a long, satisfied-baby sigh. I could have sat beside that sweet, giant lump of a baby all day, just rubbing his ears and patting his face while he blinked up at me in thanks.

The goal of these orphanages is to raise the rhinos until they're sufficiently independent to live on protected lands in the wild; in the meantime, they're getting as much love, support, and kindness as their rescuers can offer. Everybody involved knows there's nothing we can do that's truly a substitute for these babies being raised by their mothers, but that doesn't stop the conservationists from striving every day to offer the next best thing.

Full-Moon Heartache

A lot of my experiences in South Africa have stuck with me, and they're part of the reason I've been back several times since that first visit. I offer a veterinary assist when I can, and bring as much publicity as possible to the organizations that are fighting every day to save the rhinos. On my first visit—my first day, actually—one of the rangers told me something that has stuck with me ever since. It was an overcast morning, and we were talking about the provisions the landowner had in place for nighttime security. The ranger looked around and nodded, assuring me that the rhinos were as safe as they could possibly be for the night. Then he told me that dark nights aren't the ones he worries most about. "It is the poachers' moon," he said, glancing up at the sky. "That's the one we hate to see coming."

The poachers' moon? What the hell was that?

Turns out, it's the mysterious, sometimes spooky, sometimes romantic thing most of us call a full moon. I used to love full moons and even thought they had a little bit of a call-to-the-wild effect on me. But now I know that poachers love them, too. Offering the equivalent of dim stadium lighting over the bush, a full moon provides a perfect opportunity to steal onto protected property and savage the rhino population while South Africa sleeps. Factor in that some of these poachers even charge a premium for a rhino horn acquired during a full moon because it's supposedly imbued with extra-strong powers, and you've got all the makings of a disaster. During a supermoon in September 2015, eight rhinos were killed in a single night in a single park. During a full moon in May 2017, another nine lost their lives. Rangers know these nights are coming, but even with staffing up and prepping to the best of their ability, they simply don't have the manpower or the resources to protect all the rhinos who unknowingly rely on them to stay safe.

10

Uganda

I've seen the biggest waterfalls in the world—including Victoria Falls in Zambia and Iguazu Falls in Brazil—but I've never seen a display of water as aggressive as the one at Uganda's Murchison Falls. To create the falls, the three-hundred-foot-wide Victoria Nile grudgingly funnels itself until it's narrow enough to thunder through a twenty-three-foot-wide stone gap, after which it rockets down 145 feet with a world of pent-up force behind it. Ugandans sometimes describe the falls as a war between rock and water, and when you see and hear eleven thousand cubic feet of river per second slamming through this pass, it's hard to believe that the rock has held its own for so long. God forbid you ever went over: those falls would kill you three or four times before you hit bottom. And once you reached the placid water beyond the base, you'd likely be consumed by the gnarly Nile crocodiles that bask in the sun on the banks below the falls. These guys deserve a wide berth in the water and on land, as they weigh in as heavy as a ton and are known man-eaters.

Standing at the top of those falls after a trip that took me from

California to Illinois, Illinois to Belgium, Belgium to Rwanda, and finally Rwanda to Uganda was the perfect antidote for my jet lag. It's a place where you can truly feel *alive*.

Blast from the Past

The first time I traveled to East Africa, I was barely an adult, and every new encounter blew my mind and increased my fascination with the place. The semester I spent in Tanzania as an undergrad was a game changer in my life—cementing my desire to travel, work with animals, and document my adventures. In late October 2019, I traveled back to the region on my first-ever trip to Uganda. I'd visited several countries in Africa by then, but this trip brought me back to the quintessential East African landscape of broad lowland savannah dotted with wooded copses, all of it super green in the wet season. Seeing that distinctive natural beauty felt like a trip back to a favorite memory. This time, though, instead of being a kid taking my first safari, I was there to help with the process of translocating a small group of young giraffes so they could become a new seed population in a protected national preserve. One of my conservation heroes, Ivan Carter, who co-runs the Ivan Carter Wildlife Conservation Alliance, had invited me to come lend a hand as the Giraffe Conservation Foundation worked with Ugandan authorities to tackle the daunting task.

I'd never moved a giraffe before—most people, even veterinarians and conservationists, never do—but I knew a little about the logistics. By any measure the job was going to be monumental, complicated, and infinitely challenging. By the time my five days of work were through, I expected, the process would have kicked my ass, physically and mentally, but that didn't matter—I was just eager to be part of such a huge, potentially game-changing mission.

Robo-Dino-Bird

Of course, no great road trip goes in a straight line, and on my way to meeting the giraffe-translocation team, I had another stop I was excited about. The Uganda Wildlife Conservation Education Centre in Entebbe is an animal sanctuary that does amazing work in its community, and it just happens to be home to an animal that's always been on my bucket list to meet: the shoebilled stork. These birds are actually in the pelican family and are among the coolest, craziest birds in the world. An aquatic carnivore, the shoebill looks like a mix of dinosaur, robot, and Muppet, with a humongous gray head, wide yellow eyes, a sloping beak ending in a curved hook, and wings that could come straight out of a field guide to dinosaurs (check out the pterodactyl). We don't know if they're actually prehistoric, but these birds are definitely ancient, with records of them going as far back as ancient Egypt. At an average of five feet tall with an eight-foot wingspan, they're physically intimidating. Plus, they're so dinosaurish they look like they've been walking the earth for eons—the kind of creature you instinctively know to regard with a healthy respect.

The shoebill I met at the Education Centre is named Sushi. He's a quirky, intelligent bird—one with surprisingly polite manners when it comes to people. He bows his head toward newcomers, and if you bow back and are patient, he might let you get close to him. In the wild, you'd likely never manage to approach a bird like this (and if you did, you'd regret it if the shoebill decided to lay down the law). Pelicans and other long-billed aquatic birds can be extremely dangerous, especially because one of their first defenses is to peck at the eyes of anything they deem to be a threat. I've worked with aquatic birds and pelicans in wildlife rescues, and for the big ones you have to wear full face masks. When I met Sushi, I knew he had come to the Education Centre decades ago as a rescue and had gotten comfortable with people. Based on his reputation, it was unlikely he'd go for my eyeballs, but I intentionally kept a little distance between my face and his beak at first. As expected, he turned out to be 100 percent agreeable and showed zero signs of aggressive behavior. This is a special bird who's become an effective ambassador for his species, inspiring people to learn about, respect, and even protect these rare creatures.

In the wild, birds like Sushi are deadly hunters. They wait for their prey, standing motionless in shallow water for as long as it takes for a meal to come to them. When it happens, the stork snaps up the fish, rodent, turtle, or even smallish monitor or croc in his huge beak, pulls its head off with the bill's sharp edge, and swallows the rest of it whole. Knowing that, I took my time approaching Sushi, and he rewarded me with one of the coolest greetings in the bird world—clattering the top and bottom of his bill together in a unique *pop-pop-pop-pop-pop* that sounded like a large wooden box being rapidly and repetitively opened and slammed shut. Lots of long-billed birds make this sound, but in smaller species it's more of a *pip-pip-pip*. With a big bill like Sushi's, the deep, hollow beak clacking stops you in your tracks—at least until you're sure it's a friendly sound and not an angry one.

Despite the fact that shoebill storks have few natural enemies, their numbers are down because they're often poached for rare bird collectors. Since they lay just an egg or two at a time, their population continues to fall year after year. At this writing, it's estimated that there are fewer than five thousand of these rare and vulnerable birds left in the wild.

The day I met Sushi, hundreds of school-age children were at the center, too. I don't think it's possible to underestimate the importance of familiarizing kids with their local wildlife and helping them learn to respect it. Believe it or not, most children in most regions of Africa have never seen a rhino or a giraffe, an elephant or a lion in person, and many come from communities that think of these iconic African animals as "pests" that interfere with agriculture and land management. Wildlife sanctuaries and rehabilitation centers that welcome kids give them great reasons to appreciate these iconic animals as valuable parts of their communities. Imagine if every adult who's poaching vulnerable and endangered species today had this kind of opportunity to learn about (and learn to respect) animals as a child.

Giraffes on the Move

In 1968, a survey of the large mammal population at the Pian Upe Wildlife Reserve, in northeastern Uganda, found more than 2,300 plains zebras, nearly 1,600 elands (a species of antelope), and 899 giraffes. By 1996, the number of each of those species counted was the same: zero. Also gone extinct in the area since 1966? Lions. Elephants. Black rhinos. Each species had been erased from the landscape, and one of the biggest culprits was poaching.

This is a story that's taking place all over the world and that's been unfolding in many parts of Africa, one that's been compounded by wars and political unrest over the past four decades. Civil wars in Rwanda, Uganda, Sudan, Congo, and other countries saw key wildlife populations brought to—and sometimes past—the brink of local extinction, even in national parks and protected reserves.

This was the case in Pian Upe, where species that belong with the land—after living there for thousands of years—have been MIA for more than a decade.

With the political situation in Uganda relatively stabilized, the Uganda Wildlife Authority has been working with private partners like the Giraffe Conservation Foundation to start restoring these wildlife populations.

It's impossible to talk about the project that brought me to Uganda without also delving into why anybody would undertake a job as monumental as moving, say, ten giraffes to a new home.

Translocating wild giraffes involves a ton of manpower and coordination. These aren't creatures you can just throw a net over or trap in a cage and expect things to go smoothly. Plus, the process can be risky for both the animals and the people involved.

So why do it? There are three main reasons, starting with the ecological. Giraffes are a keystone species—one an ecosystem depends on—of the East African savannah. They're mega-herbivores (meaning they consume a *lot* of vegetation), they're high browsers (eating things other animals can't reach), and their digestive process is one of the main ways seeds get dispersed through the region (yep, poop). Poaching away such a critical presence means changing the entire ecosystem, from the birds in the treetops to the insects under the ground and the plant life in between. Giraffes belong in this environment, and the environment relies on them.

The second reason is less tangible but just as important. The giraffe is part of the culture of East Africa in general and Uganda in particular. It's a travesty that they could be hunted to extinction in the second-largest protected area in the country. Given that humans caused this species wipeout, it seems fair to expect us to make it right. Today the reserve is a safe environment again, one that has the protection not just of the country's own authorities but also of multinational organizations with the resources to help manage the land and ensure the safety of its animals.

The last reason for going to all the trouble to move a small herd of giraffes 250 miles to new digs is that it can increase the odds of the species' long-term survival—basically the same logic that keeps us from putting all of our proverbial eggs in one basket. The concentration of giraffes at Murchison Falls National Park and the absence of them at Pian Upe puts the entire population at greater risk than if the animals were more spread out and not all of them were susceptible to every health and security threat.

Those arguments were enough to convince me to show up at

Murchison Falls National Park on a sweltering October morning to help make the move happen.

Looking around at the site of a translocation, the first thing that strikes you about this process is just how many people it takes. The crew was close to forty strong—from representatives of the agencies and NGOs coordinating the move to American and Ugandan veterinarians and biologists, veterinary students, and national park staff. There were plenty of jobs to go around for all of us. I was fast enough, fit enough, and educated enough about the animals to be an asset in a number of different capacities, so I was able to try my hand at most of the jobs over our ten captures.

We were a small army of experts, ready to dart, immobilize, measure, examine, and prep each giraffe for its journey. I hopped into the bed of the truck at the front of the line and squeezed in with the eight riders already there. The truck eased forward and within minutes we were focused on one young male giraffe who was grazing apart from the herd. He was the right age, he looked healthy, and he was functioning independently—a perfect candidate to be part of the new herd at Pian Upe. As we neared the animals, the female closest to us took a few steps, and then a few more, away from our path. When we kept approaching, she took off at a trot, and all around her other members of the herd started moving, picking up speed as they went. Seeing giraffes in captivity is something to appreciate, but seeing them in the wild is nothing short of stunning. Within seconds, these animals were running at nearly forty miles per hour, and yet it looked like it was happening in slow motion. It messes with your mind to see them covering so much ground but looking as though they're practically hovering in the air.

In order to dart this animal, we'd have to get within about forty yards with an extreme sedative. Because of their size and metabolism, giraffes are uniquely difficult to sedate. You basically have to overdose them to bring them down, using incredibly potent pharmaceuticals that leave little margin for error. To sedate the giraffe, we'd be using a narcotic reserved for large mammal sedation that's more than a thousand times more potent than morphine. With most species, once you have them sedated, you can monitor their vital functions and then administer a reversal after you've finished your veterinary work. For a giraffe, because of the heavy dose it takes to gain temporary control of them, you've got to give the reversal as soon as the animal is down to ensure its full recovery.

That means that once you've darted one of these magnificent creatures, there's no going back, no letting it outrun you, no giving up because it takes to terrain that's not passable with a truck.

We watched and waited. Shooting a dart is not like firing a bullet. The elements, including wind, rain, and even gravity, have an effect on a dart's trajectory. And you can't hit a giraffe just anywhere and get the desired effect. If the dart goes through the leg, for example, the drugs trickle out to the ground. If it lodges in the shoulder or scapular bone, the result won't be impactful enough. The ideal shot goes into muscle in an area where it can absorb quickly and completely.

The dart was fired, and all eyes (and all wheels) turned to the giraffe, who, not surprisingly, took off running when he felt it hit. We radioed to the rest of the team that the shot was a hit, giving them the okay to close in. It would take a few minutes to be sure the sedative had done its job. If the shot was well placed, the giraffe would probably drop in five to six minutes. If not, we'd likely have to re-dart.

We raced across the savannah, keeping pace with the streaking animal. The excitement was palpable among all of us in the truck bed, but we were completely quiet, focused on our jobs. Everyone knew the meticulously devised strategy we were about to implement, and we were quietly, intently waiting to put it into motion.

The Ugandan savannah isn't overly rocky or mountainous,

but it's no highway, either. Slamming through water and across rough terrain, rocks, and vegetation in a truck bed makes for a violent ride, and each time my body collided with the metal frame, the little medical Jiminy Cricket deep in my brain kept count, no doubt muttering things like *Damn, that's gonna leave a mark*. It was all irrelevant in the moment, because the giraffe's life depended on receiving the reversal, and nothing else really felt like it mattered from the moment the sedative hit until the process was over.

Our truck stayed in tight pursuit, our driver constantly making choices about what path would allow us to keep pace with the giraffe without getting stuck or otherwise disabling the vehicle. We all knew that the key to this whole process was that when this guy started wobbling, we needed to *be there* and start work immediately.

So there we were, a truckload of hyped-up conservationists crammed together and hauling ass as we gathered ropes and carabiners, head covers and earplugs, test kits, gloves, timers—all the tools we'd need. Half a second behind us was a second truck, filled with ropers, researchers, and the all-important Ugandan veterinarian carrying the sedative's reversal.

The giraffe began to slow, his gait got stumbly, and all of us knew the time had come. We leaped over the sides of the truck bed and hit the ground running, racing toward the animal. It's a strange combination of events—rushed and borderline violent, but also calculated to the second, with every team member knowing that his or her job has to be done both quickly and precisely. We had to reach the giraffe before he fell, and just as he began to sink, we were beside him. His body lowered to the ground, but his head stayed up swinging. This posed a danger to both giraffe and relocation crew, and in order to prevent any injuries, the first of us to reach the giraffe were tasked with bringing his head down and holding his powerful frame steady by immobilizing his head and neck.

Every person on the team relies on the others to do their jobs in such a way that all of us and the animal walk away safely at the end. Before anything else, a vet gave the sedative reversal via injection. The second that was done, a flurry of simultaneous actions were in play. Someone put a mask over the giraffe's face and secured it while someone else inserted two big sock-like plugs into his ears. Those two simple steps would significantly reduce the animal's stress for the rest of the process. There were people getting blood samples, fur samples, tissue samples, and collecting insects living on the giraffe. There were people assigned to take measurements of the giraffe's body and monitor his respiration, temperature, and blood temperature—so all around me they were shouting out numbers, which were being recorded by a second circle of team members. One team member—in this case, me—had the job of giving the giraffe a series of injections: an antibiotic, an anti-inflammatory, vitamins, and an anti-parasitic.

All of this all happens insanely fast. From dart to giraffe down is a few minutes, and from down to getting the giraffe back on its feet, about ten to fifteen minutes, with everyone working in concert the entire time.

As I reached the beautiful, graceful, fifteen-hundred-pound, semi-sedated giant, I moved in to administer his injections. Around me, other members of the team were laser focused on their own jobs. I'd watched the process once before, but this was my first hands-on participation, and I was mindful as I crouched down of the number one rule of giraffe wrangling: *Stay away from the legs.* A giraffe can kick with enough force to kill—and potentially decapitate—all but the biggest mammal. That includes one of the rare predators who'd dare go after one: the lion. I glanced to my right, doing the math as I assessed his powerful body and all four legs. He was on his right side, not peaceful but no longer wildly flailing. I turned my attention to the job at hand.

Seconds later, the giraffe struggled a bit. As I glanced up, I saw his right rear hoof—propelled by all the force this massive animal could muster—cannonballing toward my face. I snapped my head back, my Ugandan adventure flashing by—how eager I'd been, how carefully I'd studied this process, how much this was gonna hurt (if I survived it). One second that hoof had been fifteen feet away; the next it was inches from my eyes.

Mercifully (because there was not a damn thing I could have done to stop it), the kick stopped just before crushing my head. My nerves reset. Everyone on the team started breathing again, and we got the work done. After that, I reminded each person working in that general area that against all odds, a giraffe can reach you *there*.

Like Dragon Wrangling

While one contingent of the team worked on the giraffe's health and wellness tasks, another was gearing up for an equally intense job. Roping a giraffe and keeping it safe and in check after a sedation has to be the closest experience to wrangling a dragon that the modern world has to offer. It takes a crew of twelve to sixteen ropers to do the job, and while we on the vet team take our samples and give our injections, these guys are securing a harness around the base of the giraffe's neck and ensuring that the huge carabiner at its front is properly attached, with three extremely long (about forty feet long) ropes extending out from it. One will eventually be used to guide the giraffe's head forward. The other two run under the animal's forelegs and out behind him on each side. Another harness is attached to a carabiner on the bottom of the face mask; its purpose is to lead the head. As with most animals, where a giraffe's head goes, the body goes, so this one is critical.

I got to do this job on a second-day giraffe capture, and all I can say is that it is a fitness and agility test like no other. My hat goes off to the workers who fearlessly tackled this job for days in a row. As soon as the veterinary tasks on the giraffe are done, four or five people line up on each of these control ropes. The head cover stays on, which is probably the biggest reason the ropers are able to keep up—if the giraffe could see a distant point to run to, it could outrun any ranger, any day. Its top speed can reach thirty-five miles per hour, and not even Usain Bolt himself could keep up with that.

It might seem that the logical thing to do when the giraffe gets to his feet is to hold him back, but this doesn't work. A giraffe is too strong, so the ropers give him a few minutes to sort his feelings out. Some animals sprint ahead; some shake their heads or kick in frustration. They buck and they jump. In the moment, they're not happy, and they make that crystal clear. Through it all, the ropers must stay with the giraffe, close enough to maintain some control yet far enough to avoid getting tangled or trampled, remembering that the end game is to move the animal—completely unharmed—into the waiting trailer for transport. The process almost looks like a synchronized dance, with the giraffe leading and a gaggle of ropers on either side of the animal reacting to maintain their distance, all while keeping their ropes from getting crossed. Even an ungainly move by the giraffe has to be met by a smooth, deliberate response from the ropers, which makes it all like a quirky, choreographed performance.

I took a mid-rope position and prepared to hang on no matter what. The blindfolded giraffe rocked his massive body forward then back, then lurched to his feet. Twenty feet back on the rope, I kept my eyes on him, my feet moving, my mind replaying my instructions: *Stay with him, but not too close. Don't let him get to a full-out run. Don't get dragged. Don't get tangled.*

The closer you are on the rope to the giraffe, the less running you have to do but the more immediate the danger is to you. At the far end of the rope, you've got a little distance between yourself and the hooves, but you've got to run like hell, especially if the giraffe turns away and you find yourself playing catch-up as if you're on the tail end in the ultimate game of Crack the Whip.

On one particular capture, our trailer got delayed during the initial chase (not surprising, given the terrain). The time we had with the giraffe down came and went, and we all knew we had no choice but to "walk" this outrageously fast, strong, displeased animal for as long as it took for the trailer to reach us. Trying to maintain a respectful distance and position (the four o'clock and eight o'clock positions behind and to the side of the giraffe are the safest) on rough terrain littered with stones and pocked with wicked acacia thorns—all while trying to keep up with an animal that can outrun you any day of your life—may be the ultimate twenty minutes of cardio. By the time the trailer arrived, the ropers were huffing and puffing, lungs on fire, long past ready to attempt to load their dragon for transport.

Of course, loading a giraffe into a trailer is a big job in its own right. By now the giraffe is a little calmer and maybe getting a little tired, and the ropers move from behind him to a little bit in front and start urging him forward, gently "steering" him toward the open deck. With most of the giraffes we captured in Murchison Falls, all of this went reasonably well—right up until the animal heard its own hoof clank against the metal of the ramp. At that point, the universal reaction from the animals was *Whoa! Back the hell up.* Giraffes are particular neophobes—afraid of anything new and different—and these guys behaved true to form. They froze in place, locked their legs, shook their heads, tried to back away—just basically offered every possible physical manifestation of *No* at their disposal.

Fortunately, even neophobes can get used to anything eventually, and after a few minutes of the unusual feel and sound of hoof on metal, each member of the new herd managed to board the trailer and make the short trip to a holding area. These were all young adults, and giraffes are naturally social creatures, so each time we introduced a new animal to the new herd, we could see they were glad to see one another. They'd look each other over, stand side by side, share food and water, and we could see them relax a little bit.

Free

When the full contingent of ten giraffes was gathered in the outdoor holding area, it was time to embark on a phenomenal parade to Pian Upe. On arrival, they were taken into the reserve, some eight hundred square miles of protected land, and turned loose. Seeing them running together out on that open savannah where giraffes were always part of the ecosystem until people poached them out made for a magical, hopeful moment. It was a testament to what people who are committed to reversing that kind of damage can accomplish. Ivan's Giraffe Conservation Foundation has agreements with at least a dozen African governments that are participating in the organization's Giraffe Action Plan, and this wild release extended their reach to no less than a hundred *million* acres of influence.

As I flew home, with sore muscles, bruised arms and legs, a sunburn that shouldn't have been, considering all the sunscreen I'd slathered on, and a big, tired grin on my face, I thought about what an awesome opportunity I'd been given. Thirteen years ago, the first time I set foot in Africa and almost immediately came down with a case of dysentery I thought might kill me, I could not have dreamed of coming back as a team member for such a challenging and inspiring conservation program. Every passing year working with animals and raising awareness about conservation issues teaches me a little more deeply, though, that there is room for anyone who wants to be a part of this movement. For me, respecting, admiring, and understanding wildlife has become a key piece of who I am and who I want to be. I can't wait to see what gnarly adventures still lie ahead.

11

Philippines

In early 2018, my old pal Joey Brown had moved from Fiji and its crested iguanas to a new and even more endangered species: the Philippine crocodile. These animals are the rarest crocodilians (a term that includes all crocodiles, alligators, gharials, and caimans) and one of the most endangered species in the world. Their numbers aren't even in the thousands—they're in the low hundreds. In order to keep these animals from going extinct, Joey had partnered with the Mabuwaya Foundation through his master's program at the University of Oklahoma to learn more about the crocs' movements, diets, reproductive cycles, and nesting habits. Like with the iguanas, knowing where they were going, what they were doing, and what they were eating would help people keep them safe. The foundation already had an established Head Start program to capture and foster newly hatched crocs for their first one to two years of life, so they'd get their first true tastes of the world when they were bigger, stronger, and a lot less vulnerable than they'd be as hatchlings. This was one more facet of the great work this organization is doing.

If there is any cause I can fully get behind, it's definitely croc conservation. As soon as Joey invited me, I started shuffling my schedule to make sure I could travel there.

Luzon is the largest and most heavily populated island in the Philippines, the top of a cluster of islands in the Pacific shaped like an inverted V. Joey's base was in the Northern Sierra Madre Natural Park, in the northeastern corner of Luzon—a remote rural area that encompasses the largest protected forest in the Philippines.

Before I could observe and pitch in with Joey's conservation work, we had to cover a couple hundred miles, taking us from huge, vibrant, urban Manila far up into the mountains.

The first thing you have to do to travel efficiently in the Philippines is forget everything your mom or dad ever taught you about vehicle safety. By the time I arrived, Joey had made arrangements for us to ride in (actually *on*) a jeepney. The gist of this mode of transportation is that you, your gear, and the spare tire ride on the roof of an old truck, bus, or army jeep. You sit within the perimeter of a low-slung metal frame bolted to the roof—basically a luggage rack. On a fancy jeepney, it might have two rungs and rise eight inches off the frame. Many have just a single rung—more a formality than a security feature. I guess it goes without saying that jeepneys have no seat belts (even on the inside) and no emission standards. The Philippine government has been trying for years to limit these vehicles, to keep people from riding up top, and to retire the older models and get them off the road, but this mode of transportation is cheap and deeply ingrained in the society, so it's definitely not going away without a fight.

We started out in heavy traffic, but it didn't take long for the pavement to give way to dirt roads. Small sections where the ground had washed away were patched with boards, and there were countless tarps covered in drying rice grains along these rural byways. Our route was, to put it generously, one lane wide, so when we met another jeepney coming our way, both vehicles had to edge as far over as possible, and one had to stop completely while the other eased by. We could have high-fived the passengers on the roof of the other truck.

The farther north we traveled, the more lush and green and unspoiled the scenery got, until we finally reached the Philippine Sierra Madres, the natural park's unspoiled primary forest, and the Catallangan River, where we'd soon be scouting crocs. After a day of bro-ing out and catching up on what each of us had been up to since we'd hung out in Fiji a year before, we set up a sub-camp along the river near where we thought we could pick up the trail of an adult female croc Joey had fitted with a transmitter.

The logistics of this operation were *way* too much fun to feel like research. Basically, we'd hike upriver for a few hours, walking up these lush green jungle mountains, climbing over massive gray-blue boulders, and winding our way along the water. Once we'd gone a few miles, we'd throw on our snorkeling gear, wade into the water, and let the relatively gentle rapids carry us back.

So there we were, floating downriver, taking in the scenery, scouting for croc lairs. Heaven? Eden? Disneyland? All of the above. Along our way downstream, we stopped to snorkel at rocks and crevices at the river's edge. One of the things that sets the Philippine crocodile apart from so many other crocodilian species is its preference for clean, running water. Typically I'd expect to be pursuing crocs in murky, still swamps and ponds, but these guys like it right along the edges of the river. So each time we found a good rocky shelf—or, even better, an underwater cave—we'd hold our breath and free dive down to see if anybody was home. When we found a croc, one of us would set up the snare while the other filmed the capture. Once we had each croc subdued, we'd pull it onto the shore and assess it for Joey's database. We carried a scale, measuring tapes, a data log, and duct tape, to temporarily secure the crocs' dangerous jaws shut.

If a croc was already in Joey's records, we'd update the file and do a herp lover's wellness check: a quick once-over, noting gender and taking several different measurements along the head, body, and tail. If a croc was newly caught, first we'd check it for a microchip. When we found a croc who didn't have a chip, we put one in. Joey had located crocs ranging in size from juveniles barely two feet long to a male who was a whopping three hundred pounds and three yards long—a huge specimen for this species. Even at that extreme size, though, swimming with these guys in the open water is typically safe—they're not big enough to be (or inclined to be) man-eaters. Getting bit was a remote possibility, but getting eaten was not.

In addition to recording microchip information, Joey was outfitting some of the crocs with radio telemetry trackers. Crocs that were over a yard long had trackers sutured onto the top of their tails, and for smaller crocs Joey had devised a strap—essentially a leather hip pack—to go on over their back legs, with a figure-eight belt under their thighs. It sat on their top sides, oriented down their tails, like a tiny croc backpack. The best thing about this ingenious design was that it didn't inhibit the croc's mobility at all. It's a set-it-and-forget-it fashion accessory, but one that provides the conservation world with invaluable data. Joey's little custom croc pack was so effective he was able to publish a scientific article about it. It was awesome being there to watch this unique research method unfold.

We were hot on the trail of one croc in particular during this trip, a female Joey had fitted with a satellite tracking unit who'd ventured so far upriver she was in a part of the park he hadn't yet explored. This was new territory for both of us, and it was an area of truly unspoiled (maybe even untouched) forest. Once we got close to the croc's tracker, we were able to download its data and discover where she'd been in the previous days and how she'd been moving around the park.

We never found that elusive croc during my stay, but we did come upon a gorgeous female of similar size on the way back to the village a couple nights later. She was caught in a trap that Joey's local research assistants had set very close to our base camp, and she wasn't especially happy to see us. She thrashed and whipped her tail and generally made it known that she was pissed that we were disturbing her day. A full-grown Philippine croc is definitely big enough to hurt you, but these animals are not man-eaters. This species simply doesn't look at people and see a food source. In this case, the croc just wanted to be left alone. Joey and I were happy to oblige, but first we needed some data that could help protect not just this individual but also her species. And getting that data meant doing a little bit of messy veterinary work out there in the jungle. We would have to accomplish the equivalent of pumping a croc's stomach.

Because checking to see what a croc's been eating can be a dangerous job and is a process the animal doesn't like to participate in, it's not something that's done every day. With a veterinarian helper on hand, though, it was a perfect time for Joey to investigate the diet of this animal. Using a narrow PVC tube, duct tape, and a hose, we created the kind of makeshift pump used to evaluate crocodilian diets around the world. We placed the PVC tube in her mouth and then taped her jaw securely shut around it. This allowed us hands-on access and eliminated the possibility of being bitten. However, it didn't do a thing to dull her teeth, so we needed to stay mindful that a good head thrash would cut us up. We threaded a flexible hose through the tube, past the croc's mouth and into her stomach. Keeping her head and body tilted upright, we proceeded to fill her stomach with water, using a manual hand pump, and to gently massage it as well—this was to suspend most of the food content inside her stomach. Once we got a backflow of water, we knew her stomach was full.

If you're thinking it sounds like we were out there water-boarding crocodiles, keep in mind that crocs can hold their breath for several minutes at a minimum and likely closer to an hour. A couple minutes of pumping water into this animal's stomach was not a threat to her well-being.

After she was full, we tilted her the opposite way, head down. We positioned a small-mesh fishing net in front of her mouth and started massaging her stomach again (to encourage her to vomit up its contents). And then, *voilà*, crocodile vomit poured out, just like we'd hoped it would. Gross? You bet. But for a croc, also a habitual part of digestion. They are built to digest almost anything, although there are still bits and pieces they can't process—most notably fur—and once they've gleaned all the nutritional value they can get from a meal, they puke up what's left.

This particular treasure hunt revealed a snake skeleton, monitor lizard bones, and, most interestingly, hundreds of snail shells. This was consistent with Joey's findings from other spot checks of croc eating habits. He was discovering that snails are a significant part of their diet—more than anyone had thought. Knowing what an animal eats to survive is always a key component in a plan to preserve the species. I found it fascinating and kind of adorable that these scary ambush predators weren't slashing out of their water to grab big animals, the way we see crocodiles hunting on TV. They're just gently cruising these waterways and casually nibbling on snails. I found them even more endearing after learning this fact about these somewhat peaceful predators.

With her stomach empty, her transmitter checked, and her weight and length measured, our croc captive was ready to go. Since she'd made a point of thrashing around and letting us know just how annoyed she was at our disturbance, we took a few extra seconds to set up filming for her release. I got above her and sat gently just behind her shoulders, keeping most of my weight on my own feet and holding the base of her neck to keep her from lashing out. I held my camera ready. Joey stepped into the water with his GoPro, ready to capture the moment. When I let her go, the croc leaped into the river, briefly going airborne on the way. We got video of that leap and her splashing into the water from both in the air and underwater—an awesome way to capture the moment.

One of the things you learn when you're doing conservation work is that if you aren't helping local people connect with and respect the animals, you're wasting your time. Joey and the Mabuwaya Foundation were doing an amazing job with this side of the equation in the Philippines. Joey was going into schools with juvenile crocs (and donations of school supplies) to teach students about the value of the species and how rare they are. Mabuwaya was so involved with the community that the local school had even changed its mascot to a crocodile a few years back. Joey also met with local farmers to explain the plight of the crocs and how close they are to going extinct. Rather than kill a croc that shows up on their land, where it might pose a danger, locals learn that they can contact the foundation and have it relocated. I had a chance to get out into some of these communities with my old friend and meet some of the locals during my visit, and I can honestly say that there is almost nothing more rewarding than helping to educate a local population (especially kids!) about what they can do to help save their own endangered species.

Not a Bear, Not a Cat

Palawan is the last ecological frontier in the Philippine Archipelago, a long, narrow, largely undeveloped sliver of land jutting out into the Pacific, with the South China Sea to its north and the Sulu Sea to its south. This is a place that's been ranked "The Most Beautiful Island in the World," and it lives up to that high bar not only because of its gorgeous beaches and blue water but also (at least as far as I'm concerned) because of its rugged jungle and wealth of unique endemic species. Among these are the Palawan leopard cat, the Palawan hornbill, the Palawan water monitor, and, my personal favorite, the Palawan bearcat (a.k.a. the binturong).

Talk about a species that's not on the curriculum at veterinary school. Is it a bear? Is it a cat? Um, no. It's neither. The binturong is a mammal with a big bushy tail, wide-set eyes, an open face, long whiskers, and a heavy, low body. It kind of resembles a weasel, if you can imagine a massive, sixty-pound tree-dwelling weasel with the face of a bear cub, a cat's whiskers, and a howler monkey's prehensile tail. Oh yeah, and wolverine claws. Best of all, there's something about the facial structure of these animals—mouths wide and upturned—that makes it look like they're always kind of smiling.

One last uniquely bearcat feature is that they smell, strangely and truly, like popcorn. The first time I ever got close to one in the wild, I smelled it first. I tracked it for hours that night, knowing there was absolutely nothing else in the jungle that could be emitting that particular odor. Unfortunately, I never found the bearcat—I just got to smell it.

During this trip, I visited the Palawan Butterfly Eco-Garden, where a binturong rescue program is going strong. I had been on the grounds for only minutes when one of the handlers came up with a seven-month-old female bearcat, who took one look at me and decided I'd be fun to climb. While I interacted with the handler, she crawled all over me, sitting on my shoulders, arching across my head, snarfling my ears, my neck, and my phone, and generally making me feel like the luckiest man alive.

That interaction was made all the more special when the sanctuary's owner, Roy Rodriguez, explained that the bearcat who'd befriended me was the first the facility had bred in captivity. Roy is a Philippine native who found himself struggling to accept how many of Palawan's endemic species were endangered and being taken for granted. His appreciation for wildlife was misunderstood by many of his friends and family members, but instead of stewing about it, he decided to take action and opened a sanctuary. These days, he's getting a lot more Filipinos excited about their native wildlife. The breeding program he initiated is a big step toward strengthening the numbers of these sweet and vulnerable mammals, whose population has decreased by around 30 percent in the last forty years.

Wild binturongs aren't outright aggressive, but they can and will be very dangerous if approached on their home territory. And since they're so rarely spotted in their own environment (because left to their own devices, they'd spend almost all their time high in the trees), they're coveted by poachers, who sell their parts to medicine men who believe they have healing powers (spoiler alert: they don't). These poachers also sell them as pets (another spoiler alert: they do *not* make good pets).

The sanctuary's bearcats had never seen a veterinarian, so Roy and I agreed that the timing was perfect for them to have their first checkup.

Doing an exam on a wild animal—even one as sweet as a seven-month-old captive-raised binturong—poses some unique challenges. Without the formalities of an enclosure and an exam table and a lab coat, it was pretty much a sure thing I was going to get shat on. Sure enough, as soon as I tried to direct this little sweetheart, instead of just letting her have her way with me, she dropped a massive butt-clapping fart and then splattered bearcat feces all over me. It's an occupational hazard I've gotten used to, though, and with that out of the way, we were able to get down to the actual exam.

I checked her nails and nailbeds, looking for any defects or infections. Bearcats, like many arboreal species, need to have healthy fingers and claws. I checked her teeth to ensure that none were fractured and that her gums looked healthy. I palpated her abdomen—as well as her appendages, including that long, muscular tail—and her lymph nodes. I peered into her ears, searching for parasites or signs of infection, and listened to her baby binturong heart, which had a good, strong, synchronous beat, with no murmur. The whole time, I let her play with my stethoscope and fed her a steady supply of banana bites, to keep the exam low-key and comfortable.

During my visit, Roy received a call: a few hours away, a mother binturong had been shot by poachers, and her three orphaned babies were for sale. An illegal pet trader was on his way; he would buy them, then smuggle them out of the country. We didn't want those babies to leave the country for many reasons, the first being that without a mother or anyone experienced in how to care for them, they'd all likely die. Besides that, these creatures didn't belong in Laos or Korea or China or wherever they were headed. They belonged in Palawan.

Because of that, Roy and I and the production team who was traveling with me made a controversial decision. With the clock ticking before the trader's arrival, we decided to offer the family who was holding the binturongs a reward for releasing them into Roy's protective custody. Paying for these animals might be considered an incentive for the next poacher to come along, but in this case it was the only way to ensure the survival of three innocent orphans.

I believe it was the right call. By the time we got to them, the binturongs were huddled together in a dirty potato sack on the ground, barely moving. At first we were worried that they might already be dead. But when I opened the bag and peeked inside, three pairs of eyes blinked back at me. All three babies were alive, and when they saw the light they craned and stretched my way, trying to smell me and get a glimpse of their surroundings. I'm positive they were simply looking for their mother, and there was no way to explain to them that with her gone forever, the place they were headed was the next best thing to going home to family.

Back at the sanctuary, I held each of these infants and examined them individually. They were the size of small kittens, and they mewled and cried and gently protested the handling, wanting nothing more than to snuggle up with one another and their missing mom. It was hard not to be distracted by the ridiculous cuteness of these babies—but knowing that I had just a small window to note any potential health problems they might have, I did my best to stay focused.

With the exam out of the way and a little bit of a comfort level developing between us, they started getting playful. One of these little guys flopped over on his back with all four legs up, ready to grab. He swatted at my hands and then pulled them back toward him—a sure sign that he wanted to keep playing. And when the kits weren't playing with me, they were rolling around with one another—wrestling and snuggling and nuzzling each other's necks and ears, occasionally taking snack breaks to eat some of the fruit we'd put out for them. Honestly, on the cuteness scale, Pooh Bear himself had nothing on these little guys.

Roy's plan was to raise the binturongs to maturity, breed them with his existing population, and ultimately release more bear-cats onto protected lands. His commitment to strengthening the numbers of these creatures is the kind of step that may one day play a part in preserving the species.

Batting 100,000

The western coast of Palawan is home to one of the most magical national parks I've ever seen: the Puerto Princesa Subterranean River National Park. Aboveground, the place is gorgeous, with massive limestone columns jutting up out of the sea, clear blue water, white sand, and not a man-made structure in sight. It's largely made up of densely lush jungle hills that feed into the tropical ocean—one of my favorite vistas on the planet. But where things get even more interesting is underground.

What you can't see from a flyover or a boat trip past it is that Puerto Princesa contains one of the largest and most impressive cave systems on the planet, including a five-mile-long underground river that's been named one of the Seven Natural Wonders of the World. The river starts on the island but ultimately empties out into the ocean, creating what's called a mountain-to-sea ecosystem. It is incredibly rare to find everything in this ecosystem in one place: the limestone formations, old-growth forest, swamp, beach, mangrove forest, fresh water, brackish water (a mix of fresh and seawater where almost any kind of marine life-form can crop up), and a massive cave system, with chambers that are more than a football field long and more than fifty yards high. All those natural elements combine to create a home for hundreds of animals and plants you'd be challenged to find living together almost anywhere else. This place is so special that scientists continue to find new species here—including a new spider and a new fly in 2018, and three new plants in 2015.

I went into the cave system in an outrigger canoe with an expert guide, Nevong Puna, a local wildlife biologist. Gliding into the cave's entry, there's only one species your senses take note of on that first impression: bats. You can hear them, see them, smell the ammonia-tinged scent of their excrement. As we passed into the cave's first big opening, we saw a few fluttering overhead. As we got deeper into the cave, their numbers increased. Finally, in a big, dark section of cavern, I shined my light overhead and realized there were not a few, not hundreds, but thousands of bats clinging to the ceiling above us. Nevong told me that more than one hundred thousand bats had been recorded in that area alone. At least eight different species of these creatures live in Puerto Princesa park, making their homes throughout the cave system. If you're afraid of bats, this is not the place for you. But if you're like me and find these flying mammals fascinating, it's incredible. It's also the reason most visitors to this area wear hard hats on their tours, and why most guides offer one major rule of cave exploration: Close your mouth when you look up! I decided to take my chances without a hat since I'm used to getting animal crap on me as part of a normal day's work. I was much more interested in maintaining good exposure for my headlamp than I was in keeping my hair clean.

Even with the rustling of the bats, the cave—like nearly every cave I've ever been in—had a uniquely quiet, solemn aura. This is the kind of place a person goes to get in touch with the deepest elements of nature and with what life is like without the warmth and light of the sun. It's like nature's own sensory deprivation tank. The place was teeming with life, but it was all understated and tucked into the shadows. It would be easy to assume that the darkness would be forbidding to cold-blooded creatures, but I figured there was no way that many bats could be living in one place without their natural predators following. Sure enough, as I tracked a single moving pair of wings along the cave wall, my flashlight caught an iridescent reflection on a rocky shelf: a snake. Some kind of colubrid, likely nonvenomous, which meant I could safely go in for a closer look.

Whether or not a snake is venomous is always the first thought that comes to mind when I spy a new animal and can't immediately identify the species. This question was especially important here because trying to grab the snake and have a look wouldn't be as simple as walking over to it. I was about to step off a small, unstable rowboat, and there wouldn't be much space between me and the snake on the cave's wall if I jumped out onto the shelf just below it. Moving quickly, I fully extended myself from the boat and reached up over the muddy shelf it was lying on (which was above my head) to capture it before it could slip away. I pulled down a beautiful cave racer, thin and more than five feet long, completely harmless to humans but a deadly and effective predator to bats.

This was my first-ever cave snake encounter. While I looked him over, this guy wrapped himself tightly around my arm, not just anchoring but actually knotting his body over me. He was probably trying to figure out what the hell was happening. I'd be willing to bet he'd never been handled by a human before—and I doubt he ever will be again. Nevong told me that in the five years he'd been visiting these caves, he'd sometimes seen snakes, but he'd never gotten close enough to catch one. He joked about being envious, although he was clearly genuinely excited that I'd gotten to have this experience on his tour.

The racer had beautiful markings that shone in the light, and he coiled calmly in my hands while I checked him out. I kept him for only a few minutes before releasing him exactly where I'd found him. Watching him glide away across the rough rocks, I could only admire this creature who'd innovated a life underground for himself, figuring out how to live without light so he could partake in the never-ending smorgasbord of Puerto Princesa bats.

Chicken Thief

While we were exploring, Nevong told me about a lizard who'd repeatedly been sighted in a local village near the park. The residents were willing to overlook the intruder's presence—until he started stealing their chickens. I headed out there, hoping maybe I could track down the thief and relocate him to a less-populated area where he'd be better able to find food that didn't already belong to someone else.

The lizard was an endemic species of monitor—the Palawan water monitor. Like all monitors, I knew, this one would be a handful to work with. Monitors are among my favorite species in the world to wrangle because they're what I consider to be nature's version of Godzilla. They can get huge (in fact, the largest lizards on earth—Komodo dragons—are monitors), and they're all muscle, with sharp claws, tails they can use like bullwhips, and some of the scariest bite-force capabilities of any reptile species.

As I walked through the village, I could see kids playing, monkeys perched up in the trees, a dog lazing in the sun outside a hut, and then, right next to one family's home, the monitor. He was nearly six feet long, head to tail, thick and heavily muscled, lying low at the base of a tree. It was really obvious which creature didn't belong in this scene—and also why the villagers were not too stoked about having this guy hanging around so close to their homes.

A lizard like that should not be handled by anybody without extensive experience. Large monitors can be aggressively defensive, and their bites can not only easily shred through multiple layers of tissue but can almost guarantee a troublesome infection to follow—one that could even, in an extreme case, be fatal. I figured that unless somebody removed this monitor from the village, it might be only a matter of time before he'd end up on the business end of a weapon. Since nobody else who'd be willing to capture him alive and relocate him was likely to come along, I decided to see what I could do.

The monitor kept a wary eye on my approach, but he didn't attempt to move away. I'm pretty sure he was used to the locals giving him a wide berth, so he probably expected me to pass on by. A monitor who wasn't accustomed to people would have been *far* more skittish. I slowly set my backpack on the ground and sidled a little closer. When I got within a couple feet—his personal space—he realized I wasn't just a random pedestrian and directed a hiss my way. When I made a move toward him, he took off running.

Monitors always surprise me with their speed, when they choose to turn it on. (The same goes for most reptiles, unless they're cold.) Within seconds we went from scoping each other out at a distance to a full-on chase. It's not easy to run in a semi-crouch, but the only way I was going to capture this monitor without hurting him was to crouch down to his level and get my hands on him. At a sprint, I made one giant leap forward, bent my knees and my back, and got a nice grip with my left hand on the monitor's tail, several inches from the end.

Man, did he not like that. The monitor arched his spine, launched his mouth wide open, and went directly for my face. When we made eye contact (and I'm sure mine were as wide as they can get), the expression on his face read, "Bro, who do you think you *are*?" He was throwing his body side to side and swinging that gaping, septic mouth in my direction the entire time, madly trying to either get loose or get even. It's a strange predicament to be holding something so dangerous and potentially destructive, but until we resolved this contest of who was going to make contact first, I had to press on.

I knew I needed to get my right hand down on him in order to stabilize him and put an end to the madness. At times like this, I am grateful for my freakishly long arms. I held the lizard as far out as I could reach, keeping my grip on his tail and bending at the hips to keep my hands as far from my body as possible, my concentration divided between *not* getting bit and finding an opportunity to get the big guy better under control.

It was a heart-pounding moment, even for someone with extensive experience handling reptiles. I've seen people who've been bitten by a monitor, including one guy who looked like his hand got caught in a paper shredder. I knew that if this lizard got hold of my flesh, he wouldn't just bite it, he'd mangle it. That's what his teeth—long, deadly sharp, recurved, and serrated—were built for, and that's one of the reasons these animals are so successful in the wild (and, as it turns out, sometimes in villages, too).

Watching for my opening, I caught a second when the monitor was facing away from me and lowered him toward the ground. In the same instant, I brought my right hand forward and clasped him around his shoulders, effectively pinning him against the ground. My hands and legs were covered with mud from hitting the ground during the capture and my breathing was heavy, but my grin was as big as my head.

"All right!" was all I managed to spit out while I tried to catch my breath, still focused on keeping the animal restrained and ensuring that this interaction remained safe for both of us. And then, as I transferred my left hand to the base of the tail, where I'd have more control, I finally got a chance to lean in and closely inspect the lizard and make an introduction, saying, "Hey, beautiful!"

When I had the monitor up close, I could see that he had an open wound with some swelling along the side of his mouth—not too bad, but possibly painful and definitely at risk of infection. Maybe it was a stretch for me to think I could be his friend after what we'd just gone through together, but whether he liked it or not, I was a veterinarian and he was a wild animal with a vulnerable spot that would benefit from treatment.

Talking to the monitor and keeping my head well back, I steadied him and gripped the back of his head and shoulders with my left hand. With my right, I reached under his jaw and eased his mouth open. If he was going to shred a piece of my face, this was going to be the moment.

Thankfully, he held still and let me have a look at his jaw, the inside of his mouth, and, specifically, the area on the inside of his gums that was of concern to me. There were no obvious signs of infection, but I figured as long as I had him in hand and that section of exposed flesh was evident outside his mouth, the least I could do was flush it with an antiseptic. Letting his mouth close, I squeezed some Betadine solution I had in my backpack over the wound and then massaged in a small amount of antibiotic ointment. The monitor, miraculously, didn't flinch.

With the treatment complete, I hoisted the monitor up and carried him out into the jungle, away from the village and the homes and the chickens. Unfortunately, I could get only a couple miles away. Monitors are smart, roving, opportunistic carnivores, and this dude probably had an even wider territory. As I let him go and he made a beeline deeper into the jungle, I held out hope that this "intervention" would deter him from wanting to head back to the village and its chickens. Watching that big, beautiful predator go, I was grateful for the opportunity to have met and interacted with him.

Moments like that, and like the others I had in Palawan—those days of adventure are what I live for. I was headed home and back to the very different joys and hardships of life in a veterinary hospital. I knew it wouldn't be long, though, before I sat down with my calendar to figure out where I could go next.

12

Rwanda and the Democratic Republic of Congo

If you could see any animal species up close and go anywhere in the world to do it, what trip would you choose? I've asked myself that question a hundred times, and in early 2018, the answer was that I wanted to see mountain gorillas. In order to do it, I'd have to travel to the Virunga Mountains, a volcanic range where the borders of Rwanda, the Democratic Republic of Congo, and Uganda meet.

Trekking with the silverbacks is the wildlife encounter of a lifetime, and even though I love traveling alone, this was something I hoped to share with a friend. It had been years since my best friend, Tim, and I had been on an adventure. By the time this trip rolled around, he was married, with two beautiful kiddos and a full-time job. Still, that January, there we were—two of Overland Park's finest, jetting over the Atlantic on our way to meet one of the greatest and rarest exotic animal populations in the world.

Wanting a Moment

Gorillas are native solely to Africa, and the two species (eastern and western) are separated by about six hundred miles of Congo basin forest in the center of the continent. Eastern gorillas are divided into two subspecies, and the critically endangered mountain gorilla was the species I hoped to see. There are only around a thousand of these gorillas left in the wild, but the existence of even that many is a conservation success story. Thanks to the aggressive efforts of organizations like the Dian Fossey Gorilla Fund International and Gorilla Doctors, there are twice as many of these amazing animals today as there were just ten years ago.

The place I chose to visit, Volcanoes National Park in Rwanda, has helped make that possible in a couple of different ways. First, they protect their gorilla population on preserved land. This isn't easy—in fact, sometimes it's literally a war for wildlife. Keeping poachers out of the park and away from the gorilla population is a full-time job, and the heroes who do it put their lives on the line. I have incredibly deep respect for the rangers who go out and defend their wildlife every day.

The second notable program at Volcanoes deserves a lot of credit for the innovative, respectful method they've devised for using tourism to benefit the gorilla population. Besides gaining funding by charging small groups of tourists to observe (but not disturb!) the gorillas in their natural environment, this program goes one step further. Knowing that poachers are one of the biggest threats to this endangered species and that most of the poachers are just trying to feed their families, the park is slowly changing local perceptions of the native wildlife by showing people that the gorillas benefit them more alive than they do dead. This sounds like an impossible task, but Volcanoes and other programs like theirs actually hire former poachers to be rangers and gorilla trackers in the park. The park helps locals tie their livelihoods to the gorillas' survival. In Rwanda, it also uses money the program makes to help build houses and villages and schools for the community's children. Every step of the way, the locals are discovering that a thriving gorilla population can help them feed their families.

This program is part of a bigger theme that's made a huge impression on me all over the world: In order to successfully conserve local wildlife, the community has to be a part of the effort and benefit from participating. Any other way of going about conservation isn't self-sustaining.

Volcanoes Park employs a team of expert trackers who keep tabs on the gorillas' locations. This process is a totally passive stakeout and a twenty-four/seven job. Trackers maintain a respectful distance, they don't approach the animals, and they don't do anything to influence the gorillas' movements. Their job is simply to report the locations while the gorillas do whatever they want to do. Guides take it from there, combining their knowledge of the animals (as most of them were previously trackers in the park), their ability to communicate (in multiple languages), their hiking strength, and their patience to bring visitors and apes together in the mountains.

If you're a tourist, the upshot of all that organization is that if you want to see these amazing animals, you not only need to get to their mountains from wherever in the world you live; you also need to strap on your boots and hike out to find them. The place may be home to some of the most outrageous and special animal encounters on the planet, but it is definitely not a zoo. These are completely wild gorillas.

On *the* morning, Tim and I arrived at the park at sunrise—a little sore from a fairly intense crater lake hike the day before, but way too excited to care. There are eleven gorilla families in the mountains, and visitors go out in small groups to visit each family. Typically fewer than a hundred people a day get to have this privilege.

Each group, led by its guides, goes looking for a single family, and each family is different from the next (and they're also always changing). The largest family had close to forty members and was, ironically, by all accounts the hardest to track. Every family has at least one male, at least one female, and a group of subadults and babies. Several families have multiple silverbacks who live cooperatively together.

Before we started moving, our guide, Timothy (pronounced "Tim-o-teh"), laid out some rules to keep us safe. I guess he wanted to be sure we heard him before we started huffing and puffing up the mountain. "When you see the gorillas," he said, "remain calm. Don't make any sudden movements. Don't look them in the eye. Keep your posture low, indirect, and nonthreatening. Don't eat. If you hear a gorilla making the low, throaty sound that's a nonthreatening acknowledgment"—here Timothy demonstrated, and we all practiced—"you may make that same sound back. Otherwise, keep quiet.

"Oh yeah," he added, "and don't beat your chest like King Kong."

Hearing that one, I couldn't help but wonder just how many tourists who'd come before me had done this. Any? Really?

Last of all, Timothy warned us not to try to get near the gorillas. *Do not approach.* But if the gorillas approached us, he said, we should stay calm and still and never reach out toward them. We should also stay where we were, since moving away could spark a pursuit.

Ha. Like I would move *away* if I got so lucky.

The family we'd be tracking was one of the smallest at Volcanoes, with just one silverback, his mate, an infant male, and two juveniles, both girls. The male in this family was around thirty-three, and the female was the oldest actively breeding female in the area. At age forty-four, she was an über-mama.

After what seemed like an eternity of getting ready, learning the rules, and eagerly shifting from foot to foot when all I wanted to do was get started, we finally set out from the base of the mountain. Regardless of when you do this trek, it is invariably uphill, and these mountains are steep. On the day we were climbing, the terrain was also crazy slippery, thanks to heavy rain the night before. We knew it would be hot, so Tim wore shorts and I wore a tank top. Ten minutes into the hike, we were both regretting those choices. The theme of the day was gorilla tracking. But the subplot was definitely going to be stinging nettles on bare skin.

As we hiked, I kept my eyes peeled for gorillas, even though our guide seemed pretty confident that we had a couple miles to go until we would find them. Looking at the stunning landscape of steep, forested mountains, I wondered if Dian Fossey had ever walked this same path in the decades she'd lived and worked inside the perimeter of Volcanoes. Fossey contributed more to the world's understanding of gorillas than any other human has. While she did it, though, she was in a constant struggle with area poachers who killed her beloved gorillas, both for bushmeat and so they could sell their heads, hands, and bones to international collectors and tribal medicine men who believed they had healing powers.

I was no expert on gorillas or on Fossey, but I had a growing base of experience with getting involved with animals whose existence is threatened by people. Conservationists who work in the field can get incredibly close to the subjects they're studying—especially animals with high-level cognition like primates. I could only imagine how it must have felt, for Fossey, to study a family every day for years and then find a gorilla she'd built a bond with dead at the hands of poachers.

Just over an hour into our hike, Timothy got word from the trackers that we were near the gorilla family and they were coming toward us. We were along the edge of a steep ridge, and he told us to sit and wait. We sat in a spread-out line across a ledge and waited. Tim and I kept glancing at each other and then up and down the mountain. Where were they? Then, about twenty feet below us, we spotted a black mass moving our way. *This is it!* We kept watching it as it approached. A lone male, an actual silverback in the wild. I was willing that gorilla to come to our end of the line, to walk next to Tim and me, so I could see him up close and smell him and study how he moved. He was coming right toward us, and I had my camera ready. And then he veered toward the other end of our line, walked up to the people there, looked them over, and kept right on going.

As he walked away, I realized I'd been holding my breath. I don't think I was the only one. All eight members of our group sat silently staring after the silverback as he continued on his way. It felt as if a giant, furry, silver angel had walked among us.

The mature, adult, educated part of me was thinking, *That was incredible. I'm so grateful I got to see it.* But the juvenile part of me was in a little different mood: *Damn, I wish I'd been sitting over there!*

I had wanted that engagement in the worst way, wanted the gorilla to look at me, and I had *just* missed it.

The guide told us that the rest of the family had gone a different way but that the whole group seemed to be heading to the same location farther up the mountain. We decided to hike a little longer in the area in case we could get lucky with another sighting.

Hiking away from the ridge, we had to cross over another steep hill, and it was taking a long time for the entire group to get through. Tim and I were the first across, so we started making our way ahead a little bit. The guide came with us, leaving his assistants to bring the rest of the group along. We were approaching the next ridge, an extremely steep drop, and getting ready to make our way over it when Timothy stopped us.

"Hang on," he said. "He's close."

There was no question about who the *he* in that statement was, and I thought to myself, *Yessssss!*

Within seconds *he* was there. Steadily, easily covering the steep terrain on all fours, the three-hundred-pound silverback pushed toward us until he was directly in front of me—and then he stopped. He was so close I could have reached out and touched him. He was so huge, so majestic, so wild. Total beauty and total danger. With my heart slamming in my chest, I was eyeing this guy's physique and was blown away by the sheer power of his musculature. I lift weights, I've been a personal trainer, and I studied anatomy extensively at veterinary school, so I have a solid understanding of body structure and physical development. The gorilla in front of me was easily one of the most freakishly strong creatures I'd ever seen. Head to toe, he was built of well-developed, symmetrical muscles. He was strong enough to effortlessly climb that mountain every day; to tear down banana trees with his bare hands; to lift as much as ten times his weight; and, undoubtedly, to shred me if he wanted to.

His eyes darted around, taking in me, Tim, and Timothy. I was too excited to be scared, but I was trying to stay nonthreatening. Eyes down, no sudden movements, no squaring off against the big guy. I knew that of the tourists to go up the mountain that day, Tim and I were two of the youngest and biggest males. I wondered if perhaps we were being perceived as some kind of intrusion, if maybe he didn't want us there. I hunched my shoulders, bent my knees a little, tried to look small.

And then, after eyeing me and my friend for one very long minute, this giant ape who's known not just for being powerful but also for being territorial, flopped down on the ground. He was maybe three feet from me. While I was still trying to process what this might mean—and wondering if I should get lower, too—the silverback eased over so that he was lying down in the scrubby grass and then *rolled over onto his back.*

I looked at Tim and saw the same expression that must have been on my face: eyebrows up, eyes wide, mouth gaping. The universal look of *WTF is happening right now.*

The gorilla is BELLY UP?!

As a veterinarian, if you want to do your job well and not get bitten every day, you learn very quickly to read a few body language cues that are nearly universal among animals. Three things that are clear signs that a creature is feeling relaxed and not threatened: (1) they're eating; (2) they're sleepy and relaxed; (3) they show you the belly.

I knew for sure this was not submission. After the way the silverback had rushed toward us and stopped to size us up, there was zero chance that he was intimidated. Even as I was thinking this, he took one long arm, stretched it up, and laid it across his forehead. Total relaxation. He glanced my way, and I lowered my eyes again. There's no way to know 100 percent what an animal is thinking, but I was pretty sure this whole show was his way of letting us know we were not important enough to be considered a threat. His total comfort in his dominance was staggering.

While Tim and the guide and I stood watching in awe of the giant ape's display, his family caught up to him. One by one they walked right past us—first the two juveniles, then the mom, carrying her baby. My emotions were all over the place. Joy, mostly. Excitement. Awe. Gratitude. The silverback lay there on the ground watching us, watching his family. When they'd passed us, he stretched, got up, and wandered off after them.

As soon as he was gone, I hustled over to the spot where he'd been and lay down in it, copying his posture, putting my hand over my head. He had just been there on that same grass. I was blown away. I had *so* wanted a moment, and we'd gotten that. It was like winning the lottery.

Family Affair

Volcanoes National Park limits the amount of exposure the gorillas have with humans to no more than an hour a day, and no family is observed every day of the week. The program treads a fine line in order to bring in significant funds to help promote conservation and protection for the gorillas without imposing on their families any more than necessary. The small groups of tourists who do trek out to see them tend to become ambassadors on behalf of the species—because we almost universally find the experience life-altering. On this day, the trackers had radioed our guide that the entire family was together in a clearing nearby, saying that we still had time on our hour-long clock if we wanted to observe them from a distance. With our group finally back together, we took a short walk to where the family was hanging out.

I didn't think it would be possible to top the moment I'd just had with the silverback on the mountain, but what we were seeing there was a perfect complement to it. The family was acting like—well, a lot like a human family. The two subadult females were playing, wrestling, picking each other's boogers, bickering, and just basically being gorilla kids. The mom sat nearby, nursing the baby and keeping an eye on her rowdy girls. The baby was adorable—big baby eyes, pudgy baby belly, a little wisp of hair on his little baby head.

But it was the dad, again, who snagged my attention and surprised me. While the mom nursed, he sat beside them, his giant hands gently grooming the baby. His face was so intent and caring. It was one of the sweetest moments I've seen in nature—the perfect juxtaposition of power and tenderness. This gorilla could crush my skull with just one of those hands, but he was simply hanging out, being a father, in a completely unguarded moment that I'd have climbed ten mountains to see.

Gorillas share 98 percent of our DNA, and it shows. We each have ten fingers and ten toes. We have the same musculature in our faces. We make similar expressions, we bond in similar ways, and we experience the same emotions. Seeing this gorilla be tender and affectionate and totally relaxed with his kiddos was like seeing any dad, any man, any family.

And then something shifted and this was a wildlife experience again. One of the guides made a move the silverback didn't like, and the gorilla's attention snapped to the small group of humans standing near the clearing. In a fraction of a second, he went from lying on his side, gently grooming his baby boy, to postured up on all fours with his head high and defiant. Those cannonball-sized deltoids, the forearms thicker than my thighs, the lats twice as wide as mine, and the glute muscles that originated halfway up his back made for a sobering sight, one that commanded deference and deep respect. In an instant, I went from holding myself back from trying to join in the family's cuddle to holding myself back from shitting my pants.

Almost every kid thinks, *My dad can beat up your dad*, but *this* dad, he was not freaking kidding. The entire family looked up at us, and the mood of the visit turned. Everyone, almost in sync, started putting away cameras, looking down and to the side, prepping to quickly and quietly leave. We had been lucky enough to be guests at this party, but we'd worn out our welcome. The silverback was letting us know in a way only a gorilla can that it was time for us to pack up and go home. There's a scene in *The Terminator* when Arnold Schwarzenegger gets into some guy's semi-truck and confidently orders him to "Get. Out." It was like that. Nobody had to say *NOW*. We all heard it loud and clear.

Hiking and sliding our way back down the mountain, Tim and I got lost in our recollections of the day (while trying to keep our footing on the steep trails). Seeing a gorilla family going about their business, doing the things that families do, had been magical. It was also a testament to all the people who have refused to let the giant apes die out. Gorilla Doctors has been providing protection and veterinary care to these animals for more than three decades. The group's origins date back to 1984, when Dian Fossey requested help from the Colorado-based Morris Animal Foundation by saying, "There are 248 gorillas in the world and they're all going to die."

And then she asked if they'd send a veterinarian.

Providing veterinary care to creatures in the wild is a practice some people find controversial. After spending a lot of time in recent years seeing some of these programs up close, my own view of it is simply this: If people have been directly responsible for damage to a species or a habitat, then we have the duty to take direct responsibility for contributing to a recovery—even if that demands measures that push back against the order of the natural world. The care and protection the Volcanoes gorillas receive seem like the least humankind can do for a species we single-handedly nearly wiped off the face of the earth.

The Other Side of the Mountain

When you stand on a peak in the Virunga Mountains in Rwanda and look out, you're gazing at the southwestern corner of Uganda and a vast expanse of the Democratic Republic of Congo. The DRC is more than eighty times bigger than Rwanda, with about seven times as many people. But it wasn't the view from the top of the mountain that had drawn me to the DRC, or even the fact that it is one of only three countries in the world where you can still find eastern gorillas (the third is Uganda, which also borders the Virungas). Instead, the idea for my trip was hatched when I saw a viral video of a pilot named Anthony Caere transporting an orphaned chimpanzee named Mussa to the Lwiro Primate Rehabilitation Center, near the DRC's eastern border. In it, the chimp sits, naps, and plays on Caere's lap; Caere grooms him, nuzzles him, and shows him the controls. They gaze out the window together. It is the kind of captivating and heartbreaking moment that happens every day in wildlife rescue. The chimp is obviously looking for comfort and companionship from the man, which he gets—but the only reason he needs it is because some other human murdered his mother and the rest of his family.

I reposted that video and reached out to the pilot to say I was moved. I told him how much I admired his work—basically just

sent a fan note. After that, Anthony and I got chatting about conservation and became friends. He put me in touch with the rehab
center, and the director invited me to come out and see the place
for myself.

Meeting my new pilot pal and visiting a chimp sanctuary in
the DRC? I couldn't pack my bags fast enough.

Or get my shots. I'd had all kinds of injections and oral vac-
cines for travel in the past—for hepatitis A, hep B, yellow fever,
and typhoid, plus a full series of rabies shots. But I'd never had
to get a cholera vaccine, until I learned that the DRC has 10 percent of the world's cases and that the area I'd be traveling to is
a hot spot for it. This particular vaccine came in a form I hadn't
had before—a powder you mix with water and then drink. Many
countries don't bother to confirm that visitors have had their vac-
cines, but when I finally made it to the border of the DRC, not
only did the customs officer insist on seeing proof of a yellow
fever vaccine, he also scanned my forehead with a temperature
sensor to be sure I wasn't arriving in his country sick with Ebola
or anything else.

After flying to Kigali, Rwanda; connecting to Kamembe; and
then riding to the Congolese border crossing, I spent ninety minutes in a truck to finally make it to the Lwiro Primate Rehabilitation Center. In contrast to the noise and chaos of the border
crossing, this place, with its Belgian colonial, cottage-like build-
ings dating back to the 1960s and its quiet grounds, felt like an
oasis. I was dead tired—but definitely *not* too tired to start meeting the center's residents.

Lwiro's director, Itsaso Vélez del Burgo, led me to the one
place that could definitely keep me wide awake: the nursery. And
when I say "nursery," I'm not kidding. These chimps are between
six months and three years old, and they truly look and act like
human toddlers in chimpanzee suits. They're a little stronger and
a little rougher than children, but the way they laugh and play
and interact with one another, the way they get sleepy or grumpy

or snuggly—it's like looking at any other bunch of "kids" at pre-school.

The chimps have caretakers with them all the time, feeding the babies, cuddling the youngsters who need loving contact, redirecting the troublemakers, and constantly steering all of them to form bonds with each other. The caretakers do their best to mother the orphans so they can survive, heal, and become part of the chimp family at the center. If these animals are ever going to be able to be released into the wild, they need to have a bonded family of their own. Since every one of these chimps has a story similar to Mussa's—a violent murder, a lost family, a rescue, a trip to Lwiro—the only way they're ever going to have those bonds is by building them with each other.

I desperately wanted to go into the enclosure and play, but since these babies are meant to return to the wild, it's best to limit human contact. Itsaso also reminded me that even though the chimps were mostly gentle with the teachers who were with them every day, they would probably want to play rough with me. Primates all over the world typically perceive me as a big, sturdy male, suitable for climbing and poking and roughhousing. Chimps in general, even juveniles, are much stronger than humans—typically about four times stronger. The secret to that difference in strength is in the way their muscles are constructed, with the fibers closest to their bones longer and denser than ours. And while those muscles pack a lot more punch than ours, the delivery is not as finessed—meaning sometimes a chimp swats at something (or somebody) and hits it (or me) *much* harder than is necessary to make their point. Even these young chimpanzees could harm a person if they wanted to, and even their "play" bites can inflict gnarly injuries.

So I sat outside the enclosure, and it turned out that I still had whatever "it" factor it is that makes so many of these guys want to be my friend. After just minutes of waiting, a young chimp with huge eyes waddled my way, gave me a wide-open gummy smile, and eased up to the other side of the fence. Itsaso warned me that this little girl was usually shy, so I just watched and waited. She was pretty subtle about it for a baby chimp, but she did want to get close to me, and I spoke softly through the fence to her until the other babies got curious about the new person in their home. The second was a lot bolder, demanding my attention instead of politely asking, and blocking the rest of the chimps from getting too close until the novelty of holding my attention wore off. When he finally got tired of me, a third chimp approached. He leaned toward the fence, resting his head against it, and looked straight into my eyes with his stern baby face. Itsaso, behind me, quietly said, "This is Mussa."

This was the chimp from Anthony Caere's video, the chimp who'd sat on his lap and cuddled him and won the heart of the world with how adorable and vulnerable and trusting he was on his way to the rescue. This completed the full circle for me. In the months since I'd seen that video, the sweet, gentle chimp who'd watched the clouds go by in the cockpit had come into his own. Mussa had actually become quite a little handful for his caretakers at the rehab center. He loved to engage and was an instigator, looking to get attention any way he could.

I said, "Hey, Mussa, it's great to meet you, man," and in response, he pushed his hand through the fence, reaching for my hand.

Looking at this playful, trusting little guy, I could still make out the marks where he'd been tied up as a captive. On arrival, the majority of the chimps at Lwiro have open wounds, scabs, and scars from being bound with rope around their waists. Some have also been tied around their necks. Many of the chimps suffer psychological damage, so some don't want to be touched and others pull out their hair or, at first, refuse to eat. As they realize that they are going to be treated gently and given their independence, most of them start to bond, sometimes first with each other, sometimes with the caretakers who feed them.

But like Mussa, some of these chimps actually arrive completely open to being loved. While I was at Lwiro, a new chimp was rescued and brought to the center. Her arrival will stick with me forever. This little girl, orphaned and alone, had traveled for hours in a plastic crate. Watching that crate be unloaded, I wondered what could be going through her mind. She looked so patient—waiting and wondering. We know chimps grieve and experience complex emotions, but she looked calm.

I don't know what I was expecting when the door of this crate was opened. Maybe that the chimp would cower in the corner, afraid to come out. Maybe that she'd come barreling through and try to get away. Or maybe that she'd be angry and fly at the face of the first person she saw, swinging her little limbs and baring her teeth in rage and frustration.

None of those things happened. Instead, a young veterinarian on the Lwiro team knelt down in front of the crate, reached up and unclasped the door, then sat back and waited. The door swung open and this little chimp eased slowly out, tilted her head to look up at the man, opened her arms wide, and reached up for a hug. This chimp leaned all the way into the embrace of the rescuer who'd freed her, resting her head on the man's chest, nuzzling against him.

Take my heart and stomp on it. After all the bullshit and agony my own species had put this baby girl through, she still just wanted to be loved.

I knew the chimp would be loved and taken care of at Lwiro, but the question that kept hitting me over and over again was *Why can't she just be with her mom?*

Standing by my side, witnessing the welcome of this chimp to her new home, was Anthony Caere. Of course he'd been the pilot to fly her to safety.

We sat down to get to know each other. In that place and in those circumstances, however, it was almost impossible to turn our thoughts to anything but the chimps.

The illegal pet trade in this species is a sick, ridiculous machine, built on the idea that apes make desirable pets or that they're great entertainers. News flash: chimpanzees may just be the worst pets on the planet. Yes, they are unbelievably endearing when they're babies. But by age five (if not sooner), most chimps (still juveniles) are stronger than most adult humans. Soon after that, they reach sexual maturity, and high levels of sexual hormones like testosterone make them all the more dangerous.

FYI: sexual maturity is the most common period when young wild and exotic animals (primates but also raccoons, wild cats, and so many others) stop being passive and rapidly grow out of their cuteness. They start having minds of their own and resenting being told what to do. They play rough; they break things. They shit wherever they feel like it, and they have a nasty habit of throwing that shit around—playfully, angrily, or out of boredom. Chimps bite. They slap. They hit. They can purposely or accidentally hurt or even kill a human owner.

Of all the creatures on earth, the one I'd least want to be trapped in a small space with is a chimp, because they're the reason the expression "Go ape" exists. Jane Goodall even noted in her books that chimps appear to have very little empathy. They are capable of violent and horrifying treatment of one another. I'd rather be up against a big cat or a bear or a hippo. Any animal can be ruthless when it's being territorial, but there's a logic to that. Grown chimps, though, are capable of flat-out sadism and have been witnessed cruelly taunting and even torturing others of their kind. At least any of those other dangerous animals would kill you fast.

Oh yeah: and they live, on average, about fifty years.

Why on earth would anybody want one of these creatures for a pet? Because they saw a picture of a baby chimp sitting on someone's lap, playing with a child's toy, or wearing a child's clothes. Adorable? You bet. Good idea? Absolutely not.

Awesome Alpha

Lwiro has two huge enclosures for its growing chimp population. The first is for adolescents, and as we walked along the outside of it, Itsaso told me about the histories of some of the residents. Like people, chimps have widely varied personalities, so some of these guys came running up to the fence to see me or reach out to touch my hand. Others hung back, shy and a lot more reluctant to get close to a stranger. I'm sure there were others I didn't see at all, safely tucked back in the heavily vegetated section of the enclosure.

The second enclosure is the home of the growing Pori family. At the time of my visit, the group was thirty-five individuals strong. The enclosure itself is massive—over six acres—and it encompasses grassland, jungle, and a running stream with fresh water. It is the closest thing to being in the wild that is possible for these rescued chimps, and they have a ton of room to roam within its borders.

Some of the chimps were curious, and others were hungry, heading my way for the handfuls of corn, bananas, beans, and zucchini I had to share with them. Itsaso kept us steadily moving, though, until we stood across the fence from Kongo, the alpha. He was big for a chimp, probably weighing in at around 150 pounds. If gorillas are the championship bodybuilders of the ape world, with their imposing size and bulging muscles, chimps are the Olympic wrestlers—stout, musclebound, and athletic. Kongo's hands were a giveaway to his strength—far bigger than a man's (except for the little thumbs) and thick, with ropes of muscles extending up his arms.

Just as if she'd taken me into his house or his office, Itsaso introduced me to him. Kongo looked me over, calm and steady, and actually gave me a nod. Like, *Okay, you can hang for a while.* To be honest, standing across from this guy, looking at him with him looking at me, it felt more like I was meeting a person who didn't speak my language than it did like meeting a creature of a different species.

It's pretty obvious when you meet Kongo that he is everything we all want an alpha to be. He displayed a quiet, confident, benevolent authority. All around him, other chimps were watching to see how he'd react to me, and when they perceived that he was relaxed and cool with my visit, they relaxed, too. It was apparent that everyone under him had complete respect for him.

This wasn't an alpha who spends his time proving he's the boss—he's very secure in that. With all the posturing out of the way, he was free to be a good leader to the Pori family. After he studied me for a while, he turned his attention to engaging with one of the younger chimps. Itsaso told me he gets angrily dominant only when he absolutely has to—like to break up a fight between two junior males. Even when he scraps with the younger apes, he doesn't hurt them. This guy was mayor, coach, and dad rolled into one—all roles you want filled by someone with a steady temper. And it's worth noting that this is not typical among adult male chimps. They can be brutal to each other, especially members of other troops, and they can easily go berserk over territory and violently injure or even murder other chimps.

It's possible that Kongo's temperament is a result of his origin story. Just like the other chimps in the Pori family, he came to the center from a terrible life. In 2007, he was found bound to a post by heavy chains around his neck that were secured with a padlock. He was crouched in the full sun, with no food or water. He was so thin that his eyes and ears looked huge in his head, and his hair was coming out in patches. That was the day he was rescued.

Today, Kongo looks like a different animal. His face is full, his limbs are muscular, and his hair is thick. And his eyes look wise, not haunted, the way they do in the pictures of his rescue. His story of evolution from a broken victim to an alpha male is an inspiring example of the resilience of this species.

A Problem We Can Help Solve

Chances are, if you're reading this book you aren't saving up to get a pet chimp. But even those of us who have no interest in living with apes can unintentionally be part of the problem they face in central Africa. By responding positively to images of chimps as pets, we feed the idea that they're fun to have around. So the best thing we can do on social media is not engage with content that depicts primates as household pets. If we don't "like" or comment when we see pictures of chimps wearing clothes or doing tricks or hanging around people's houses, we won't help feed the demand that keeps poachers ripping these babies out of the wild in the DRC every day.

If you want to help promote change, make a comment about the truths of what this sort of content can lead to. It's an easy opportunity to educate someone else who might have no idea about how destructive these images can be. I really think most people who engage with this kind of content have big hearts for animals and want what's best for them. They just don't know that sharing or liking or saying "omg how cute!" or "I want one!" can lead to more poaching, more deaths, and more orphans.

13

Bahamas

Swimming with sharks in the Bahamas rocked my world. I've always loved these animals—their mouths chock-full of razor teeth, their streamlined bodies built for slicing through the water, and their dominance of their domain undisputed. They are ancient creatures—aquatic dinosaurs. The ancestors of today's sharks have been swimming in the earth's oceans for more than four hundred million years, predating actual dinosaurs by about half that time. Predating, actually, any living thing that walks on land. And through the millennia and even five mass extinctions, sharks haven't changed a whole lot. If you could time-travel back one hundred million years or more and go for a dive, you could still easily recognize a shark as a shark.

Even in a world of constant evolution, there are a few things Mother Nature seems to look at and figure, *If it ain't broke . . .*

Maybe even more remarkable than the age of some shark species are the ages of some individual fish. In 2016, scientists used radiocarbon dating to determine the age of a single Greenland shark at around *four hundred years*. That guy was practically prehistoric all by himself.

A Giant PR Problem

Two facts:

Every year a handful of people (an average of six) die as a result of interactions with sharks.

Every year approximately one hundred million sharks die as a result of interactions with humans.

So for every single person who meets a *Jaws*-like end, more than ten million sharks kick the bucket. And *we're* afraid of *them?* This is a group of species with a serious image problem. Cattle, deer, bees, dogs—they're all responsible for far more human deaths than sharks every year, but we don't shiver at the thought of any of them.

I'm a firm believer that if you don't love a creature, you won't care about conserving it. And if you don't know it, why would you love it? Sharks are the ultimate example. Almost everything most of us know about them comes from movies and headlines and Shark Week. And while we're busy not caring, the number of endangered shark species is increasing every year. Some of them—about 16 percent—are teetering on the brink of extinction.

In 2018, I got it into my head that I wanted to find a way to know these amazing animals better. I'd had encounters with several shark species by this time, but never a species that had a forbidding reputation, and never outside of a cage. My objective was to get into the water and meet one of my favorite megacarnivores, the tiger shark, and share with the world how special, beautiful, and impressive these animals are—and why we should *not* be immediately afraid of them.

And if there was any way to pull it off, I wanted to have that experience without being in a cage.

I asked around about the possibilities, and a friend in the diving community put me in touch with some fellow shark enthusiasts in Florida. These two dudes are dedicated shark conservationists, and they share a deep love of the ocean and a commitment to educating the public about the vital role sharks play in our underwater ecosystems.

Of the possible itineraries, diving at Tiger Beach in the Bahamas sounded like the perfect trip. This location is a destination for shark aficionados from all over the world, and it's the rare environment where you can consistently encounter tiger sharks within a few dozen feet of the surface. These animals are comfortable at depths over one thousand feet, but they continue to show up in the same shallow Bahamas waters year after year.

Even though their numbers rise and fall with the seasons, tiger sharks live near their namesake beach year round, so the odds of a sighting were good as we left the Florida coast before dawn, heading southeast toward the Bahamas.

I'd seen a tiger shark once, from a distance, during a dive in Fiji. That one was about six feet long—a juvenile—and he was just passing by. The experience stuck with me and kept me hungry for a real encounter with one of these massive fish.

My hosts, Chris and Mike, had been leading expeditions like mine for years, so I trusted that I was in good hands. Chris, the captain, manned the helm while Mike, the videographer, and I prepped our gear. As we suited up to dive, he told me the most important thing to remember underwater was to keep my head on a swivel. *Always* be looking, he said, because even though these sharks are not *coming* for you, they could still easily bump into you. He also warned me to pay attention to personalities. A fish is definitely not just a fish (something I did already know after years of working with fish and realizing that they do not get nearly enough credit for their individuality and intelligence). Some sharks can quickly be identified as shy, some as curious and interested in divers, others as especially skittish or bold and thus potentially dangerous.

We weren't keen on hand-feeding sharks, figuring that the practice is both unnecessary and asking for trouble. Instead, we dropped a weighted bait crate into the water at the dive site to bring the sharks closer. For some conservationists, even this method of drawing wildlife in is controversial because it facilitates contact between our species. But given how terrified people are of sharks and how rarely they hurt us, it seemed to me that helping responsible divers learn about these creatures and serve as ambassadors back to the rest of the world was probably worth putting out a snack tray once in a while.

Mike explained that once they smelled the bait, the sharks would swoop in near the crate, then swim away and circle back again and again. Oddly, the crate would never run out. One of the cool things about this whole process is that it's simply the smell of the baitfish that keeps these sharks interested. Many would come but not eat. In addition to the tiger sharks, we'd probably see reef sharks and lemon sharks. We might also see nurse sharks, more tentative bottom dwellers who'd arrive late to the party but often try to suck the fish from the small openings of the crate.

We'd see it all, but it would be the tigers we'd remember, because they're one of the largest species of any kind in the sea, and once you've seen one, you never forget it.

Out of My Element

Not very many wildlife encounters can put me on edge. Plenty of them heighten my attention and keep me dead focused, but that's something else. Heading out to meet one of the most profoundly powerful apex predators on the planet was, honestly, fine, but doing it so far out of my element—air—was enough to give me a twinge of actual fear. To get really close to sharks, I'd have to move out of the oxygen and under the water. I've done plenty of diving; still, it's always a leap to trust a machine with your breathing, and being underwater alters the way your senses process everything. Over a decade of world travel and wildlife interactions, I'd come to trust and rely on my quick reaction times, and while I was swimming with sharks didn't seem like an ideal time to start throwing all that out of whack.

When we'd finished going over the basics of equipment safety, shark etiquette, and diver behavior, Mike and I slipped off the boat's platform and started a quick descent. For the record, the moment of entry and the moment of exit are the most potentially problematic times for divers in the vicinity of large sharks. Anytime you're splashing around on the surface of the water you've got two big disadvantages. First, you're distracted and you're not seeing the full underwater picture. Second, you're likely flailing around like a potential food item. I was eager to get this step over with—and to do it without making any big splashes that might either scare a shark away or bring a hungry one to me.

I was certified to dive down to one hundred feet, but the sandbars at Tiger Beach are only about thirty feet under. The deeper a dive, and the higher the water pressure on your body, the more oxygen you consume with each breath. Less depth here meant more available breaths to work with during the dive, which meant more tank time, which was *so* fine with me.

We wore weight belts to counter the buoyancy of our wet suits and quickly dropped toward the floor. The water was warm and clear, and as we descended I focused on the sandbar that would momentarily be under me, thinking, I guess, about landing on my feet. (Generally I don't often do or think about this as a diver, because most of my dives are on coral reefs and I'm making a real effort to *avoid* touching my feet to anything.)

Whatever my thought process, it was wrong. Mike was descending at the same pace, facing me as we were just hitting the sand. One second I was looking at him like any other compadre I'd travel side by side with, and the next he was forcefully thrusting his right arm out past the left side of my face. His hand was extended like that of a testy traffic cop dealing with an especially difficult driver. I looked over my left shoulder and there, *directly* behind my head, her eye to my eye, was a fourteen-foot shark—who appeared, in that terrifying moment, to be mostly teeth.

Hello! She'd been coming straight at the base of my head. Mike's extended arm deflected her away from me. He would explain later that the goliath had probably been attracted by the glint of metal on my BCD (buoyancy control device) apparatus and its resemblance to light's reflection off fish scales, but in the moment I realized that everything he had warned me about on the boat was very, very real.

As always, adrenaline and enthusiasm make for the most epic wildlife experiences, and now I knew I was in for some real action. From that moment on, I was on an almost mechanical swivel. Look front, look left, look right, look behind. Repeat. Repeat. Repeat. I literally didn't spend more than a single second looking in the same direction for the next two hours. Keep in mind that on dives you wear a mask and that diminishes a significant amount of your peripheral vision—all the more reason to keep that head moving.

As I touched bottom, I took a minute to scan the terrain. There was a long, wide sandbar, there was the bait crate, there were just us two divers in the water, and there was a growing parade of sea life streaming our way. Dozens of lemon sharks, skittishly darting from side to side, barely steering clear of Mike and me. And from about twenty feet off, the giant tiger who'd just given me the most terrifying peekaboo of my life, making a huge arc, heading back my way. Fifteen feet, ten feet.

Mike stepped up beside me to demonstrate the move that would be key to our entire dive: the redirect. We'd talked about it, but some things you have to see to believe. As the shark closed in at about eight feet, Mike played the traffic cop again, only this time, not nearly as urgently. He casually raised one arm up, palm open and facing forward, his eyes focused on the animal, who was two and a half times longer than us and closing in. I was thinking, *Wow, okay, it's just like that?* My guide knew what he was doing, and the shark's eyes took in the outstretched hand and the obstructive arm, and as I stood there infatuated with her and excited to do this on my own, she made a small adjustment to her path that would have almost—though not quite—caused her to miss us.

I was thinking, *Nice, but not enough*, but then Mike finished this maneuver by placing his hand at the side of the shark's snout and gently easing her a hair farther from us—far enough that the shark would pass peaceably by.

As more sharks rolled in, I observed for another minute or two, all the while keeping up my *front, left, right, rear* spot checks. And then I was dying to try it, to have this amazing contact myself. I moved closer to the bait tray, kicked my fins off, buried my feet in the sand, and got down on my knees. Then I waited just seconds for the first shark to arrive. A lemon shark, small and fast and clearly not interested in having an interaction, as he stayed a foot or two away. Behind him, though, was a full-grown tiger.

This time I was ready, and I was able to focus not just on how to avoid getting a test bite on my BCD but also on memorizing the details of this magnificent creature. Like most sharks, this tiger came with minions, foot-long remoras, under her belly. Her skin shone in the water, her eyes glinted black and bottomless, and her mouth—about a foot across—was a great gash across the front of her entire face.

She approached with it slightly agape (as sharks always do), and inside I could see those big, broad, beautiful chompers. The dentition on these guys is amazing, built to allow them to eat *anything*. They can use those teeth and their powerful jaws to crack open a sea turtle shell like a nut. They can shear off great chunks of dead whales. For the most part, though, they eat—wait for it—fish.

I raised my arm, ready for this shark, and she politely adjusted her path to go around me. Inside I was bummed not to make contact, but I wanted to be respectful. The next one approached, coming from behind, and for the first time I put my hands on one of these amazing creatures, feeling the rough and stippled skin with its perfectly symmetrical pattern. Although I've put my hands on a lot of animals, the feeling of tiger shark scales was a completely new experience. Their scales (a.k.a. dermal denticles) actually feel synthetic—so much that you wonder, *How did nature create this?! Wow.* I wanted to put my nose right up to that skin, get up close and examine it, maybe rub my cheek against it for just one sec. But any of those things would have been both invasive and risky (and weird, I'm told), so instead I just watched the shark go.

For the next two hours, I was like a kid playing in the world's biggest, most action-packed sandbox. The biggest challenge, honestly, was not stopping and staring. Being up close and personal with this species I'd been dying to meet was so satisfying, I wanted to soak it all up, so that I'd remember every detail. But staring was the one no-no in the box. I needed to keep my eyes up, and my head turning, to stay safe.

Hundreds of sharks came my way (including seven or eight tigers that stuck around through the entire dive), and I felt that I was directing traffic around that bait tray like a pro (and loving every second of it). After the first few passes, I was able to distinguish some of the individuals—one with a scar over her eye, one with a chunk missing from a fin, a couple who almost seemed to want to engage. To investigate? Maybe. To hurt me? Nope, or I would have *been* hurt.

One thing was for sure, though: they were relaxed and comfortable, and none of these sharks were even the least bit hungry for me. I was no more a prey item there on the seafloor than the boat itself or my discarded flippers. They had come for the fish.

We stayed on the seafloor until the oxygen tanks started to run low. If I'd had enough air to breathe for two days of sandbox-and-shark play, I would have been all in and Mike might have had to stop me from trying to feed from the bait crate.

Breaking the surface and climbing back onto the boat and into the sun, I felt like I'd been gone for days, as if I'd made an epic trek, or aged a year. The whole experience felt that monumental. For someone who's afraid of sharks, my day would have been a nightmare; but for me, it had been a dream come true.

Can't Swim Without a Fin

It's clear at just a glance that the tiger shark is an alpha predator, perfectly evolved to be top dog in the ocean, never needing to fear much of anything. Even so, they don't target humans in the water, don't especially want to eat us, don't automatically feel threatened or defensively aggressive toward us when we dive into their realm. What other apex predator does that? Try getting between a lion or a grizzly bear or a crocodile and its food and then firmly guiding it around you by the muzzle and see how that works out.

Wait. Don't.

The fact is, of those ten or fewer human fatalities that are attributable to sharks every year, almost all of them are cases of mistaken identity—a shark taking a bite out of something it believes might be food and then tragically leaving that victim to bleed to death.

On the flip side, many of the cases of people killing sharks are deliberate predation, often of the worst possible kind. Rather than killing these creatures and then making use of the entire animal, unscrupulous fishermen who supply the demand for shark fin soup slice the fins off live sharks and then drop the rest of their bodies—95 percent or more—back into the ocean, where they, too, bleed to death.

That's not really fishing, is it? It's just wasteful, thoughtless slaughter.

Since we're so apathetic about sharks—or fearful of them—it's easy to think, *Eh, who cares?* Only not caring about sharks is getting us into trouble. I know the day is never going to come when everybody wants to snuggle a tiger shark as badly as I did, but we are way overdue for adjusting our mind-sets from *fear* of these amazing creatures to *respect*. We can all respect how powerful they are. How durable. How effectively they do their jobs in ecosystems all over the world.

Without sharks to keep other species in check, the delicate balance of sea life experiences a ripple effect, with the sharks' direct prey thriving and consuming more of what's below them on the food chain. When the numbers of a single hammerhead species plummeted due to overfishing, for example, the population of the rays they eat exploded. Then the supply of *their* food—scallops, clams, and other bivalves—took a dive. Sharks are also responsible for consuming a significant amount of carcasses that would otherwise spread disease and dirty our oceans. We are literally talking about the circle of life here, and when we allow somebody to hack a big slice out of it, we don't get to choose how that section gets filled in.

People have likely been fishing for sharks for as long as we've walked the earth, and that's been a part of our balanced circle. But killing one hundred million of these critical predators each year? It's unprecedented, and it's asking for trouble.

There's one other way to look at this equation, a perspective worth considering even if you don't or can't love sharks. A recent study of the economic benefits and impacts of finning and of the growing ecotourism industry found that a shark that brings in divers is about *two hundred times* more valuable alive than it is dead. If money is your only motivation—that's a ton of it.

Acknowledgments

Working with wildlife around the world has always been a dream for me, and I've been willing to do just about anything—and go absolutely anywhere—to make it a reality. I've also had a ton of guidance and support along the way from people who believed in me, taught me, invited me along to learn and experience, and shared my observations and enthusiasm. I owe each of them my gratitude. I especially want to thank my family and friends, who never questioned my pursuit of this vision (or the outcomes so far). That goes double for my mother and father, who've encouraged and cultivated my passion for the natural world all my life. To my partners and mentors at Conejo Valley Veterinary Hospital, thank you for your unwavering support of even my most unconventional goals, and for letting me call such an outstanding facility my professional home.

Being an animal lover puts me in the company (and in the social media feeds) of like-minded people around the world, and I'm grateful to every reader, follower, and contributor who has supported my work. Even if we haven't met, your engagement and support have been significant to my wild pursuits.

Writing a book is a different kind of adventure from the ones

I usually take. The process was, in part, a fantastic trip through nearly fifteen years of memories, taking me back to many favorite moments and reminding me how much I appreciate each trip and wildlife encounter. It was also a long and winding trek, one that required an expert guide—or in this case, an experienced and dedicated publishing team—to lead the way. I'm grateful to this team for embracing my stories and priorities and helping me capture on paper the places and the animals, and the pains and joys I've experienced with them. Many thanks to my literary agent, Cait Hoyt, for encouraging me to get started on a book and for setting me up with my publisher; to editor James Melia for his enthusiasm for my work and expert guidance throughout this process; to Kerry Cullen for her careful and thoughtful review; to Bonnie Thompson for her concise copyedit; to Brendan Murphy for checking my facts; and to the entire amazing team at Henry Holt, including Amy Einhorn, Maggie Richards, Kenn Russell, Caitlin O'Shaughnessy, and Carolyn O'Keefe for their generous and professional support. And of course thanks to my writer, Jana Murphy, who helped me find my voice and elegantly transformed my stories into a book of which I'm extremely proud.

Everybody knows choice of travel companion can make or break the experience, and I've been lucky to see the world with people who share my adventurous spirit, my passion for wildlife, and even (sometimes) my willingness to go without creature comforts to access some exceptionally exotic locations. Among them, I want to thank Timothy Diggs for literally being down for anything, even when he has no idea what wild or legitimately dangerous situation we may find ourselves in. And Joey Brown, who's devoted his education and career to learning more about our wildlife and how to protect it—and has generously included me on many of his most significant projects. And I especially want to thank Nathalie Basha for seeing my vision from day one, for actively supporting it as my camera operator and video editor and for sharing some of my favorite adventures.

Works Consulted

"100 Million Sharks Killed Every Year, Study Shows on Eve of International Conference on Shark Protection." National Geographic.com. https://www.nationalgeographic.com/culture/onward/2013/03/01/100-million-sharks-killed-every-year-study-shows-on-eve-of-international-conference-on-shark-protection/

"2018 State of the Rhino." International Rhino Foundation. https://rhinos.org/2018-state-of-the-rhino/

"769 Rhinos Poached in South Africa in 2018." Save The Rhino. https://www.savetherhino.org/africa/south-africa/769-rhinos-poached-in-south-africa-in-2018/

Addley, Esther. "Epidemic of UK Rhino Horn Thefts Linked to One Criminal Gang." *The Guardian* (U.S. Edition). https://www.theguardian.com/environment/2011/aug/08/rhino-horn-thefts-chinese-medicine

"Almost All Snakes Have the Same Mindboggling Superpower." BBC News. http://www.bbc.com/earth/story/20160511-almost-all-snakes-have-the-same-mindboggling-superpower

Alvarado, Laura. "Be on the Lookout for Crocodiles in Costa Rican Beaches." *Costa Rica Star*. https://news.co.cr/be-on-the-lookout-for-crocodiles-on-costa-rican-beaches/74010/

"American Crocodile." National Geographic.com. https://www.nationalgeographic.com/animals/reptiles/a/american-crocodile/

"Anxiety." Inner Mammal Institute. https://innermammalinstitute.org/anxiety/

"Binturong." IUCN Red List of Threatened Species. https://www.iucnredlist.org/species/41690/45217088

"Biodiversity." Galapagos Conservancy. https://www.galapagos.org/about_galapagos/about-galapagos/biodiversity/

Bittel, Jason. "How Nile Crocodiles Are Bigger and Badder Than Alligators." National Geographic.com. https://www.nationalgeographic.com/news/2016/05/nile-crocodiles-florida-reptiles-science/

Boback, S. M., et al. "Snake Constriction Rapidly Induces Circulatory Arrest in Rats." *Journal of Experimental Biology.* https://www.ncbi.nlm.nih.gov/pubmed/26202779

Boulos, Nick. "Cambodia's Cardamom Mountains, Full of Secrets." *Washington Post.* https://www.washingtonpost.com/lifestyle/travel/cambodias-cardamom-mountains-full-of-secrets/2012/08/09/0b63cf10-d837-11e1-b360-33e7ac84e003_story.html

Bowen, Devon. "Evolution's Ultimate Predators." Two Oceans Aquarium. https://www.aquarium.co.za/blog/entry/top-10-prehistoric-sharks

Bradford, Alina. "Sloths: World's Slowest Mammals." Live Science. https://www.livescience.com/27612-sloths.html

"Camp Leakey." Orangutan Foundation International. https://orangutan.org/our-projects/research/camp-leakey/

"Chimps as Pets: The Reality." Jane Goodall Institute UK. https://www.janegoodall.org.uk/chimpanzees/chimpanzee-central/15-chimpanzees/chimpanzee-central/28-chimps-as-pets-the-reality

Chow, Lorraine. "It's International Gibbon Day!" EcoWatch. https://www.ecowatch.com/international-gibbon-day-2614836646.html

"Darien National Park." United Nations Educational, Scientific and Cultural Organization. http://whc.unesco.org/en/list/159

"Dong Phayayen-Khao Yai Forest Complex." United Nations Educational, Scientific and Cultural Organization. https://whc.unesco.org/en/list/590/

"Eastern Gorilla." IUCN Red List of Threatened Species. https://www.iucnredlist.org/species/39994/115576640

Eastman, Quinn. "Learning from Lampreys." *Emory Medicine.* http://news.emory.edu/features/2018/02/lampreys/

"Elephant Herd." Elephant Nature Park. https://www.elephantnaturepark.org/category/elephant-herd/

"Facts About Manta Rays." Manta Ray World. https://www.mantaray-world.com/facts-about-manta-rays/

Fairclough, Caty. "Shark Finning: Sharks Turned Prey." Smithsonian Ocean Portal. https://ocean.si.edu/ocean-life/sharks-rays/shark-finning-sharks-turned-prey

"Fijian Crested Iguana." International Iguana Foundation. https://iguanafoundation.org/information-by-species/fijian-crested-iguana/

"Fijian Crested Iguana Reintroduction." Iguana Specialist Group. https://www.iucn-isg.org/latest-news/fijian-crested-iguanas-reintroduction/

Formoso, Celeste Anna. "New Spider Species Found in Puerto Princesa Underground River." Philippine News Agency. https://www.pna.gov.ph/articles/1045595

Gabbatiss, Josh. "Why Pairing Up for Life Is Hardly Ever a Good Idea." BBC Earth. http://www.bbc.com/earth/story/20160213-why-pairing-up-for-life-is-hardly-ever-a-good-idea

"Galapagos Giant Tortoise." Galapagos Conservation Trust. https://galapagosconservation.org.uk/wildlife/galapagos-giant-tortoise/

"Galapagos Islands." United Nations Educational, Scientific and Cultural Organization. https://whc.unesco.org/en/list/1/

"Gibbon Basics." Gibbon Conservation Center. https://www.gibboncenter.org/gibbon-basics.html

"Gorilla Doctors Timeline." Gorilla Doctors Mountain Gorilla Veterinary Project. https://www.gorilladoctors.org/about-us/history-past-gorilla-doctors/

"Gorillas." Endangered Species International. https://www.endangeredspeciesinternational.org/gorillas.html

Gospodinova, Ayo. "The Story of Little Mussa." Africa Geographic Editorial. https://africageographic.com/blog/the-story-of-mussa/

"Green Anaconda." National Geographic.com. https://www.nationalgeographic.com/animals/reptiles/g/green-anaconda/

"Green and Black Poison Dart Frog." Potter Park Zoo Docent Manual 2017. https://potterparkzoo.org/wp-content/uploads/2017/06/Amphibian_Green_Black_Poison_Dart_Frog.pdf

Harrison, Emma. "Leatherback Nesting Trends in Costa Rica and Panama." Sea Turtle Conservancy. https://conserveturtles.org/11427-2/

Hessel, Matthew, and Scott McAninch. "Coral Snake Toxicity." National Center for Biotechnology Information. https://www.ncbi.nlm.nih.gov/books/NBK519031/

"Hippopotamus Attacks and Kills 13 in Boat in Niger." ABC Australia. https://www.abc.net.au/news/2014-11-20/hippopotamus-attack-kills-13-in-boat-in-niger/5904646

Hoffman, Sarah. "Ape Fracture Patterns Show Higher Incidence in More Arboreal Species." *Discussions*. http://www.inquiriesjournal.com/articles/799/2/ape-fracture-patterns-show-higher-incidence-in-more-arboreal-species

"How Much Milk Does a Baby Need?" Baby Rhino Rescue. https://www.babyrhinorescue.org/wp-content/uploads/2018/07/Rhino-Milk-Fact-Sheets-RSA.pdf

Hrala, Josh. "This Is the Horror Sloths Go Through Every Time They Have to Poop." Science Alert. https://www.sciencealert.com/this-is-the-horror-that-sloths-have-to-go-through-every-time-they-poop

"Humpback Whales." NOAA Fisheries. https://www.fisheries.noaa.gov/species/humpback-whale

Hunowu, Iwan. "Saving Species in Sulawesi." Conservation Leadership Programme. http://www.conservationleadershipprogramme.org/interview/saving-species-in-sulawesi/

Imster, Eleanor. "Humpback Whale Population on the Rise." EarthSky. https://earthsky.org/earth/humpback-whale-population-on-the-rise

"Indonesian Rainforests." Rainforest Action Network. https://www.ran.org/indonesian-rainforests/

"Information About Sea Turtles: General Behavior." Sea Turtle Conservancy. https://conserveturtles.org/information-sea-turtles-general-behavior/

"Kakadu National Park." Australian Government Department of Agriculture, Water and the Environment. https://www.environment.gov.au/topics/national-parks/kakadu-national-park

"Kimberley Geikie Gorge to Return to Its Indigenous Name." ABC Australia.

https://www.abc.net.au/news/2016-06-13/kimberley-geikie-gorge-to-return
-to-its-indigenous-name/7506256

Kiprop, Victor. "The World's Loudest Animals." World Atlas.com. https://www
.worldatlas.com/articles/the-world-s-loudest-animals.html

"Komodo Dragon." National Geographic.com. https://www.nationalgeographic
.com/animals/reptiles/k/komodo-dragon/

"Komodo Dragon." Smithsonian's National Zoo & Conservation Biology Institute.
https://nationalzoo.si.edu/animals/komodo-dragon

"The Life of a Newborn Humpback Whale." https://whaletrust.org/the-life-of-a
-newborn-humpback-whale/

Lwiro Primates. https://www.facebook.com/lwiroprimates

"Mangrove Snake." Smithsonian's National Zoo & Conservation Biology Institute.
https://nationalzoo.si.edu/animals/mangrove-snake

"Mantas-at-a-Glance." Manta Trust. www.mantatrust.org/about-mantas/mantas
-at-a-glance/

Mey, Wolfram, and Hendrik Freitag. "New Species of Caddisflies (Insecta: Trichop-
tera) from Emergence Traps at Streams in Central Palawan, Philippines." *Aquatic Insects*. https://www.tandfonline.com/doi/abs/10.1080/01650424.2019.1617423

"Marine Iguana." National Geographic.com. https://www.nationalgeographic.com
/animals/reptiles/m/marine-iguana/

"More Than Half of Amazonian Armadillos Carry Leprosy." Science Daily.
https://www.sciencedaily.com/releases/2018/06/180628151918.htm

Mosher, Dave. "Gorillas More Related to People Than Thought, Genome Says."
National Geographic.com. https://www.nationalgeographic.com/news/2012
/3/120306-gorilla-genome-apes-humans-evolution-science/

"Murchison Falls National Park at a Glance." Uganda Wildlife Authority. https://
www.ugandawildlife.org/explore-our-parks/parks-by-name-a-z/murchison
-falls-national-park

Myers, Ransom, et al. "Cascading Effects of the Loss of Apex Predatory Sharks
from a Coastal Ocean." *Science*. https://science.sciencemag.org/content/315
/5820/1846.full

Nielsen, Julius, et al. "Eye Lens Radiocarbon Reveals Centuries of Longevity in the
Greenland Shark." *Science*. https://science.sciencemag.org/content/353/6300/702

Nuwer, Rachel. "When Becoming a Man Means Sticking Your Hand into a Glove
of Ants." *Smithsonian Magazine*. https://www.smithsonianmag.com/smart
-news/brazilian-tribe-becoming-man-requires-sticking-your-hand-glove-full
-angry-ants-180953156/

"The Phajaan Ceremony: Why You Should Never Ride an Elephant." Nomadic
Planet. http://www.nomadic-planet.com/2017/01/23/why-you-should-never
-ride-an-elephant/

"Poison Frogs." Smithsonian's National Zoo & Conservation Biology Institute.
https://nationalzoo.si.edu/animals/poison-frogs

"Puerto-Princesa Subterranean River National Park." United Nations Educational,
Scientific and Cultural Organization. https://whc.unesco.org/en/list/652/

"A Rhino Nightmare: The Blood Moon." Save The Rhino. https://www.savetherhino
.org/our-work/protecting-rhinos/rhino-nightmare-the-blood-moon/

"Ring of Fire." U.S. Geological Survey. https://earthquake.usgs.gov/learn/glossary/?term=Ring%20of%20Fire

Ringler, Eva. "Revelations in the Way Poison Frogs Care for Their Young." National Geographic.com. https://blog.nationalgeographic.org/2018/01/09/revelations-in-the-way-poison-frogs-care-for-their-young/

Salahi, Lara. "Chimpanzees vs. Humans: Sizing Up Their Strength." ABC News. https://abcnews.go.com/Health/Wellness/chimpanzees-humans-sizing-strength/story?id=16696826

Smith, P. D. "Tasty Tale of the Tortoise." *The Guardian*. https://www.theguardian.com/books/2004/jul/31/featuresreviews.guardianreview7

Solly, Meilan. "Why Otters Disembowel Toads Before Eating Them." *Smithsonian Magazine*. https://www.smithsonianmag.com/smart-news/why-did-mysterious-predator-turn-toad-inside-out-180971841/

"Southeastern Asia: Southern Cambodia stretching into Thailand and Vietnam." World Wildlife Fund. https://www.worldwildlife.org/ecoregions/im0106

"Species Fact Sheets: Rhincodon Typus." Food and Agriculture Organization of the United Nations. http://www.fao.org/fishery/species/2801/en

Sundstrom, Bob. "Snake Eagles Are Serpents' Worst Nightmare." National Audubon Society. https://www.audubon.org/news/snake-eagles-are-serpents-worst-nightmare

"Ta Prohm." Atlas Obscura. https://www.atlasobscura.com/places/ta-prohm

Thaitrakulpanich, Asaree. "Rare Tiger Cubs Spotted in Khao Yai Signal Hope for Vanishing Species." Khaosod English. http://www.khaosodenglish.com/news/2017/03/29/rare-tiger-cubs-spotted-khao-yai-signal-hope-vanishing-species/

"Tiger Shark." Oceana. https://oceana.org/marine-life/sharks-rays/tiger-shark

"Two-Toed Sloth." San Diego Zoo. https://animals.sandiegozoo.org/animals/two-toed-sloth

Westhoff, Guido, et al. "Target Tracking During Venom 'Spitting' by Cobras." *Journal of Experimental Biology*. https://www.ncbi.nlm.nih.gov/pmc/articles/PMC2871007/

"What Are the World's Deadliest Animals?" BBC News. https://www.bbc.com/news/world-36320744

"Where Do Orangutans Live?" World Wildlife Fund. https://www.worldwildlife.org/stories/where-do-orangutans-live-and-nine-other-orangutan-facts

"Why Hippos Are Spraying Their Dung." Science and Technology News. https://www.technology.org/2018/12/05/why-hippos-are-spraying-their-dung-like-agricultural-machines/

Worm, Boris, et al. "Global Catches, Exploitation Rates, and Rebuilding Options for Sharks." *Marine Policy*. https://www.sciencedirect.com/science/article/pii/S0308597X13000055

Yamaguchi, Adam. "The Darien Gap—A Desperate Journey." CBS News. https://www.cbsnews.com/news/darien-gap-dead-end-desperate-journey/

Zwick, Karen, et al. "Pian-Upe Wildlife Reserve: Biological and Socio-ecomonic Survey." Society for Environmental Exploration. https://web.archive.org/web/20130823034504/http://frontier-publications.co.uk/reports/Uganda/GameReserves/170PianUpeReserve.pdf

About the Author

Dr. Evan Antin originally hails from Kansas City, Kansas, where he grew up spending the majority of his childhood in search of native wildlife, including snakes, turtles, and insects. He went on to study evolutionary and ecological biology at the University of Colorado at Boulder and veterinary medicine at Colorado State University. For fifteen years Evan has traveled the world, working with wildlife in ecosystems on six continents. In addition to his wildlife veterinary and conservation work he is a practicing veterinarian in Thousand Oaks, California.